Brasil

A Concise Thematic Geography

Phillip Vaughan-Williams

Head of the Geography Department,
Gowerton School, West Glamorgan

University Tutorial Press

Published by University Tutorial Press Limited
842 Yeovil Road, Slough, SL1 4JQ.

ISBN 0 7231 0813 7

Published 1981
Reprinted with minor revisions 1981
Reprinted 1982 (twice)

Photoset and printed in Great Britain by
Redwood Burn Ltd., Trowbridge, Wiltshire and
bound by Pegasus Bookbinding, Melksham, Wiltshire

Preface

The Brasilian sub-continent provides the geographer with a remarkable opportunity for understanding the characteristics of the underdeveloped and developed worlds, within a single vast nation state. Brasil is a dynamic country which has experienced rapid change in recent years, and now bridges the development gap. Regional contrasts in development are considerable. Amazonia is one of the last frontier regions of the world whilst Greater São Paulo is the largest and most diversified manufacturing complex in the developing world. Thus within Brasil, geographical interrelationships can be analysed at different levels of complexity and at varying scales.

The major aims of this book are to achieve a comprehensive geographical 'over-view' or synthesis of Brasil's problems, progress and potential, and to present an objective account of national and regional development programmes. It should prove suitable for a number of 'A' level courses and should also provide a useful introduction for more advanced studies.

The approach is essentially thematic. Both systematic and regional themes are presented in a logical sequence. Where appropriate, basic concepts are explained through the use of simple models. The numerous maps, diagrams, tables and photographs are intended to complement the text, and should therefore be referred to frequently. Many of the maps are capable of being simplified by the student. Tables are not listed separately, but are numbered in sequence with the maps and diagrams, to facilitate the reading of the text.

Though the early chapters are mainly systematic, the regional synthesis is maintained throughout. In the chapter on physical geography, the regions are formal in nature; in the chapters on population, urbanisation and economic development, they are functional; in the sections on regional imbalances and regional development, the emphasis is on planning regions.

The student has the option of following the chapter sequence as it stands, or can alternatively select regional case-studies from Chapters 9 and 10 to illustrate many of the themes discussed at an earlier stage. In the text frequent reference is made to other related sections, though the student is encouraged to consult the contents list and index to gain a fuller understanding of specific topics.

Brasil is used rather than Brazil, as it is the Brasilian's name for his country. A number of Brasilian terms are also used, because they are distinctive, and add 'flavour'. A glossary of all major terms is included, and this also gives a guide to pronunciation.

Every effort has been made to use the most recent data available at the time of writing. Most data is for the late 1970s, and in some cases the most reliable estimates and forecasts are used. The author is particularly indebted to the *Instituto Brasileiro de Geografia e Estatistica*, Rio de Janeiro, and the Brazilian Embassy in London, for the use of many of their recent publications.

The author also wishes to express his gratitude to Chris Kington for his faith in teachers, to Simon Boyd for his detailed and meticulous editorial work, Tina Dutton for the artwork, and Rosamonde Lynch for her help in the search for photographs. Thanks are also due to J. F. Lee and the other readers of the manuscript, and to the staff and students of the Geography Department at Gowerton, who have all made significant contributions. The book would not have been conceived or completed without the unfailing support and encouragement of Ann Vaughan-Williams.

December 1980.   P. V-W.

Contents

List of Maps, Diagrams and Tables

Note that all maps, diagrams and tables are numbered together in sequence. Photographs are listed separately.

List of Plates

Introduction

Brasil has suffered for many years from a narrow and stereotyped international image. It is not merely the country of coffee, nuts, jungle, football and carnival. The 'Federative Republic of Brasil' is a vast, dynamic, and rapidly developing country, which has already emerged as a leading commercial and industrial power within the developing world.

Brasil's territory is of sub-continental proportions, covering an area of 8 500 000 km² —forty-seven per cent of the area of South America—and extending through thirty-nine degrees of both latitude and longitude. Not only is it the largest tropical country, and the largest in the Southern Hemisphere; it is also the fifth largest in the world. Brasil occupies a strategic position within South America, sharing common borders with ten of its twelve nation states.

Brasil's unique culture and distinctive national identity is the result of many factors. It contrasts with the rest of the continent in its Portuguese heritage and language. Brasilians are a blend of European, Amerindian, African, and other peoples with diverse ethnic and cultural backgrounds. They are proud of their hybrid origins, so much so that racial harmony and cultural unity—*convivência*—is virtually a national cult.

Throughout the colonial period, and especially since the establishment of the republic in 1889, Brasil has experienced many rapid changes. During the twentieth century, its population has grown so rapidly that Brasil is now the world's seventh most populous country. Its estimated population in 1980 was 123 million. There has also been a dramatic urban transformation which has had considerable social repercussions. In 1940, two-thirds of all Brasilians were rural, but today over two-thirds are urban. Greater São Paulo is South America's most populous metropolitan region with over 11 million inhabitants, and is also its major industrial centre. If it continues to grow at present rates, by the year 2000 it would have a population of over 25 million and would rank second in the world behind Mexico City. It is already larger than Greater London.

One of Brasil's major characteristics is its great internal diversity, and marked regional contrasts. In part this results from the variety of physical environments, but it also owes much to the cyclical nature of economic development over four centuries. New commodities for export were produced in different parts of the country, so that distinctive regional economies developed. This in turn led to distinctive regional populations, because the source of immigrant labour varied considerably at different times. For instance, sugar-cane was at first produced in the North-east by African slave labour, whereas coffee was later cultivated in the South-east by a predominantly European labour force.

In spite of improved transport and communications, and the drift to the cities, Brasilians still refer to each other as *Paulistas, Mineiros, Nordestinos* and *Suleiros* (inhabitants of São Paulo, Minas Gerais, the North-east and the South respectively). Most Brasilians also have a distinctive mental image of the remote, underpopulated, and underdeveloped, interior backlands of the country. They refer to these areas as the *sertão*, in much the same way that Australians refer to the 'outback' and Americans referred to the 'wild west'. The *sertão* is still regarded as being a mystical, primaeval region, and a world apart from the densely populated eastern regions of the country.

Brasil's well defined regions offer a remarkable opportunity to study the 'underdeveloped', 'developing' and 'developed' worlds, and their respective problems rates of progress and potentials, within a single nation state. Indeed, Amazonia and the western interior are in economic terms still the 'colonies' of the developed South-east region.

The map on page ix shows the states and territories of Brasil, and the most common grouping of these into five *grandes regiões* (major regions). These are: (i) the *Norte* (North) which corresponds to Amazonia; (ii) the *Centro-oeste* (Central-west) which is largely tropical grassland; (iii) the *Nordeste* (North-east)—the by-passed and overpopulated region which prospered during the colonial period, but which is now chronically overpopulated; (iv) the *Sul* (South) which is the temperate region of Brasil; and (v) the *Sudeste* (South-east) which is the most developed region, with many characteristics similar to those of advanced countries. The map also shows the location of the state capitals, and the Federal District. Brasília became the new capital city in 1960. The location of this purpose-built capital in itself reflects the contrasts and rivalries between the major regions.

It must be emphasised that Brasil is still a developing country, though by no means a typical 'third world' country. As such, it faces a variety of problems, as did the advanced countries in their formative period of economic expansion. Poverty is still widespread, living standards are generally very low and many still live at subsistence level. There are also gross inequalities in personal incomes. Many aspects of existing development programmes and government policies are problematic. But it is important to place those problems in perspective. Considerable progress has already been made in the provision of social services, as well as in achieving economic growth. Many deep-rooted problems are incapable of being solved by instant remedial action, and their solution must be regarded as a long-term objective. Likewise, the authoritarian political regime, which seized power in 1964, has many opponents; yet from

i. Administrative Divisions.

ii. Brasil in a World Perspective: Selected Statistics for Ten Countries, (Mid-1970s).

Country	Area in '000 km²	Population in millions	Annual rate of population increase (%)	Per capita GNP in US$ per annum	Numbers of Doctors per million people
U.S.A.	9 363	212	0.8	6 640	1 572
Brasil	8 512	110	2.8	900	443
Mexico	1 973	62	3.5	1 000	655
Venezuela	912	12	2.9	1 710	935
Zaire	2 345	26	2.8	150	34
Nigeria	924	65	2.7	240	37
Japan	372	112	1.2	3 800	1 122
India	3 288	621	2.0	130	191
Italy	301	56	0.8	2 770	1 806
United Kingdom	244	56	0.1	3 360	1 107

Note that the countries are not ranked in any way.

Source: *United Nations Statistical Yearbooks* (New York).

1967 to 1973 it achieved average annual growth rates above ten per cent. Brasil's economy now ranks eighth in the 'free world'.

This dramatic growth was highly concentrated in the South-east; so much so, that in recent years major regional development and industrial decentralisation programmes have been established. It is still too early to assess the achievements, but it is clear that the potential of Amazonia and the Central-west is great, and that if Brasil's full potential is to be realised, these regions must make a greater contribution to the national economy in the future. The major problem lies in the selection of appropriate development programmes, and the use of appropriate technologies.

Some idea of the scale of the problems can be given by reference to the overpopulated North-east. This region alone has over 36 million inhabitants; there are more *Nordestinos* than there are Argentinians or Colombians. The question arises as to whether Brasil as a whole is overpopulated. In this context, a country's population must be related to the level of exploitation of resources and the level of economic development. If overpopulation is defined as a state where a reduction in the number of people would result in an increase in the average standard of living, then Brasil must be considered to be overpopulated, because a significant proportion of those Brasilians of working age are unemployed and underemployed, and others live a self-sufficient existence at or near subsistence level. However, there is no doubt that Brasil has the resource potential for a much higher population. It is significant that both the other Latin American countries given in the table have a higher per capita Gross National Product than Brasil. In the case of Venezuela, massive oil revenues contribute greatly to this. However, both have much smaller populations than Brasil, which substantially accounts for their larger per capita GNP.

Brasil's economy continues to grow rapidly, in spite of the country's low petroleum reserves and the continuing world energy crisis. Agriculture has generally lagged behind the manufacturing sector, but both are becoming increasingly diversified. Manufactured goods are today the major exports. Brasil even exports automobile components to the United States of America, and produces more motor vehicles each year than the U.S.S.R.

1 The Physical Environment

The interaction between man and the physical environment is one of the central themes in geography. The environment provides man with a great variety of organic and inorganic resources, which he can exploit and develop in a number of different ways. The aggregate stock of environmental resources has a significant effect on a country's potential for economic development. But the rates and levels of exploitation are themselves dependent on the growth and development of the country's economy, and on the level of technological progress.

The physical environment also imposes a variety of constraints on development, which can be severe in regions subject to major environmental hazards. Whilst Brasil is a predominantly tropical country, with less extreme environmental contrasts than many countries, the physical environment is far from being homogeneous. There are significant local and regional contrasts in the 'lithosphere' (the rocks of the earth's crust), in the 'troposphere' (the lowest zone in the earth's atmosphere within which variations in climate and weather occur), and in the 'biosphere' (the zone of life). Many of these have a major effect on human activity.

The potential of Brasil's physical environment is great. As yet, because of a relatively low level of exploitation of many resources, much of it is still to be realised. However, the pressure on these resources is increasing rapidly, and in some cases mismanagement has already caused irreversible damage. The biosphere is especially at risk because of the lack of knowledge about the delicate balance of nature within the fragile tropical ecosystems, and because rapid economic growth frequently demands short-term gain at the expense of long-term conservation. These man–land interactions will be recurring themes in this and later chapters.

The Lithosphere: Structure and Relief

About sixty per cent of Brasil's territory is highland, between 200 m and 1 200 m in altitude. The highlands of the *Planalto Brasileiro* (Brasilian Highlands) and the *Planalto Guiano* (Guiana Highlands) consist of ancient Pre-Cambrian 'shield' rocks. They are separated by the vast riverine lowlands of the Amazon basin.

These ancient shields, together with those of Africa, India, Australia, and Antarctica, once formed the single southern continent of 'Gondwanaland'. The breaking up of this continent about 125 million years ago, and the westward drift of the crustal 'plates' of the Americas, caused the opening of the Atlantic Ocean basin. It also resulted in the formation of the fold-mountain ranges along the western leading edge, and was probably the major factor responsible for the down-tilting of the *Planalto Brasileiro*. These highlands are generally highest in the east, and terminate in the great escarpment which dominates much of Brasil's coastal region. The escarpment is in places step-faulted, and also intruded by large rounded 'sugar-loaves' of granite and gneiss (see **1.5** on page 5). It is predominantly an erosional rather than a structural feature. Differential erosion of varied rock types, and erosion along fault lines, has resulted in discontinuous and narrow coastal plains. The sugar loaves are exhumed igneus intrusions often following major fault lines. They are being exfoliated by the chemical decomposition of the crystalline rocks and the peeling of sheets of rock. The sheets are detached by the mechanical stresses caused by alternate heating and cooling, and the weathered rock debris is then removed downslope by wash and creep.

The Guiana Highlands—which contain Brasil's highest peak (*Pico da Neblina*, 3 014 m)—consist almost entirely of the most ancient Pre-Cambrian rocks. The Brasilian Highlands are more complex. Here, ancient crystalline rocks form a number of mountain ranges, whilst the younger Pre-Cambrian metamorphic and sedimentary rocks outcrop along a series of major anticlinal structures known as geanticlines. Three major geanticlines converge in the state of Minas Gerais to form the highly mineralised area of the 'Iron Quadrilateral' which is Brasil's major source of many metallic and non-metallic minerals (see **7.3** and **7.5** on pages 94 and 96).

Within the shield are three large structural basins which contain more recent Palaeozoic and Mesozoic rocks, and also several down-faulted troughs or rifts, as shown by **1.1** and **1.2**. The rifts of the coastal zone of the North-east also extend into the narrow offshore zone, and contain Brasil's largest proven petroleum reserves.

Brasil's southern plateau is very different, as it is the result of a massive Triassic lava flow. The basaltic

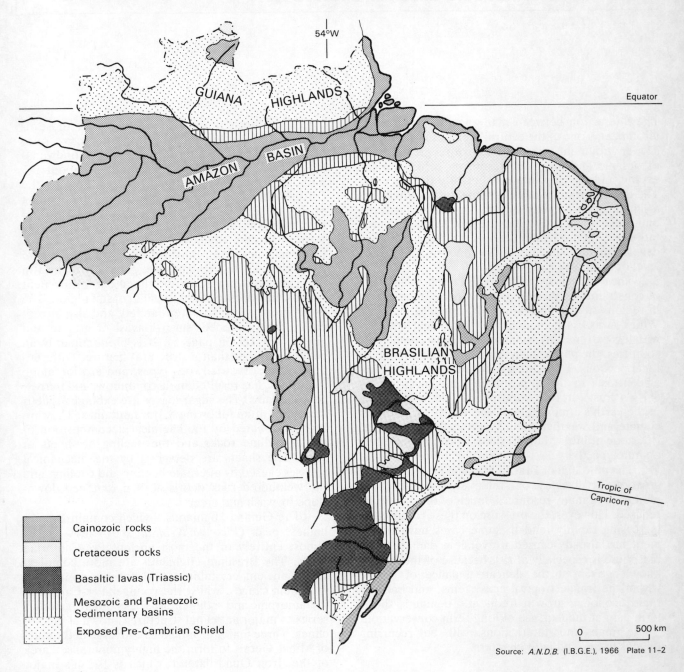

54°W

GUIANA HIGHLANDS

Equator

AMAZON BASIN

BRASILIAN HIGHLANDS

Tropic of Capricorn

Cainozoic rocks

Cretaceous rocks

Basaltic lavas (Triassic)

Mesozoic and Palaeozoic Sedimentary basins

Exposed Pre-Cambrian Shield

0   500 km

Source: *A.N.D.B.* (I.B.G.E.), 1966   Plate 11-2

1.1. Geology.

lavas are up to 600 m thick, cover an area of about 90 000 km², and terminate in a series of scarps. These are the most prominent landscape features and also form a series of waterfalls along the rivers of the Paraná system. The most famous are the 80 m high Iguaçu and Sete Quedas falls.

The landscape of the shield areas consists of mountain ranges and wide table-lands (*tabuleiros*) separated by scarps. These highlands have been sub-

jected to many millions of years of uninterrupted terrestrial weathering and erosional processes. The erosional history—denudation chronology—of the highlands is complex. Not only does much of this highland region experience a tropical continental climate with alternating wet and dry seasons, but in the past it was also subjected to climatic change. There is evidence to suggest that the *Planalto Brasileiro* experienced a more humid climate during the

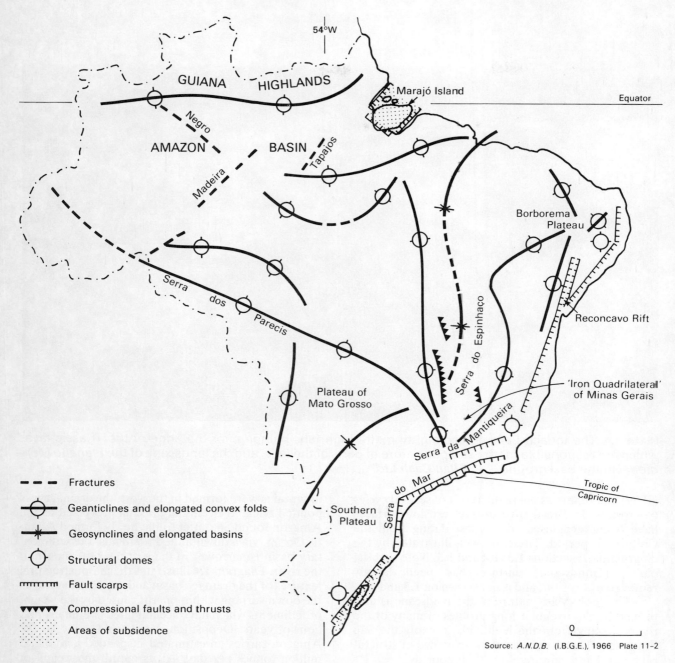

Legend:

- - - Fractures

⊖ Geanticlines and elongated convex folds

✳ Geosynclines and elongated basins

○ Structural domes

⊓⊓⊓⊓⊓ Fault scarps

▼▼▼▼▼ Compressional faults and thrusts

⋮⋮⋮⋮⋮ Areas of subsidence

Source: *A.N.D.B.* (I.B.G.E.), 1966   Plate 11–2

1.2. Major Structural Features.

glacial advances of the Pleistocene period, when the earth's latitudinal climate zones were compressed towards the equator.

It is probable that the dominant process in the formation of the table-lands is 'pediplanation' caused by scarp retreat. Pierre Birot (1960) regards the tropical continental climate and savanna vegetation as providing conditions very favourable to scarp retreat. He explains that the plateaus have degraded

soils with grassland vegetation, whilst the scarps have younger soils and are forested. Erosion is most rapid on the scarps because of the moister micro-climate under the forest cover, which also increases the rate of chemical decomposition. The parallel retreat of the scarps is maintained by the removal of the rock debris by sheet-wash during the wet season.

The landscape of the highlands of Brasil and Africa have been interpreted by Lester C. King

Plate 1.   The Iguaçu Falls. These eighty metre high falls plunge over the edge of the Triassic lavas which are responsible for the stepped nature of parts of the falls, and the landscape of the *Planalto Meridional* in the background.   ***J. Allan Cash Ltd.***

(1959) and others as being the result of several cycles of erosion. In Brasil, five distinct erosion surfaces have been recognised, the oldest dating from the Cretaceous period. These are well illustrated by the diagrammatic sections **1.3**, **1.4** and **1.5**. Note that the oldest (Gondwana) surface has been largely removed by erosion, and is not shown on **1.3** and **1.4**.

The 'polycyclic' nature of the landscape is also proven by the irregular long profiles of many of the rivers flowing from the highlands, notably the São Francisco. The rivers also show evidence of structural control and capture along their courses.

The Brasilian and Guiana Highlands are separated by the great geosynclinal basin occupied by the Amazonas/Solimoẽs river and its numerous tributaries. The basin is widest and deepest in the west, in the trough between the foothills of the Andes and the tilted shield. It contains great thicknesses of Tertiary and Quaternary deposits derived from the erosion of the Andes. Whilst these deposits are mainly the result of fluvial deposition there is evidence that some are lacustrine in origin. It is probable that the proto-Amazon flowed westwards, but as the fold-

mountains were formed in the west, the drainage was ponded back. It eventually became reversed as the Amazon found an outlet to the newly formed Atlantic Ocean, via a downfaulted rift. Thus, the sedimentary basin is narrower in the east near the mouth of the river. Diagram **1.4** illustrates the major structural features of the drainage basin and in particular shows the downwarping within the rift caused by the weight of sediments which have accumulated over many millions of years. Deposition is still rapid today, as the Amazon carries an estimated suspended load of 1.3 million tonnes per day. At its mouth the weight of sediments is great and causes crustal subsidence over a wide area (see **1.2**). This in part explains the lack of a true delta, but the redistribution of sediments by longshore drift to the north-west is the major factor; it is also responsible for the depositional coast of the Guianas to the north-west.

Along its longest tributary, which has its source above 5 000 m in the Peruvian Andes, the Amazon flows 7 200 km to the Atlantic. Its course within Brasil has an extremely shallow gradient, in the order of 1 in 100 000 over 3 200 km. The drainage

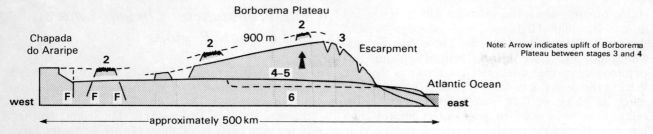

1.3. Diagrammatic Section across North-east Brasil.

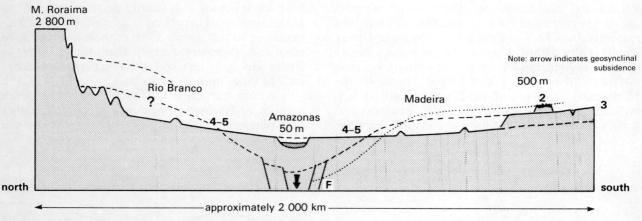

1.4. Diagrammatic Section across the Amazon Basin.

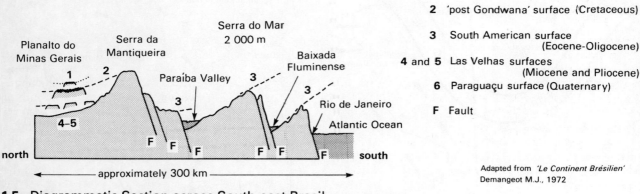

1.5. Diagrammatic Section across South-east Brasil.

1   Gondwana surface (Triassic/Jurassic)

2   'post Gondwana' surface (Cretaceous)

3   South American surface
        (Eocene-Oligocene)

4 and 5   Las Velhas surfaces
        (Miocene and Pliocene)

6   Paraguaçu surface (Quaternary)

F   Fault

Adapted from *'Le Continent Brésilien'*
Demangeot M.J., 1972

basin is much larger than the sedimentary basin, and includes large areas of the *planalto* in the states of Mato Grosso do Norte, Goiás and Pará. That part of the drainage basin within Brasil accounts for about fifty-six per cent of national territory and contains seventeen tributaries over 1 600 km in length.

A major characteristic of the river is its great depth, over 100 m in its lower reaches. Thus it is tidal as far west as the Xingu confluence, and is navigable by 10 000-tonne ships as far as Manaus, and 4 000-tonne ships to Iquitos in Peru. It results from channel entrenchment during the glacial periods of the Pleistocene, when sea level was considerably lower, and the phenomenal discharge which averages 160 000 m³ per second.

The present regime of the Amazon is complex. The drainage basin is so large that it contains regions of varying annual rainfall, and there are variations in the duration, severity and seasonality of the dry season. The Andean tributaries have a relatively stable regime, whilst the southern tributaries, rising in the Brasilian Highlands, experience a 'winter' drought of three to four months. The northern shortest tributaries, rising in the Guiana Highlands, experience a 'spring' drought. The result is that the level of the river fluctuates; at Manaus the range is as much as 12 m, so that floating quays and flexible ramps have to be used. In recent years deforestation has also affected the regime, increasing and speeding up surface run-off, and causing flooding.

Brasil's two other major river systems are the Paraná and São Francisco, whose basins account for 10.5 per cent and 7.4 per cent of Brasil's territory respectively. The São Francisco is the largest river wholly within Brasil; like the Paraná it has a highly seasonal regime, but it is even more extreme because it flows through Brasil's semi-arid region in the North-east. The uses of Brasil's rivers are varied, including irrigation, hydro-electricity, transport and fishing. These aspects are discussed in later chapters.

The Troposphere: Climatic Controls and Climate Regions

Over ninety per cent of Brasil's territory lies within tropical latitudes and experiences mean annual temperatures above 22°C, but there are considerable regional and local variations in climate and weather. In the temperate south the mean annual temperature range varies from 16° to 20°C, contrasting with the equatorial region where it is below 1°C in places. Latitude is not the only factor affecting temperature. In the South-east in particular, altitude modifies temperature, so that above 1 000 m there is a true *zona temperada* (temperate zone). However, nowhere in Brasil are there marked altitudinal climatic zones such as those in the high Andes.

Within tropical Brasil, spatial variations in the amount and seasonal incidence of rainfall, rather than temperature variations, have the greatest effect

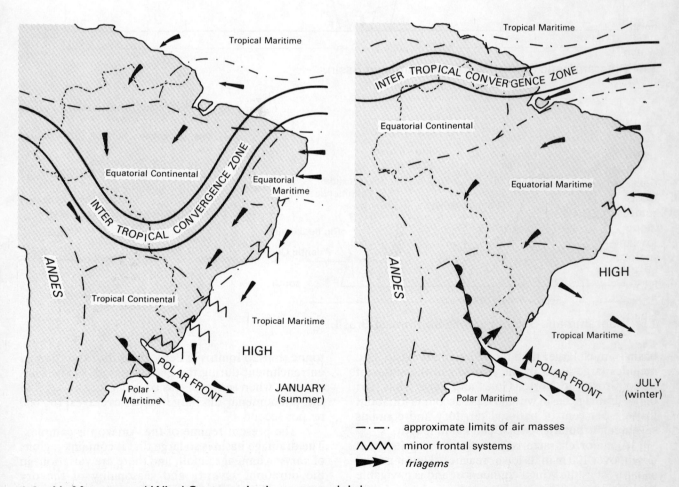

1.6. Air Masses and Wind Systems in January and July.

on human activity. This is true even in parts of the equatorial region.

The Andean cordillera forms an effective barrier within the troposphere, so that the effects of Pacific air masses are excluded. Brasil's climates are therefore chiefly affected by only three major air masses, as shown by **1.6**. The western interior region of Amazonia is dominated by the relatively static and unstable equatorial continental air mass, and consequently this region experiences little seasonal variation. Eastern Brasil is affected by the seasonal movements of the inter-tropical convergence zone, and the sympathetic movements of the equatorial maritime and tropical maritime air masses. The movement of this equatorial low-pressure belt also determines the positions of the moisture-laden north-east and south-east trade winds.

In January the inter-tropical convergence zone bulges southwards over Brasil, so that western Amazonia is dominated by equatorial continental air whilst eastern Amazonia and the *planaltos* experience their rainy seasons. The coastal areas south of Salvador also experience a 'summer' rainfall maximum. In July the maritime air masses migrate northwards with the inter-tropical convergence zone, which then straddles the Guiana Highlands. Much of Brasil is now dominated by the equatorial maritime air mass. The interior and south-east plateaus experience a 'winter' drought, though this is less severe towards the Atlantic coast. The temperate south has well distributed rainfall throughout the year. In the 'winter', polar maritime air migrates northwards over Argentina, and occasionally cold waves migrate northwards from the polar front. These *friagems* frequently cause temperature inversion and killing frosts. The southern plateau—*Planalto Meridional*—retards the cold waves so that they are channelled along the coast, and more significantly, along the lowlands of the Paraná river basin. Frosts are a major hazard in the south, and in several years such as 1908, 1963, 1975 and 1976, have devastated the coffee plantations of northern Paraná state. The effects of this climatic hazard are discussed in Chapter 6.

The Causes of the Drought Hazard

Whilst much of the tropical plateau experiences a 'winter' drought from June to August, the semi-arid plateau of North-east Brasil—which has been designated the *Poligono das Secas* (Drought Polygon)—has an annual rainfall less than 1 000 mm. At the dry core, annual rainfall is less than 500 mm. Here rainfall is not only low but also unreliable from year to year. It frequently occurs as short torrential showers which cause flash-floods. The droughts have had a catastrophic effect on the inhabitants of this *sertão*

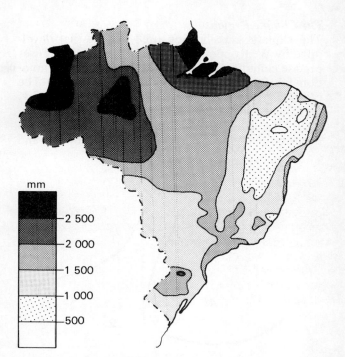

mm

— 2 500

— 2 000

— 1 500

— 1 000

—500

1.7. Average Annual Rainfall.

region. They have disrupted agricultural colonies, caused famine, malnutrition and death, and have frequently forced the survivors—the *flagellados* (beaten ones)—to abandon their farms and to migrate to the already overcrowded cities of the coastal zone.

The factors responsible for this anomalous semi-arid climate are complex. The major cause is that the 'hump' of North-east Brasil projects eastwards into the South Atlantic high pressure system, much further than is the case with other equivalent regions. Thus, the North-east plateau is greatly affected by the stable descending air of this anticyclonic system. This is even the case in 'summer' when much of the interior experiences its rainy season, and the polygon receives most of its limited annual rainfall. The anticyclone, though weaker in summer, persists in the North-east, so that as the inter-tropical convergence zone migrates south in 'summer', it is retarded over the semi-arid region. Thus, the polygon never comes directly under the influence of unstable maritime air masses. This explanation is supported by the fact that 'spring', the period of maximum aridity, is the very time when the anticyclone is strongest over the region.

The coastal area between Cape São Roque and Fortaleza (see **9.5**) is also semi-arid and within the *Poligono das Secas*. It is clear, therefore, that the drought is not primarily the result of orographic influences.

The Climate Regions

The climatic classification used here is that developed by W. Köppen. It is quantitative in that it uses precise climatic data, and employs a shorthand notation for the climate regions as shown by **1.8**. The capital letters A, B and C refer to Tropical rainy, Dry, and Temperate rainy climates respectively, whilst the other letters are the initials of German terms referring to the seasonal incidence of rain and seasonal temperatures. The major characteristics of the climates are as follows:

Af—the humid tropical climate of western Amazonia, with no dry season.

Am—Humid tropical with a short dry season. These 'equatorial' climates experience little or no seasonal variation, the diurnal temperature range being

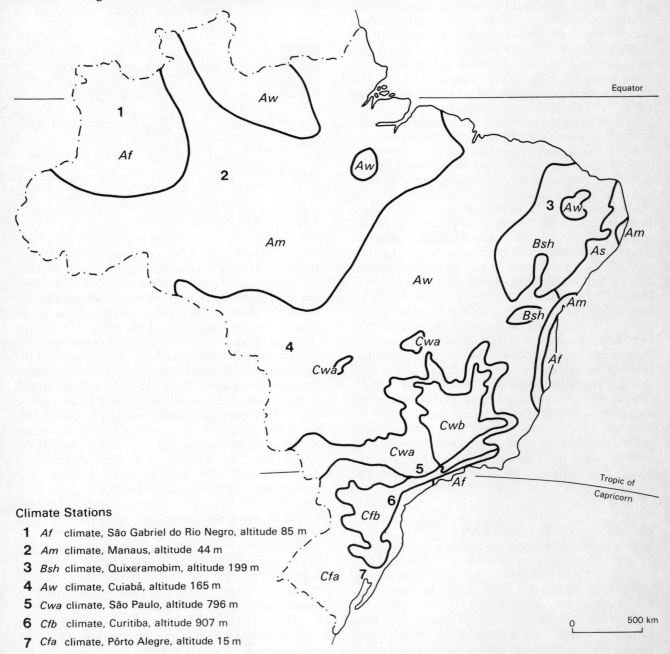

Climate Stations

1 *Af* climate, São Gabriel do Rio Negro, altitude 85 m

2 *Am* climate, Manaus, altitude 44 m

3 *Bsh* climate, Quixeramobim, altitude 199 m

4 *Aw* climate, Cuiabá, altitude 165 m

5 *Cwa* climate, São Paulo, altitude 796 m

6 *Cfb* climate, Curitiba, altitude 907 m

7 *Cfa* climate, Pôrto Alegre, altitude 15 m

1.8. Climate Regions after W.Köppen, and Selected Climatic Statistics. (See text for explanation of notation).

greater than the average annual temperature range in many places. Annual rainfall exceeds 2 000 mm, except in part of Pará state which has a dry season (see **1.7**). Rainfall results from convectional downpours in the early afternoon when evapotranspiration is greatest. Rapidly ascending thermals of hot air carry water vapour to very high altitudes, forming massive cumulo-nimbus clouds which cause torrential showers. The rain-forest has a considerable effect on rainfall; it has been estimated that up to fifty per cent of total rainfall results from recycling of moisture by evapo-transpiration. The *Af* and *Am* climates also occur along parts of the Atlantic coastal region where aspect is important, as the great escarpment and coastal mountain ranges concentrate the rainfall associated with the trade winds.

As—The humid tropical, dry 'summer', climate of much of the North-east coast north of Salvador.

Aw—The tropical continental humid climate, with a marked dry season in 'winter', which dominates much of the tropical highlands. Annual rainfall varies from 1 000 mm to over 2 000 mm. The effectiveness of rain in raising soil moisture content is greatly reduced by rapid surface run-off and high rates of evaporation.

Bsh—The semi-arid tropical climate of the North-east plateau, where annual rainfall is below 1 000 mm, and which experiences severe droughts.

Cw—The *Cwa* and *Cwb* climates are the humid subtropical or warm climates, with dry winters. They are those of the highlands in the South-east where altitude lowers temperatures. The '*a*' type has hot rainy summers, whereas the '*b*' type has cool rainy summers, the latter being at higher altitudes.

Cf—The *Cfa* and *Cfb* climates are those predominantly in sub-tropical latitudes. They are both humid and warm, with no dry season. The '*a*' type occurs in lowland areas which have hot summers whereas the '*b*' type occurs on the southern plateau which has cool summers.

The Biosphere

Soil moisture content is probably the most significant single factor affecting plant growth, and also has a major role in soil development. It is therefore essential to discover the spatial patterns and variations in soil moisture. The extreme contrasts in moisture regimes are shown by **1.10**; Taracuá within the *Af* climate region has a wholly humid regime, whilst Soledade within the *Bsh* climate is almost entirely dry. The temperature and rainfall scales on the graphs have been calibrated so that the mean monthly rainfall and temperature curves can be compared one with the other to define the moisture regimes.

Of fundamental importance are the number of 'botanically dry' days in the year. Gaussen has developed a 'xerothermal index' to quantify this, and this is mapped in **1.9**. The map is very effective in explaining variations in vegetation because climate and vegetation regions rarely coincide exactly. Vegetation is also affected by factors other than climate, such as landscape, rock-type, altitude, aspect, and human activity.

Spatial variations within the biosphere are generally gradual rather than abrupt, so that many major vegetational types grade into marginal types. This is the case with both of Brasil's major ecosystems—the *selva* rain-forest and the *campos*

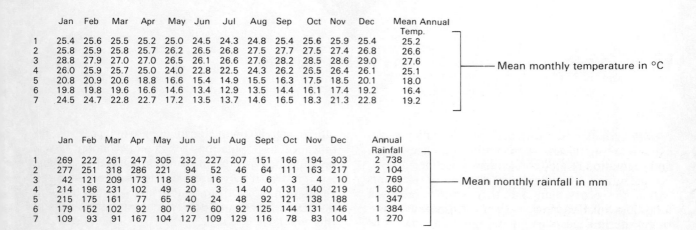

	Jan	Feb	Mar	Apr	May	Jun	Jul	Aug	Sep	Oct	Nov	Dec	Mean Annual Temp.
1	25.4	25.6	25.5	25.2	25.0	24.5	24.3	24.8	25.4	25.6	25.9	25.4	25.2
2	25.8	25.9	25.8	25.7	26.2	26.5	26.8	27.5	27.7	27.5	27.4	26.8	26.6
3	28.8	27.9	27.0	27.0	26.5	26.1	26.6	27.6	28.2	28.5	28.6	29.0	27.6
4	26.0	25.9	25.7	25.0	24.0	22.8	22.5	24.3	26.2	26.5	26.4	26.1	25.1
5	20.8	20.9	20.6	18.8	16.6	15.4	14.9	15.5	16.3	17.5	18.5	20.1	18.0
6	19.8	19.8	19.6	16.6	14.6	13.4	12.9	13.5	14.4	16.1	17.4	19.2	16.4
7	24.5	24.7	22.8	22.7	17.2	13.5	13.7	14.6	16.5	18.3	21.3	22.8	19.2

Mean monthly temperature in °C

	Jan	Feb	Mar	Apr	May	Jun	Jul	Aug	Sept	Oct	Nov	Dec	Annual Rainfall
1	269	222	261	247	305	232	227	207	151	166	194	303	2 738
2	277	251	318	286	221	94	52	46	64	111	163	217	2 104
3	42	121	209	173	118	58	16	5	6	3	4	10	769
4	214	196	231	102	49	20	3	14	40	131	140	219	1 360
5	215	175	161	77	65	40	24	48	92	121	138	188	1 347
6	179	152	102	92	80	76	60	92	125	144	131	146	1 384
7	109	93	91	167	104	127	109	129	116	78	83	104	1 270

Mean monthly rainfall in mm

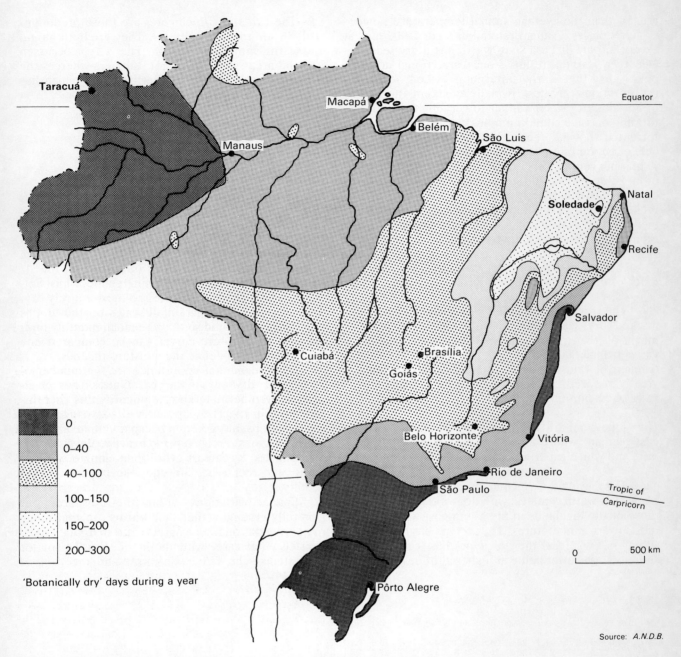

■	0
(grey)	0–40
(dotted)	40–100
(light)	100–150
(dotted)	150–200
(white)	200–300

'Botanically dry' days during a year

1.9. Brasil's Dry and Humid Areas: Gaussen's 'Xerothermal Index'.

Source: *A.N.D.B.*

cerrado grasslands. However, on a smaller scale, catenas are significant; these are local changes in soil and vegetation related to the factors outlined above.

Diagram **1.11** illustrates the major elements within the ecosystem, and the possible feedback loops and linkages between them. In different ecosystems the linkages vary in strength. The effects of

human activity on the biosphere are of increasing significance, as population growth and economic development increase the pressure on natural resources. Even in Brasil there are today few areas of 'natural' vegetation, apart from remote areas of rain-forest in Amazonia. These effects will be discussed later in this chapter.

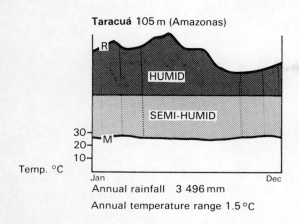

Taracuá 105 m (Amazonas)

HUMID

SEMI-HUMID

Temp. °C

Annual rainfall   3 496 mm

Annual temperature range 1.5 °C

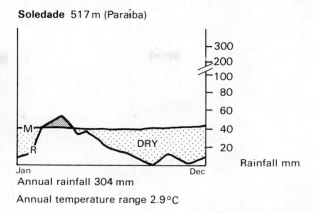

Soledade 517 m (Paraíba)

DRY

Rainfall mm

Annual rainfall 304 mm

Annual temperature range 2.9 °C

M – mean monthly temperature curve
R – monthly rainfall curve

Note: see 1.9 for location of climate stations

Source: *A.N.D.B.*

1.10. Contrasts Between Humid North-west Amazonia and the Semi-Arid North-east.

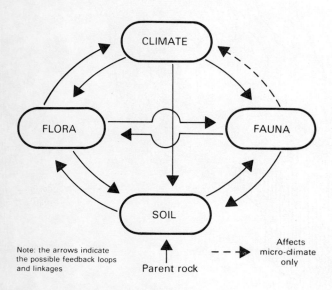

Note: the arrows indicate
the possible feedback loops
and linkages

Parent rock

Affects
micro-climate
only

1.11. A Simple Ecosystem Model.

The Selva *Ecosystem*

The Amazon basin contains the world's greatest and least modified tropical rain-forest. Its latitudinal position enabled it to survive the major effects of the Pleistocene glacial periods, though the lower sea levels must have had an effect on the water-table. So great is its 'biomass' (quantity of organic material) and so rapid the rates of photosynthesis, that it has been estimated that it may contribute as much as fifty per cent of the world's atmospheric oxygen. The survival of the forest also owes much to the low human population density of the region, and the agricultural practices of the Amerindian inhabitants. Their activi-

ties are in sympathy with the delicate ecological mechanisms which maintain the balance of nature within the forest.

The *selva* (rain-forest) displays considerable botanical diversity. Over ninety per cent of the flowering plants are evergreen trees, and there are over 2 500 species of these alone. The *selva* on *terra firme* (dry land) is typically stratified, consisting of three or more foliar layers as shown by **1.13**. The fauna of the forest is just as diverse, and many animal species are so highly adapted that they live entirely within a single foliar layer. Emergent trees are typically straight and slender, with buttressed lower trunks for support as they are mostly shallow-rooted. They are highly adapted to the search for light, with wide canopies. They are also adapted to the hot, wet climate as their leaves are very broad so as to maximise transpiration, and often have 'drip tips' which shed rainfall quickly. The main canopy is virtually continuous, with interlocking crowns, but the lower crowns are conical or strongly tapered because of the limited light. From about 5 to 10 metres above the forest floor there is a dense canopy formed by the crowns of saplings and shrubs. Beneath this the levels of sunlight are so low that there is little growth on the forest floor. It is littered with the rapidly decomposing remains of vegetable matter. Within the forest are many other plants. These include climbers, such as the lianes; epiphytes, such as orchids, which grow on the trees but do not feed on them; parasitic plants; and saprophytes, such as fungi, which live on decaying organic matter. Many plants produce toxic chemicals as defensive mechanisms, and some are sources of drugs such as quinine and cortisone. Because of the great variety of species, dif-

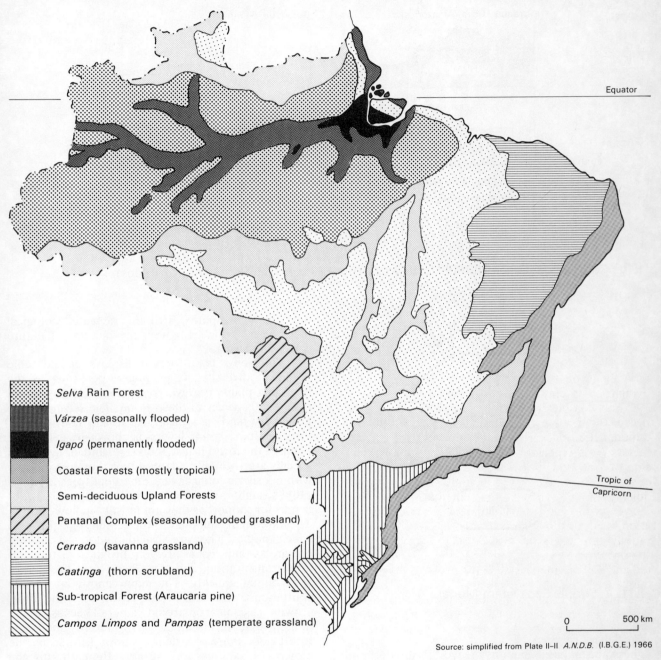

Selva Rain Forest

Várzea (seasonally flooded)

Igapó (permanently flooded)

Coastal Forests (mostly tropical)

Semi-deciduous Upland Forests

Pantanal Complex (seasonally flooded grassland)

Cerrado (savanna grassland)

Caatinga (thorn scrubland)

Sub-tropical Forest (Araucaria pine)

Campos Limpos and Pampas (temperate grassland)

Equator

Tropic of Capricorn

0   500 km

Source: simplified from Plate II–II *A.N.D.B.* (I.B.G.E.) 1966

1.12. Vegetation.

fering nutrient requirements, and the intense competition for space and light, individual species do not grow together in 'stands', but are usually dispersed. Stands only occur where there are atypical soils, or in areas with a marked dry season.

The luxuriant *selva* vegetation is almost entirely the result of the lack of seasons and the resulting continuous growth in a constantly humid environment. It has little to do with the underlying soils. The *selva* 'latosols' are strongly leached by groundwater, which

removes the soluble minerals and nutrients. The soils are strongly acidic, and often contain a lateritic horizon composed of sesquioxides of iron and aluminium. This massive compact laterite can be up to 10 metres thick, and it effectively limits root growth and drainage when fully developed. The vegetation is maintained by rainwater-borne elements, such as nitrogen, calcium, iron and phosphorus, and by a direct nutrient cycle involving the decaying forest litter. N. Stark (1970) has shown that fungi and bac-

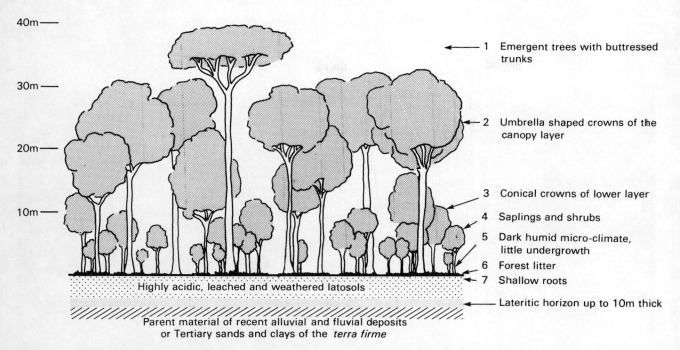

40m—

30m—

20m—

10m—

← 1 Emergent trees with buttressed trunks

← 2 Umbrella shaped crowns of the canopy layer

3 Conical crowns of lower layer

4 Saplings and shrubs

5 Dark humid micro-climate, little undergrowth

6 Forest litter

← 7 Shallow roots

Highly acidic, leached and weathered latosols

← Lateritic horizon up to 10m thick

Parent material of recent alluvial and fluvial deposits or Tertiary sands and clays of the *terra firme*

1.13. A Diagrammatic Representation of the *Selva* and Underlying Latosols.

teria living on the litter pass nutrients directly to living root systems.

The complexity of the *selva* is even greater because of internal and marginal variations and gradations. Internal variations result from two major factors. Some species became isolated by the extension of grasslands into the *selva* during the Pleistocene period, and failed to colonise the grasslands quickly enough when normal conditions returned. However, the major factor influencing internal variation is low soil-moisture levels, caused either by rapidly draining sandy soils or by a marked dry season. Where these occur, the forest cover is depleted and there is an increase in the proportion of deciduous trees, shrubs and grasses. There are several examples of such areas, including the *cerrado* grasslands which have developed on wet 'hydromorphic' latosols, north of the Amazon river in the state of Pará.

The major variations in the *selva* are marginal rather than internal. There is an infinite variety because of gradual as well as abrupt changes. However, several major types can be recognised.

Along the courses of major rivers more complex vegetational distributions occur. These are the result of the greater sunlight, the soil variations on the seasonally flooded *várzea* floodplain, and the variations produced by a rapidly changing drainage pattern. Generally, ground cover is denser, and the density of trees is much reduced. Many tree species are highly adapted to the *várzea* swamplands, with respiratory

aerial root systems which support the short trunk above flood level. In some places on the floodplain, true grasslands occur, known as the *campinas de várzea;* they are very well developed in the area south-west of the Amazon–Xingu confluence. East of this area, around the mouths of the Amazon and Tocantins rivers, the floodplains experience river and tidal flooding. Here, the effects of the Amazon 'bore'—the *pororoca*—are very important. It is caused by the counter-effects of the river discharge and spring tides. The wall of sea-water can reach a height of 10 m above river level, and has a devastating effect on the floodplain. In this region the typical vegetation type is the *igapó* swamp forest, a virtually impenetrable chaotic jumble of trunks, climbers and floating plant debris. Many plants are adapted to the brackish water, whilst others are less salt-tolerant. In predominantly salt-water coastal environments, a *mangue* (mangrove) vegetation develops. This is similar to the *igapó* in many ways, with aerial root adaptations. However, the *mangue* does not have to cope with the *pororoca*, only with tidal changes. Regular tidal flooding restricts methods of plant reproduction, so that many trees propagate by developing saplings from lateral root systems under the mud-flats. In many places a succession of plants is discernible, with 'pioneer' species along the seaward edge. These are capable of extending the mud-flats by accretion. Further inland, accretion eventually results in a change first to brackish water, and then to freshwater swamp.

Plate 2. The *selva* rain-forest. This oblique aerial view of the *selva* illustrates the continuous canopy which characterises much of the *terra firme* of the Amazon Basin. **J. Allan Cash Ltd.**

The boundary between the *selva* and *cerrado* grasslands is highly irregular. There is usually a gradual transition from evergreen rain-forest to semi-evergreen forest, through deciduous seasonal forest, and eventually to grassland. The transition involves a reduction in tree stratification and density, a change to deciduous species, and an increase in shrubs and grasses. The reduction in the biomass is considerable. Along the major rivers, *galeria* (tunnel) forest penetrates the *cerrado*, particularly along the rivers Araguaia and Tocantins. The term *galeria* is very appropriate because in places the crowns of trees on both banks interlock to form a tunnel of foliage.

On the flanks of the Andes in many South American countries, a montane forest develops with increasing altitude. However, in Brasil this is rarely the case because variations in altitude are not so great. There are, however, similar gradations in parts of the state of Acre, and occasionally on the flanks of the higher *planaltos*. The effects are broadly similar to those brought about by a dry season, but

evergreen trees predominate, and occasionally different species are involved such as mosses and giant shrubs.

The Cerrado Ecosystem

The tropical grassland ecosystem exhibits even greater spatial diversity than the *selva*. The *cerrado* has a much smaller biomass and generally consists of varying proportions of deciduous trees, grasses and sedges. It is generally found in areas with a drought of from two and a half to five months duration, but its distribution does not correlate precisely with any climatic characteristic. Theories attempting to explain the nature and distribution of the *cerrado* are controversial.

Goodland (1970) outlines three major factors that could explain the characteristics of the *cerrado*, but he also adds that once established, the *cerrado* could be maintained by other factors.

The 'climatic theory' is now largely discredited because *cerrado* is found in several different climatic regions such as Köppen's *Aw* and *Cfb* types.

Plate 3. The *cerrado*. This view of the *cerrado* in the Federal District shows the scattered trees, and ground cover of grasses and sedges. ***Tony Morrison.***

However, the seasonality of rainfall must be significant. Most species were initially considered to be 'xerophytic', i.e. highly adapted to the drought, but recently many researchers have cast doubt on this. Many tree species are very deep rooted, and such is the slow downward percolation of water on the *planaltos* that these trees may receive most of their ground moisture from four to six months after the rainy season.

The 'anthropic theory', which emphasises the role of man's activities, has gained considerable support. In many savanna regions man has had a considerable effect through pastoralism, silviculture, deforestation, cultivation and burning. Whilst grazing and burning need not necessarily be the result of human activity, there is no doubt that the *cerrado* has been extensively burned by the Amerindian for centuries. It is a means of encouraging the growth of grasses and is still a common practice today, even in areas of commercial farming. The main period of burning is from June to September, at the end of the dry season; burning destroys the seeds

of annual plants and the lowest branches and foliage of trees, and it forms a layer of sooty ash which is rich in nutrients. Many trees show evidence of being adapted to burning; one type in particular has a sinuous subterranean trunk from which the branches grow vertically upwards. Many species are woody and thorny, and are protected from burning and grazing.

The 'edaphic theory', which emphasises the correlation between *cerrado* vegetation types and varying soil types, has most support. It has been lent particular weight by detailed studies, which have shown great local variations in the *cerrado* to be the result of changes in landscape, lithology and related soils.

As previously stated, the *planaltos* are the product of several cycles of pediplanation over many millions of years. Consequently, the soils are generally degraded. They are mainly ferruginous and weathered ferrallitic latosols, consisting of red and yellow clays and sands. They are moderately acidic, and are lacking in humus and nutrients such as phosphates and nitrates. These coarse textured 'auto-morphic' plateau soils contrast with the 'hydromorphic' soils along watercourses. Near rivers, 'gley' soils predominate; these are grey clays subjected to either permanent or seasonal waterlog-ging.

The *cerrado* soils, therefore, seem to offer the best explanation of the *cerrado*'s characteristics, whilst burning would seem to be the major factor in maintaining the ecosystem.

1.14. A Catena in the *Cerrado*, showing landscape-soil-vegetation relationships.

The great variations in soils and vegetation within the *cerrado* can best be explained by reference to a typical catena, as shown in **1.14**. A catena illus-trates the effects of landscape and slopes on soil de-velopment, and can also be used to show the relationship between these and vegetation. The diagram is self-explanatory, but it is worth emphasis-ing the salient points. The densest forest—the *mata*—is only found on the scarps where active erosion is taking place. This produces young soils, relatively rich in nutrients and with a high moisture content. On the *planalto* there is a general succession from dry to relatively wet forms: from *Campo limpo*, a completely open grassland with no trees; to *Campo sujo*, with scattered trees; to *Campo cerrado*, with more complete tree cover; to *cerradão*, where tree cover is over fifty per cent. The major factor increas-ing the proportion of trees towards the scarp edge is ground-moisture content. On the *planalto*, laterites and duricrusts restrict ground-water percolation; but near the scarp edge, the steeper slopes and the influence of the scarp in lowering the water-table result in rapid ground-water movement.

As has been shown, contrasts between the *selva* and *cerrado* are considerable, and each offers very different potentials for human activity. The great contrasts between the nutrient cycles are shown by **1.15**.

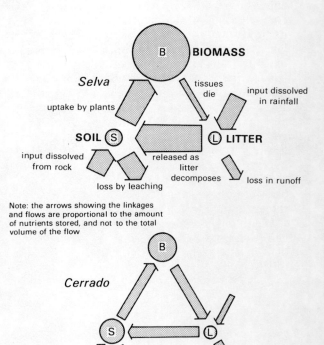

After Hilton (1979), based on Ghersmehl (1976)

1.15. The Contrasting Nutrient Cycles of the *Selva* and *Cerrado*.

The Caatinga

The semi-arid plateau of the North-east has a unique tropical thorn scrub vegetation, referred to as the *caatinga*. The low and unreliable rainfall results in xerophytic species such as cacti, 'bottle' trees, shrubs such as mimosa, and palm trees in the moister areas. The term *caatinga* literally means 'white bush'. The region is a parched upland, with bare rock pavements and coarse soils which are for the most part saline. Only on the low damp areas on the floodplains of seasonal streams—the *vazante* regions—does green predominate.

The palms are used intensively by the *Nord-estinos*. The Carnauba palm supplies a great variety of useful materials, such as the hard white wax yielded by the young shoots which is used as a primer for polished wood. The palm is also used for timber and thatching. The Babaçu palm yields a very high quality vegetable oil.

The *caatinga* has been vividly described by Euclides da Cunha in *Os Sertoẽs* (1902):

'The *caatinga* stifles the traveller; it cuts short his view, strikes him in the face, stuns him, enmeshes him in its spiny woof, and holds out no compensating attractions. It repulses him with its thorns and prickly leaves, its twigs sharp as lances; it stretches out in front of him, for mile on mile, unchanging in its desolate aspect of leafless trees, of dried and twisted boughs, a turbulent maze of vegetation standing rigidly in space or spreading sinuously along the ground all having the same appearance of moribund vegetable growths. The sun is the enemy whom it is urgent to avoid, to elude, or to combat; the burning air is sterilised, the ground parched and cleft becomes petrified . . . and like a lacerating haircloth, the *caatinga* extends over the earth its thorny branches.

Climb any elevation whatsoever and let your gaze wander, and it will encounter the same desolate scene: a shapeless mass of vegetation, the life drained from it, writhing in a painful spasm.'

Plate 4. The *caatinga.* This view of the open caatinga of Northern Bahia illustrates the discontinuous ground cover, thorny scrubland and xerophytic species. ***Dr. P. A. Furley.***

Southern Brasil

Whilst the *cerrado* extends southwards into northern Minas Gerais, much of the vegetation of the Southeast was originally semi-deciduous upland forest, though much of this forest and the tropical maritime forest of the coastal plains has now been deforested (see **6.1**). The well distributed rainfall of the *planalto meridional*—south of the Tropic of Capricorn— results in a humid sub-tropical mixed forest, dominated by the Paraná pine (*Araucaria angustofolia*). This *Pinheiras* region is the nation's most exploited source of timber. Along the Serra Geral, which marks the edge of the plateau, higher rainfall results in a sub-tropical rain-forest; this type of forest is also found on the coastal lowlands.

South of the plateau, lower altitudes and higher latitude results in a change to temperate grasslands similar to the pampas of Argentina and Uruguay. The region is called the *Campanha*. It has silty soils, rich in humus which support high quality grazing land.

The Management of the Biosphere

Whilst the potential for the development of the biosphere is great, the management of the complex and delicate mechanisms within the ecosystems must involve the use of appropriate methods and technologies. However, Brasil has a long history of ecological mismanagement which in extreme cases has caused irreversible damage.

Ecological research in the tropics is still in its infancy, and only relatively small areas of the biosphere have been mapped in detail. The low density interaction between the Amerindian and early colonists with the biosphere had little effect, but through the nineteenth and twentieth centuries the pressure has increased.

Massive deforestation in the east, especially in the Paraíba valley and near Belém, to clear land for coffee and food crops respectively, resulted in severe soil erosion and soil exhaustion. Similarly, the sugar lands along the north-east have suffered from centuries of monocropping.

Even more disturbing than this is the exploitation and colonisation of the *selva*. Goodland and Irwin (1975) believe that the *selva* could be transformed from, 'green hell to red desert'. Since the mid 1960s, Amazonia has suffered considerable deforestation as a result of a number of pressures, including the exploitation of newly discovered mineral reserves, speculative road construction programmes, and the establishment of vast cattle ranches. Some areas to be cleared were so vast that illegal napalm bombing was used.

Small-scale deforestation can seriously deplete the animal and insect populations which maintain ecological equilibrium, but massive deforestation can have even more serious repercussions. It could result in a decrease in atmospheric oxygen and a corresponding increase in carbon dioxide; an increase in mean annual temperatures; a decrease in rainfall; an increase in surface run-off; and widespread soil exhaustion and erosion. Many of these could have global repercussions.

This theme will be expanded in later chapters, but it is appropriate to elaborate further at this stage. In 1975 alone, deforestation claimed an estimated four per cent of Amazonia's trees. In 1976, SUDAM—the development agency for Amazonia—licensed and helped finance the deforestation of 3.5 million hectares. In an attempt to conserve the *selva*, the Brasilian government introduced the 'fifty-percent forest rule', which required each colonist to preserve half his lot. This was widely violated; but even the rule itself is of dubious value, as it resulted in the isolation of small patches of forest and disrupted the internal balance within the forest. The forest became incapable of self-regeneration. The Amazonia experience has been that most small-scale projects have been highly successful, especially on the *várzea*, but many large-scale projects have proved less productive than envisaged.

Goodland and Irwin regard the large-scale development of Amazonia as unnecessary. They argue that, 'The *cerrado* is endowed with more amenable agricultural conditions ... and that ... conventional agriculture in the *cerrado* is even now at least as

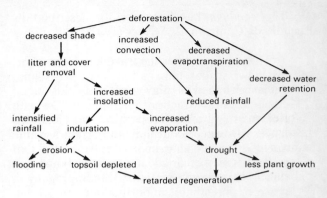

After Goodland, R.J.A. and Urwin, H.S. (1975)

1.16. The Environmental Disruption caused by Deforestation.

successful as in Amazonia ... requires less research ... and provokes less environmental damage'.

Unfortunately, the mismanagement of the *selva* is likely to continue; widespread human poverty deserves a higher priority in a developing country with limited means.

Accelerated research and investment is, however, vital. Following the UNESCO Conference on the Environment at Stockholm in 1972, the federal government selected a site in Mato Grosso do Norte for the establishment of Humboldt City. This is a research centre for experimental studies related to the occupation of virgin tropical areas. It is ideally located to study the *selva* and *cerrado*. Some long-term survey projects are in progress or are being planned, such as aerial infra-red photography of the entire *selva*, and constant remote sensing from a satellite in geo-synchronous orbit directly above Brasil.

The problem is 'time'. Currently, rates of exploitation and development are higher than rates of the discovery of new technologies and methods appropriate to tropical environments. Recently the Brasilian government in its third development plan has recognised the potential of the *cerrado*, and is now attempting to re-direct new colonisation towards the *cerrado* and away from the *selva*.

2 A Concise Historical Perspective

A brief analysis of Brasil's political and economic history is necessary to explain the root causes of many contemporary geographical patterns and processes, and in particular the contemporary regional imbalances in development.

The Colony

In 1494, six years before Admiral Pedro Alvares Cabral claimed the Brasilian coast for Portugal, the 'New World' was divided between Portugal and Spain by the Treaty of Tordesillas. Portugal received that part east of the meridian 370 leagues west of the Cape Verde Islands—which corresponds with longitude 48°W. The colony was first named 'Vera Cruz' and 'Santa Cruz', but then 'Brasil' after the first exploitable resource, the red dye-wood *pau-brasil*. Trading posts were established at several coastal sites, but by the mid-sixteenth century over-exploitation around these small ports had virtually exhausted the accessible reserves.

The first organised occupation of the coastal region began in the 1530s, in an attempt to consolidate Portuguese territorial claims and to exploit the resources of the colony. It was during this period that the first permanent towns were established, the first being São Vicente in 1532. They were strategically located at defensive coastal sites, and functioned as ports through which the primary products of their hinterlands were exported to Portugal. As Portugal was a relatively small country with limited wealth, the development of the colony was entrusted in 1534 to a number of hereditary captaincies granted to wealthy nobles (see **2.1.**). This policy failed and the Portuguese crown reassumed responsibility in 1594. Relics of the captaincies remain in the names and boundaries of some of Brasil's eastern states, particularly in the North-east.

In the mid-sixteenth century, sugar plantations were established along the coastal plain of the North-east—the *zona da mata*—which was the closest region to Portugal. The relatively few coastal Amerindians were enslaved to supply the labour. But the expansion of sugar-cane cultivation necessitated the import of African slave labour. An estimated 3 500 000 survived the passage; they were from diverse ethnic backgrounds, and included Islamic Sudanese groups as well as Bantu peoples.

The region became the world's major sugar producer for two centuries, its success resulting from the rich red clay *massapé* soils, and previous experience in sugar-cane production and slave labour on São Tome island. Salvador developed as the major port and administrative centre of the colony, and like most other colonial towns was planned around a centre *praça* (square), flanked by the churches and administrative buildings of the colonial elite. The architecture and decoration of these buildings was typically 'baroque' in style.

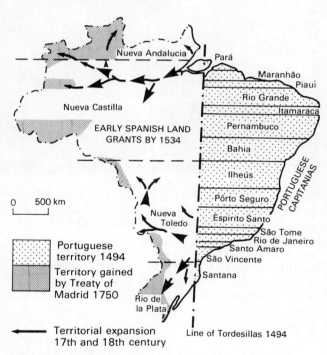

2.1. Colonial Brasil: Early Portuguese and Spanish Land Grants

The plantation system resulted in a strongly patriarchal society which was conservative, feudal and predominantly rural. It was controlled by the land-owner—the *senhor de engenho*. The *engenho* (plantation) was the economic and social focus of the colony, and thus the colony offered little opportunity for independent immigrants, or for innovation and technological improvement. The monocropping of the ratoon sugar-cane led to falling yields at a time

Plate 5. Ouro Prêto. Formerly the state capital of Minas Gerais, and the centre of the eighteenth century 'gold rush', the magnificent baroque architecture of Ouro Prêto is now preserved as a monument to colonial Brasil. ***J. Allan Cash Ltd.***

when the region faced increased competition from the plantations of the West Indies. This problem was aggravated by the Dutch invasions of the mid-seventeenth century. The *zona da mata* (forest zone) began to experience economic stagnation and widespread poverty—problems from which it has still not fully recovered.

Following the death of King Sebastião of Portugal, Philip II of Spain successfully claimed the Portuguese throne in 1580. The union of the Iberian kingdoms and their colonies for a period of sixty years had major repercussions, as the line of Tordesillas lost its significance. The union enabled Portuguese pioneers—*bandeirantes* (literally flag bearers)—to penetrate the interior from their bases at São Vicente and São Paulo. It was these expeditions which were responsible for extending Portuguese control over a large part of what is now the Central-west region of Brasil. Pedro Teixeira also claimed the Amazon for Portugal. Following the return of Portugal's independence under João IV in

1640, the new territories were claimed under the right of '*uti possidetis*', the right of useful possession.

Many of the *bandeirante* expeditions established temporary settlements which later became the sites for Brasil's first inland towns, but it was their discovery of gold at Ouro Prêto in the 1690s which transformed the economy of the colony. Thousands of colonists were lured from the coastal settlements, and during the following century an estimated 800 000 immigrants joined Brasil's 'gold-rush'. For the first time the colony offered opportunities for poor Portuguese immigrants. The temporary mining camps were replaced by a profusion of permanent settlements, and so numerous were the mines that the region became known as Minas Gerais (general mines). Vila Rica do Ouro Prêto became the colony's major settlement. Its baroque churches were lavishly decorated in gold leaf and by the soapstone sculptures of Aleijadinho (the little cripple). Ouro Prêto is now preserved as a monument to colonial Brasil.

The growth of Rio de Janeiro as a major port and commercial centre owed much to the gold exports, over which it had a monopoly. The easiest natural route to the coast along the Doce Valley was then blocked by hostile Amerindians, otherwise Rio would not have become the main outlet. Much of the gold was used to purchase textiles from Britain, a commitment of the Methuen Treaty of 1703. Rio's new wealth and rapid growth led to its replacing Salvador as the colonial capital in 1763, emphasising the shift in the colony's economic centre of gravity from the North-east to the South-east. However, the mining boom of Minas Gerais did not lead to industrial development, and so in the nineteenth century, when the boom was over, the region reverted to beef rearing which had developed during the boom to feed the mining regions.

In the second half of the eighteenth century Brasil's territory began to take on a more recognisable form, though it was still only about half its present area. Spain's main interest was the Andes, which provided both precious metals and a large Amerindian labour force. The Treaty of Madrid (1750) ceded Spanish rights to Amazonia, and the treaties of El Pardo (1761) and San Ildefonso (1777) consolidated Portuguese control over much of the territory claimed by the *bandeirantes*. The northern limits of the colony were well defined, following the watershed within the Guiana Highlands which effectively separated it from the British, Dutch and French Guiana colonies. To the west, the colony stretched to the foot-hills of the Andes, but in the south the temperate grasslands of the *pampas* were disputed. Eventually, Uruguay was established as a 'buffer' state between Brasil and Argentina.

By the end of the eighteenth century, the colony seemed to offer little potential for future development. The revenue from sugar and gold exports had not been used for investment in industry. In 1597 the first commercial iron works in the 'New World' had been established near Sorocaba (São Paulo state), and a number of charcoal-fired iron furnaces had been constructed in Minas Gerais. But the domestic market for their products was limited to the needs of mining and the plantations. A Portuguese decree—the *Alvara* of 1785—ordered the destruction of the colony's infant manufacturing industries in order to protect those of the 'mother' country, and the British monopoly of cotton textiles. When the *Alvara* was revoked in 1808, new furnaces were established in Minas Gerais using European technology and technicians. But within twelve years they had all closed. J. P. Dickenson (1962) attributes these early failures to the departure of the foreign iron-masters, an increasing shortage of timber, and the absence of a skilled indigenous labour force.

Brasil's Independence

Economic stagnation, and the limited opportunities offered by the colony towards the close of the eighteenth century, resulted in increasing political unrest and a growing nationalist movement. The most significant revolt was the Minas Conspiracy of 1789, which attempted to establish a republic in Minas Gerais. It was put down in 1792, and its leader Tiradentes (the 'tooth-puller') was executed. The transformation in the political status of the colony was not to be achieved through major internal pressures, but as a direct result of the Napoleonic Wars in Europe.

In 1808, King Dom João II of Portugal was forced to transfer his court from Lisbon to Rio to escape Napoleon's invasion of Portugal, and as a result Brasil became the only colony to gain some political superiority over its mother country. In 1815 Brasil became part of a united kingdom with Portugal. Following Dom João's return, Dom Pedro the prince regent initiated a number of political and economic reforms, and on 7th September 1822 he proclaimed the independence of the Brasilian Empire. Thus, in contrast with the Spanish colonies, Brasil had achieved political independence without bloody revolution, major political unrest, or territorial fragmentation.

Dom Pedro's control over the empire was short-lived, as he was increasingly opposed by the parliamentary government he established in 1824. His rule was further undermined by the war with Argentina, resulting in the loss of the territory in the south which is now Uruguay. In 1831 he abdicated in favour of his five-year-old son, Pedro de Alacantara. Pedro II's reign finally received parliamentary support in 1840, and resulted in immediate social and economic progress. The most significant of these was the abolition of the slave trade in the 1850s (though not of slavery itself) against the wishes of the élite plantation owners. Their conservatism and self-interest had been largely responsible for the deepening malaise and economic crisis in the sugar zone of the North-east. The crisis of the North-east was compounded in the late nineteenth century by the droughts of the *sertão* interior plateau, which had developed as a supplier of livestock. The *sertanejos* were accustomed to the region's unreliable and low rainfall, but the *grandes secas* (great droughts) of 1877 and 1879 ravaged the region, causing an estimated 500 000 deaths in Ceará alone. Many fled to the increasingly overcrowded cities of the coast.

However, the major economic developments of the nineteenth century affected new areas of the empire. From 1850 to 1910, Amazonia experienced a short-lived rubber boom. This fragile boom was

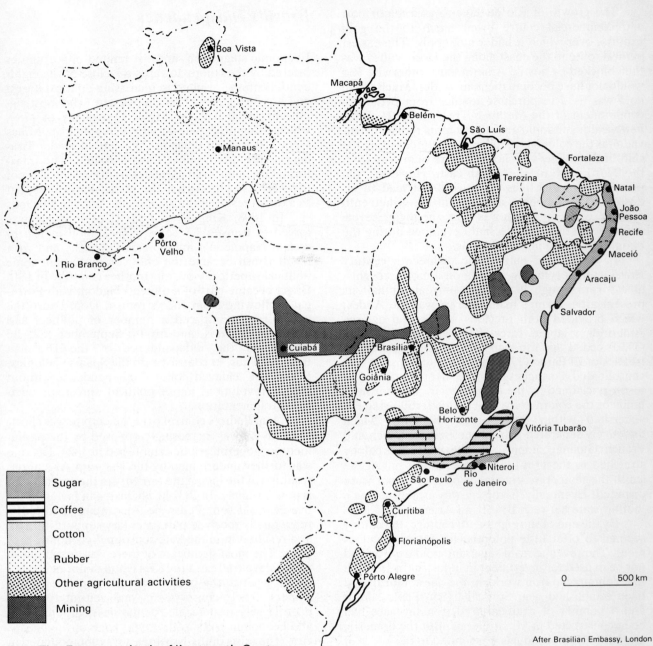

Sugar

Coffee

Cotton

Rubber

Other agricultural activities

Mining

After Brasilian Embassy, London

2.2. The Economy in the Nineteenth Century.

based on the exploitation of widely-spaced wild rubber trees, and cheap labour from the North-east. The lack of planned development resulted in the collapse of the region once rubber plantations had been established in South-east Asia, and Amazonia reverted to an economic backwater. Coffee cultivation was introduced into the South-east early in the nineteenth century and, as soon as it spread to the fertile *terra roxa* (red earth) soils of the São Paulo plateau in the 1820s, it began to dominate the national economy. Its success led directly to the re-emergence

of the iron smelting industry, to supply the iron needed for the rapidly expanding rail network of São Paulo. However, the furnaces were still manned by slave labour, and still used the traditional direct-smelting process fired by charcoal. Coffee export revenues provided the investment necessary for further economic development, and the further expansion of coffee cultivation initiated several waves of immigration from Europe and Japan. An estimated five million immigrants entered Brasil from 1874 to 1957.

Tariff reforms were introduced to encourage the development of a domestic textiles industry. The first cotton mills were established in Bahia in 1844 to provide the coarse materials for the clothing industry which supplied the new immigrants. The industry was boosted by the decline of the cotton states of the Confederacy in the U.S.A., during and after the American civil war of 1861 to 1865. By 1881 there were forty-four mills in Brasil.

From the mid-nineteenth century, coffee exports contributed over sixty per cent of the total by value and led to the dramatic growth of São Paulo city. It began to emerge as the leading commercial and industrial centre, and reinforced the economic dominance of the South-east region. The temperate South also experienced agricultural development and immigration. Here, the colonisation of virgin lands was well organised and the farmscape was highly planned. German and Italian immigrants settled the southern plateau, and effectively diversified the agricultural sector by cultivating temperate crops, and by using new techniques. The southern *minifundio* (small farm) farmscape contrasted markedly with the *latifundio* (plantation/estate) farmscape of tropical Brasil.

The Republic and Twentieth Century Brasil

The collapse of the empire was caused by several factors, including the growing importance of the military, the unpopularity of the heiress to the throne, and the antagonisation of the clergy. But the single most important factor was the abolition of slavery in 1888, as the influential land-owners were not compensated for the loss of an estimated 700 000 emancipated slaves. In 1889 a military coup d'état was successful and the republic was declared on 15th November. The early years of the republic were a period of political turmoil, resulting from widespread opposition to the military leaders who had adopted dictatorial powers. A further military revolt lasted from 1893 to 1895, and this was followed by the revolt of the *sertanejos* led by the religious fanatic Antonio Conselheiro. This ended with the massacre of the group at the village of Canudos in 1897. It was this revolt that inspired one of Brasil's greatest literary works—*Os Sertões*—by Euclides da Cunha, from which the quotation in Chapter 1 was taken.

Plate 6.   The Opera House at Manaus. This was the symbol of the wealth generated by the nineteenth century rubber boom of Amazonia. Manaus is today experiencing another boom because of its 'free port' and tourism.   *Tony Morrison.*

The first republic lasted until 1930. It was a period of financial crisis, which began with the disruption of the plantation system in the North-east caused by the massive drift of the emancipated negro population to the coastal cities. The crisis was compounded by the disruption of world trade during and after the First World War. This period was also characterised by a wave of economic nationalism, strengthened by industrial growth which gradually gained momentum. At the end of the nineteenth century, industrial growth had been stimulated by protective tariffs and currency devaluations. These measures, coupled with the importance of coffee export revenues, further strengthened the industrial dominance of the South-east, although it did not result in much diversification of industry. By 1919 there were over 13 000 industrial establishments as compared with 636 in 1889.

These early attempts to achieve economic independence were centred on the development of food processing and textiles production, but the iron and steel industry also expanded. Brasil's first ingot steel was produced in 1917, and in 1925 South America's first 'integrated' steelworks was completed at Sabara near Belo Horizonte. By 1920, São Paulo had emerged as the leading industrial centre because of the investment of coffee revenues and the development of hydro-electricity stations at Cubatão at the foot of the great escarpment. The 1920 census shows that forty-seven per cent of the nation's industrial workers were employed in the food processing and textiles industries, and that the South-east contained over two-thirds of the industrial labour force. However, this period of industrial growth without true industrialisation had little effect on employment. The agricultural sector still employed over two-thirds of the total labour force, and the vast majority of the population lived as subsistence farmers in rural areas. The level of technology was still very low.

Outside the dominant centres of Rio and São Paulo, industrial growth was limited, although the iron smelting industry had begun to prosper in the *Quadrilátero Ferrífero* (Iron Quadrilateral) around Belo Horizonte. This was as a result of the area's high quality haematite iron ores, manganese ores, local supplies of charcoal and of the increased demand for iron, primarily as a result of railway construction. Equally important was the establishment of the Ouro Prêto School of Mines in 1876 which provided the first Brasilian technicians and technologists.

Throughout the late-nineteenth and early-twentieth centuries, coffee revenues were maintained at a high level. Fluctuations in the harvest caused by frosts and pests had little effect, as Brasil's monopolistic position enabled her to control world market prices. But in 1906 a massive harvest forced the government to initiate a 'valorisation' scheme; this involved the government purchasing a third of the harvest by means of a foreign loan which was repaid by 1914. Three valorisation schemes were necessary up to 1924, when a permanent control scheme was established.

The trade disruptions of the First World War, inflation, and the effects of the inter-war world depression, profoundly affected economic thought in Brasil. This led to political changes and the increased involvement of the government in economic development.

During the mid-1920s there was increased criticism of the constitution, mainly by the military. This culminated in the revolution of 1930 which ended the first republic. The 1930 election had failed to reflect the demands of the military, and Getulio Vargas, one of the military leaders seized power. Vargas initially attempted to increase democratic political representation, but widespread chronic poverty and financial crises led to clashes between extreme 'communist' and 'fascist' groups. In 1937 Vargas declared a state of emergency and, under the *Estado Novo* (New State) constitution, became a dictator. During the 1930s and early 1940s, he achieved a relatively stable political climate and significant advances were made not only in social welfare and education, but also in the growth and diversification of manufacturing industry. Vargas also increased the power of central government at the expense of the state governments, and transferred power from the rural aristocracy to the new urban élite.

From 1930 to 1945, Brasil lost its comparative advantage in coffee cultivation as Colombian and African producers increased their share of the world market. The equivalent of three years' coffee production had to destroyed when four massive harvests coincided with the great world depression of the 1930s. Coffee was dumped at sea, burned and even used to fuel locomotives. During the same period, industrial production expanded at an average annual rate of over five per cent but this growth was almost entirely concentrated in the South-east. São Paulo had attracted the great majority of recent skilled immigrants, had become the focus of domestic and foreign investment, and had developed into the major market. In contrast the North-east declined, and its share of industrial employment fell from 27 per cent in 1920 to 17 per cent in 1940.

Vargas was forced to resign by the military in 1945. Under the presidency of General Dutra, a new constitution was written which allowed representative democracy, a multi-party system and increased civil liberties. However, the military maintained their control as guarantors of the constitution. Dutra also attempted to improve the economy of the North-east, by initiating the first phase of the Paulo Afonso hydro-electricity project on the Rio São Francisco, and by linking the region to the South-east by a new highway. The new state steelworks was also inaugurated at Volta Redonda in 1947.

The 1951 election resulted in the return of Vargas as elected president. The shortage of imported goods during the Second World War had stressed the need for industrial self-sufficiency, and a second phase of industrial growth was initiated. The basis of this growth, and of the subsequent diversification of industry, was the adoption of an 'import substitution policy' in the early 1950s. Domestic industries were encouraged to produce goods which had formerly been imported. However, rapid industrialisation required massive capital investment in the infrastructure which resulted in increased public spending, higher taxation, and borrowing from abroad. This led to large balance of payments deficits and self-perpetuating inflation.

During the presidency of Juscelino Kubitschek (1955–61) a decision was taken to expand high-technology industries, in an attempt to encourage the development of ancillary industries. The motor vehicles industry was given priority and was established in the south-eastern suburbs of São Paulo city by three of the major world motor vehicle corporations. They were attracted by low wages, government incentives and high profit margins. Within a year production had soared to 30 500 vehicles, with fifty per cent of the components being produced domestically. Between 1947 and 1961, industrial growth reached an average annual rate of about ten per cent, and the volume of industrial production trebled. Brasil's planned reduced dependence on imported manufactured goods, and the increased production of capital goods as well as consumer goods, had proved highly successful. In 1958 Brasil became South America's leading industrial country.

Kubitschek's presidency also achieved other major developments, including the formation of the state-controlled petroleum company PETROBRAS, and the construction and inauguration of the new national capital of Brasília. However, this dramatic growth and these expensive projects had been achieved at great cost. Industrial activity had become grossly over-concentrated in Greater São Paulo, and agriculture had been neglected. Agricultural production had increased at a rate less than half that of industrial production. Regional inequalities had thus become more exaggerated. Moreover, Brasil had become the world's single largest debtor, and inflation had reached intolerable levels. By 1963 the economy had stagnated and, despite desperate attempts by the Goulart administration, inflation reached the equivalent of an annual rate of 150 per cent. Unemployment increased, poverty became even more widespread and critical, and the already crowded cities were flooded by more rural migrants. Social and political unrest reached a level which the military considered could lead to a communist revolution.

The structural weaknesses of the economy and society had been exposed. There was clearly a marked division of the country into three distinct Brasils: a developing South-east and South, a grossly overpopulated and underdeveloped North-east, and an underpopulated and underdeveloped North and Central-west.

The Military Coup d'Etat and the New Political Order

The political events up to 1945 have been interpreted by O. Ianni (1970) as being related to two main factors: (i) a need to curb the political and economic power of agricultural exporters and importers of manufactured goods, who formed the wealthy élite; and (ii) the conflicts between the aims of political democracy and economic development. From 1945 to 1964, industrialisation had created the conditions necessary for the emergence of a 'middle class'. It also increased tensions within the peripheral rural areas which had been by-passed during this phase of rapid economic development. Economic stagnation in the early 1960s set the scene for a new political crisis.

The military seized power on 31st March 1964, and imposed a three year period of austerity, authoritarian constraint and political repression. They attempted to achieve political stability so that a new phase of economic growth could be initiated. The price of controlling hyper-inflation was heavy, since real wages and average living standards fell. They also developed a new model of economic growth, based on modernisation. Modernisation was facilitated by state control over the key sectors of the economy; and this was achieved because authority was centralised, and the executive was pre-eminent.

Since 1964, the military government has attempted to encourage greater links between the Brasilian economy and the world economy—a doctrine of 'interdependence'. It was vital to attract massive foreign investment, rather than rely on loans as had previously been the case; and so a system of state and private joint participation with foreign corporations was developed. The new joint corporations were all to have Brasilian majority control. This policy was very successful. Foreign and multi-national corporations were attracted to Brasil by government incentives, political stability, the prospects of high profits and the great potential for expansion. Thus, Brasil's recent economic growth has been aided by the advanced technology of the foreign participants.

This has also meant that decision-making and investment is now controlled by a political and economic élite, and that foreign corporations have a greater say in Brasil's internal policies.

During the so-called 'Golden Age' from 1967 to 1973, dramatic rates of economic growth were achieved. The Gross Domestic Product grew at an annual rate of over ten per cent, and exports by an annual rate of twenty-four per cent. Real wages increased and new employment opportunities expanded at a higher rate than the rate of population growth. The federal government hailed these achievements as an 'economic miracle'. There were also significant structural changes in the economy. For the first time in Brasil's history, the export revenue from manufactured goods exceeded that from the agricultural sector. Even within the agricultural sector, coffee temporarily lost its position as the leading export to sugar and soya.

The rapid economic growth of the 'Golden Age' was slowed down by the quadrupling of world crude oil prices in 1973 and 1974. This emphasised the economy's great dependence on imported fossil fuels. The ensuing energy crisis and world economic recession, together with the continuing need for imported petroleum, has resulted in large trade deficits. High rates of domestic and foreign investment are mainly in high technology capital-intensive industries. This does little to reduce the structural and regional imbalances in the economy. It also means that many new employment opportunities can only be filled by highly skilled workers. These are a very small minority, and consequently most Brasilians still lie outside the money economy.

Since the military coup d'état, three five-year development plans have been prepared with the aims of correcting strucural imbalances, and initiating a new 'Golden Age'. The plans also contain policies for social development and regional development. Programmes of regional development and industrial decentralisation lie within the general framework of the National Integration Programme (PIN). Many projects have had considerable success, but they are still in their infancy and cannot be expected to have a major short-term economic impact.

Today, in gross terms, the Brasilian economy ranks eighth in the 'free world', alongside that of many 'middle income' European countries. Brasil can no longer be considered a typical 'third world' country. However, regional contrasts are so great that the South-east region contains the major share of commercial agriculture and manufacturing industry, whilst Amazonia and the Central-west are virtually a separate 'third world'.

3 The Brasilians

There are a number of important and interrelated topics involved in understanding Brasil's population geography. They include the problems of the declining Amerindian minority, demographic characteristics, immigration and miscegenation (racial mixing), rapid demographic growth and rapid urbanisation. The effects of these on social development are also significant. The process of urbanisation will be discussed separately. It is sufficient to note at this stage that from 1940 to 1980 Brasil has experienced a dramatic transformation in its population, from being two-thirds rural to two-thirds urban. The growing economic dominance of large cities has been the major factor influencing the rapid rates of rural depopulation.

Whilst immigration is discussed separately from demographic growth, it should be appreciated that immigrants have made a major contribution to population growth. This is far in excess of the estimated 3 500 000 African slaves, and the 5 000 000 'new' immigrants that settled in Brasil between the late-nineteenth and the mid-twentieth centuries. Their descendants have contributed directly to subsequent demographic growth, and have also made a major contribution to Brasilian culture and society.

Population Distribution and Density

It is clear from the population density map (**3.1**) that the spatial distribution of Brasilians is markedly uneven. This is well illustrated by the need to adopt irregular class limits on the map. The map uses the estimated population of the 361 'micro-regions' as devised by the Institute of Brasilian Geographers, rather than fewer and larger administrative units. The '250/km^2+' class is sufficiently high to define the major urban agglomerations, but in reality urban population densities are much greater—the highest density in 1975 was over 10 750/km^2, in the urban municipality of São João de Meriti in Greater Rio.

The broad pattern is, firstly, that of a relatively densely populated eastern zone which parallels the coast, averaging about 500 km in width; secondly, there is a grossly underpopulated western interior and north which corresponds with the regions of Amazonia and the Central-west. If the eastern zone is defined as that area with an average density of over 10/km^2, then it accounts for only 25 per cent of

Brasil's territory but for about 90 per cent of the population. It also contains all nine metropolitan regions, and virtually all Brasil's other large and medium-sized cities and towns. It is clear that this zone also contains all the 'secondary' concentrations—areas with high rural population densities. These are closely related in space and economy with the 'primary' (or major) urban concentrations.

The broad distributional pattern has remained relatively stable over a considerable period. The root cause of this lies in the nature of Brasil's economic development and, in particular, the continuing important role of exports and the dominance of the ports. Of the ten major urban agglomerations defined on **3.1**, eight are ports, and the two exceptions—Greater São Paulo and Belo Horizonte—are themselves both 'twinned' with major ports. Despite its name, Pôrto Alegre has ceased to be a significant port—Rio Grande and Pelotas at the mouth of the lagoon are better sited, and have deeper water. The details of Brasil's development are discussed elsewhere, so that here it is only necessary to summarise the major causal factors.

The concentration of population and economic development in the east is largely the result of the orientation and accessibility of the region; the formidable barrier of the Andean cordillera in the west remained under Spanish colonial control, and subsequently became part of the distinctive Hispanic republics. The Andean barrier and remote Pacific coast deterred major population movements to the west, and the great escarpment effectively limited early colonial development to the littoral *zona da mata* sugar lands. The first major movements onto the plateau resulted from the 'gold-rush' of Minas Gerais and the establishment of coffee cultivation on the *terra roxa* plateau soils of São Paulo state. Both stimulated immigration from abroad, and internal migration from the North-east, whilst the South was colonised by later waves of immigrants.

The dominance of the South-east in terms of mining, commercial farming, and later manufacturing, resulted in its emergence as the nation's 'core region', so that its population grew dramatically. The region's population now exceeds that of the North-east—in 1980 it contained an estimated 42 per cent of Brasilians as compared with 30 per cent in the North-

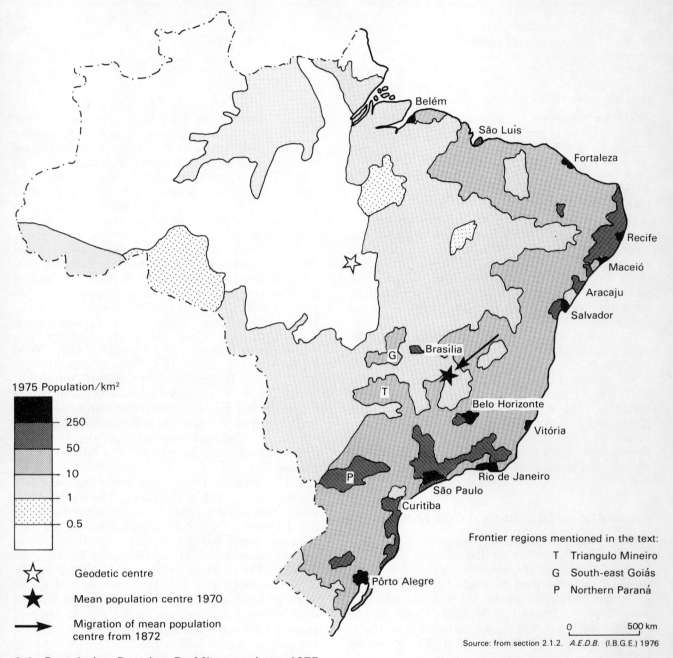

1975 Population/km²

- 250
- 50
- 10
- 1
- 0.5

☆   Geodetic centre

★   Mean population centre 1970

➤   Migration of mean population centre from 1872

Frontier regions mentioned in the text:

T   Triangulo Mineiro
G   South-east Goiás
P   Northern Paraná

0   500 km

Source: from section 2.1.2.   *A.E.D.B.*   (I.B.G.E.) 1976

3.1. Population Density: By Micro-regions, 1975.

east. The migration of the mean population centre from 1872 to 1970 is also shown by **3.1**; it is significant that the movement was generally parallel to the coast, showing that population movements into the interior have been relatively insignificant. It is also significant that the mean centre lies almost exactly central within the eastern zone, between Fortaleza in the north and the Uruguayan border in the south.

The map (**3.1**) also shows that the eastern zone is widest—i.e. the frontier of colonisation is most advanced—in areas peripheral to the South-east. The two major areas of colonisation are, firstly, the *Triangulo Mineiro* of Minas Gerais, and south-east Goiás, which have been reinforced since the establishment of Brasília, but which were developing frontier regions even before 1960. Secondly, there is the more recently colonised and flourishing region of northern Paraná and south-west São Paulo, which is now the main coffee producing region.

The spatial concentration of population can also be illustrated graphically by the 'Lorenz curve', produced by plotting the cumulative percentages of area and population (**3.2**). A perfectly uniform distribution would be represented by a straight diagonal, thus it is possible to compare Brasil's Lorenz curve with the diagonal. The curve can also be quantified by the 'Gini coefficient', which is calculated by dividing the area between the diagonal and the curve by the total area under the diagonal. In 1970 Brasil's Gini coefficient was 0.71, a very high value, but slightly lower than that for 1872 (0.74), indicating a very slight dispersal of population since 1872.

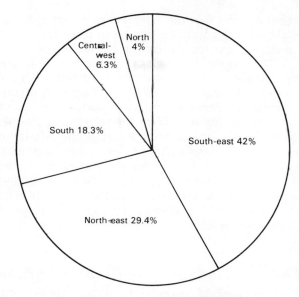

3.3. The Regional Distribution of Brasil's Population (1980 est.)

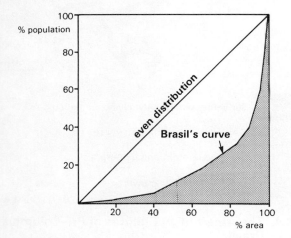

3.2. The Lorenz Curve of Brasil's Population

One of the most remarkable characteristics of the density/distribution pattern is the very steep density gradient, decaying from over 5 000/km^2 in the eastern urban centres to below 0.5/km^2 in Amazonia. This raises the question of the causes of the gross underpopulation of the North (Amazonia) and Central-west regions; together they account for 64 per cent of Brasil's area but only about 10 per cent of the population. The average population density of these regions combined is a mere 2.3/km^2. But even this average figure is misleading, as over half the population in these vast regions is urban and therefore concentrated, so that rural population densities are extremely low.

The causes of this 'human vacuum' as Pierre Gourou described it, are not as obvious as a simplistic 'deterministic' appraisal of the environment would suggest. In the past the environment has been blamed: the *selva* in particular was regarded as inhospitable and even dangerous. It has been shown in Chapter 1 that the *selva* and, especially, the *cerrado*

ecosystems could support much higher populations, as both offer a variety of possibilities for development. Similar ecosystems in other continents support larger populations without irreversible ecological damage. The answer must lie in the nature of the processes of colonisation and development in Brasil since the earliest times.

Brasil, like the rest of the 'New World', was late to be colonised by Amerindians and Europeans alike. In pre-Columbian South America, the main concentrations of the aboriginal indian population were in the temperate altitude zones of the Andes. The Brasilian Amerindian, like his counterparts, adapted his economy and society to his environment. This very close, almost 'symbiotic', relationship between man and his environment was to their mutual advantage, and it contrasted markedly with the 'exploitative' attitude of the early Europeans who neither had, nor wanted to develop, a knowledge of the environment. The Amazon river system offered a more than adequate means of access, but was only used as a means of exploiting the biological resources such as rubber. This contrast between 'exploitation' and 'development' will be more fully discussed in Chapter 7.

Brasil's economic development has long been characterised by limited capital resources, so that the East monopolised economic activity, and the more remote and vast interior and North have never made a major contribution to the national economy. It is also significant that the early economic development of the South-east involved the exploitation of its own mineral, biological and energy resources. It is only in recent decades that the resources of the interior and North have begun to be tapped, and much of these are either exported, or used in the South-east.

The regional imbalances in population are becoming even more pronounced, despite the inauguration of Brasília in 1960, the major road construction programmes, and the comparatively recent efforts of the regional development agencies. Brasília has had some success in accelerating the 'March to the West' (*O Marcha Para O Oeste*); many new agricultural colonies have been established along the new roads which converge on the federal district, but as yet the numbers involved are relatively small. The cities of the South-east still exert a strong centripetal pull on people and economic activity.

The Amerindian: The Problems of the Aboriginal Minority

Brasil's first inhabitants were groups of Amerindians who became culturally adapted to diverse tropical environments over thousands of years. The earliest archaeological evidence is in the form of heaps of discarded mollusc shells, which occur along the southeast coast and testify to the predominantly fishing economy of the *Sambaqui* (literally 'the oyster people'). These remains date from about 10 000 years ago—the end of the Pleistocene's last glacial advance. This suggests a similar origin to other Amerindian groups who are believed to have migrated from East Asia during the Pleistocene, when lower sea levels formed a land bridge across the Bering Strait. Thus the 'New World', and in particular South America, was colonised at a much later stage than the rest of the inhabited world. Unfortunately much of the archaeological record has been obliterated by intense tropical weathering and decomposition.

At the time of European discovery, Brasil probably contained up to four million Amerindians. They were subdivided into four major linguistic groups—the Tupi-Guarani, the Arawak, the Carib and the Gê. The first three groups were predominantly sedentary, practising a highly developed agriculture in the Amazonian and coastal rain-forests. The Gê, on the other hand, were nomadic and semi-nomadic hunters and gatherers, occupying the *cerrado* and some eastern regions (see **3.4**). The sedentary groups became dominant and pushed the more technologically primitive peoples to less favourable isolated interior regions. Their success resulted from the cultivation of manioc, which is easily cultivated in forest clearings and is the highest-yielding tropical food crop by weight. Manioc's protein deficiency was rec-

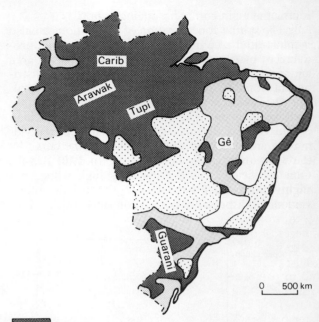

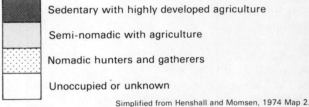

■ Sedentary with highly developed agriculture

▨ Semi-nomadic with agriculture

⠐ Nomadic hunters and gatherers

□ Unoccupied or unknown

Simplified from Henshall and Momsen, 1974 Map 2.

3.4. The Amerindian Cultures of Pre-Columbian Brasil.

tified by the products of hunting and fishing. The abundant food supply led to a highly developed social organisation, high population densities (especially in the *várzea* and littoral *baixada* (lowland) regions), and some nucleated settlements of up to 3 000 inhabitants.

The Tupi-Guarani group shared a common language, and they initially welcomed the first colonists in what has been described as 'a spirit of innocence and curiosity'. Later, many tribal groups became hostile as a result of attempts to enslave them. The Palaeo-American hunters and gatherers were traditionally hostile, and fought each other, the sedentary peoples and Portuguese colonists with equal ferocity. Some small groups are still totally isolated today even after 470 years of European colonisation.

Brasil's Amerindians have experienced a series of disastrous 'culture shocks' through contact with the colonists, and as a result their total population is now estimated at less than 100 000. Many have been assimilated into Brasilian society by racial mixing, but their lack of immunity to exogenous diseases, the effects of alcohol, and the imposition of so-called 'civilised' cultural and economic values have decimated many groups. Only those protected by isolation and inaccessibility have survived intact. Some groups such as the Guarani were gathered into Jesuit missions, but paradoxically this only made their enslavement easier after the Jesuits were expelled from the colony in 1759.

The abolition of slavery, and the formation of the republic, resulted in greater official concern for the plight of the Amerindian. In 1910, the Indian Protection Service (SPI) was established under the enlightened leadership of Candido Mariano da Silva Rondon, who was himself part Amerindian. Under the motto '*Morrer, se for preciso; matar nunca!*' ('Die if necessary; but never kill') the organisation attempted to support the Amerindian way of life and liberty whilst protecting them from persecution. It attempted to pacify and to educate them to a level which would allow them to survive in the future. Rondon's death in 1958 marked the end of an era, as the SPI later became corrupt. It became incapable of stopping numerous reported atrocities, such as the use of smallpox-infected blankets, arsenic-laced sugar, and dynamite-bombing of villages from light aircraft, which were all used to clear the land of Amerindians. A government enquiry in 1967 even found that the SPI had become directly involved in some of the atrocities. Also, official funds had been embezzled, and some Amerindians had been enslaved. Following the

Plate 8. Krain-a-kores women beg for sweets on the Cuiabá-Santarem highway. Many Amerindian groups have forsaken their traditional culture after their lands have been invaded by the bulldozer, new roads, construction gangs and ranchers. **Keystone Press Agency Ltd.**

enquiry, which caused widespread international concern, the federal government dissolved the SPI in 1968 and replaced it by FUNAI (*Fundacão Nacional do Indio*), which also incorporated the National Council for the Protection of the Indian, and the Xingu National Park.

The major aims of FUNAI are to manage the indian parks and reservations—the 'indian patrimony' of 100 million hectares—and the 150 indian posts (see **3.5**). It exists also to provide medical, sanitary and educational assistance, and in the long-term to promote the integration of the Amerindians into Brasilian society by developing their economy and by pacifying the groups which are still hostile to any form of acculturation. Although FUNAI is hampered by inadequate funds and staff, so that atrocities are still committed in remote areas by

Plate 7. A Kuikuru village in the Xingu National Park. The Park established by the Villas Boas brothers provides a refuge for many Amerindian groups. *John Hemming.*

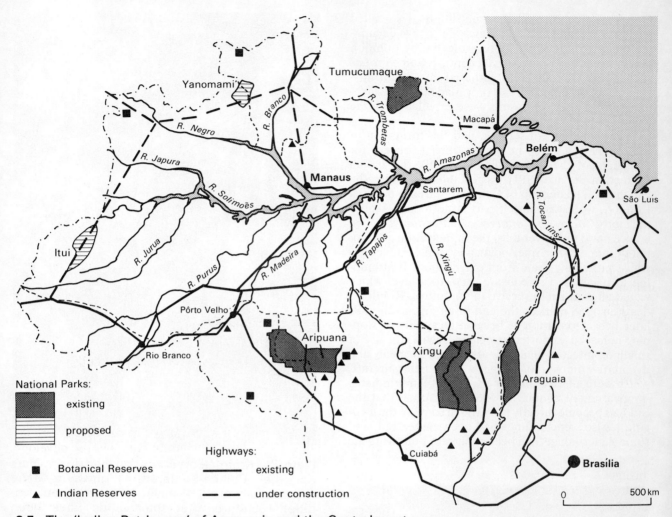

3.5. The 'Indian Patrimony' of Amazonia and the Central-west.

construction and mining gangs, ranchers and others, it has been very successful in arresting diseases within the pacified groups. Inoculation programmes have made major contributions towards the eradication of smallpox, measles, influenza, dysentery and tuberculosis, which once decimated many tribes within days of their first contact with 'civilisation'.

International criticism of the government's 'indian policies', and allegations that government officials were still involved in atrocities, led the federal government to encourage visits by international organisations in the early 1970s. Following an investigatory expedition in 1971, the Aborigines Protection Society of Britain was able to report in 1973 that allegations that the Brasilian government had either practised or connived at genocide were 'wide of the mark', and that, 'the very real pressing dangers facing the Indians of Brasil stem neither from malevolence nor from deliberate cruelty. They are due to

the ignorance and prejudice which readily ally themselves with the ruthlessness of interests whose cupidity is content to see pledges broken and even the small Indian Reserves violated rather than lose a chance of gain'. The value of indian lands to property speculators and developers is immense; land has appreciated over tenfold in value in recent years.

A major contribution to Amerindian welfare has been made by the Villas Boas brothers, whose efforts were directly responsible for the creation of the Xingu National Park by government edict in 1961. The park is run as a sanctuary for declining groups. The indians are first discovered, then pacified and brought into the park to be protected. However, even the territorial integrity of the Xingu National Park has been violated by the construction of a highway, which is part of a rapidly developing road network in Amazonia and the Central-west (see **3.5**).

The plight of the Amerindian has highlighted the whole question of the development of Brasil's few remaining undeveloped virgin regions: regions which are regarded as ripe for exploitation, and which are capable of yielding high short-term profits, if only in the form of land speculation. The future of the present isolated self-sufficient groups is problematic. Some would confine these groups to a form of 'human zoo', others would advocate that the Amerindian should be given the freedom to choose his own future. The policy of the Brasilian government is clear: the Amerindian is to be progressively integrated into Brasilian society and FUNAI is pledged to resist any forced or 'artificial assimilation'.

On 19th April 1974—the 'Day of the Indian'—the Minister of the Interior stated that, '... The basic object of the indian policy is to benefit the indian communities... It is unthinkable to integrate the indian in such a way that he becomes a racial cyst or part of a marginal community'.

Immigration and Miscegenation

The growth of Brasil from a Portuguese colony with a predominantly Amerindian population, into a mixed multi-racial nation-state with over 120 million inhabitants, owes much to what Gilberto Freyre (1946) has described as the 'Luso-Tropicalism' of the Portuguese—i.e. their adaptability to non-European cultures and environments. During the early colonial period the vast majority of immigrants were young males. The liberal attitude of the Roman Catholic Church resulted in the inter-marriage of Portuguese males and Amerindian females, producing a strong *mameluco* strain. The import of an estimated 3.5 million African slaves introduced a third element into the colony. A *pardo* strain developed from predominantly extra-marital relations between Portuguese males, and female African slaves. There was, however, little interbreeding between the Amerindian and African (*cafuso*), as the African's acceptance of slave labour conflicted with the Amerindian culture within which females were responsible for cultivating the land. Thus there was a significant cultural barrier between the two groups.

Population growth was slow during the colonial period. The tropical environment nurtures a great number and variety of diseases. These caused high mortality rates in a society with an underdeveloped social organisation and a low level of technological development. The strongly patriarchal and conservative society of the *zona da mata* sugar plantations resulted in a stagnant rural economy and farmscape, so

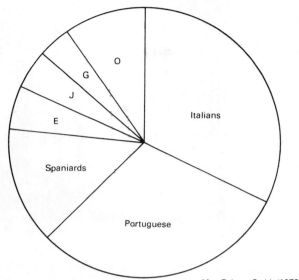

E   East Europeans (mainly Russian)
J   Japanese
G   Germans
O   Others (including Turks, Syrians and Americans)

After T. Lynn Smith (1973)

3.6. The Composition of Immigrants by Nationalities, 1884–1957.

that immigration was deterred by the lack of opportunities for the ownership of land and the development of small farms.

Following the creation of the empire in 1822, greater efforts were made to attract immigrants, as the shortage of labour was proving a brake on agricultural development. The abolition of the slave trade in 1850 initiated a new wave of immigration, which though temporarily checked by the formation of the republic in 1889, continued into the mid-twentieth century. An estimated five million immigrants entered Brasil between 1874 and 1957. Unlike earlier immigration, this phase consisted of groups from other European countries as well as Portugal, and also significant numbers from Japan (see **3.6**). Immigration was at first subsidised by the national government, but it increased considerably after these powers were devolved to state governments.

The shortage of labour was most serious in São Paulo state, because the first coffee *fazendas* (estates) had relied on African slave labour. From 1886, large sums were made available for subsidised immigration, and the state attracted over 55 per cent of all immigrants from 1878 to 1937 (see **3.7**). By 1920, São Paulo's success in coffee cultivation and subsidised immigration had been such that the state contained a very large proportion of recent foreign immigrants and had also attracted significant

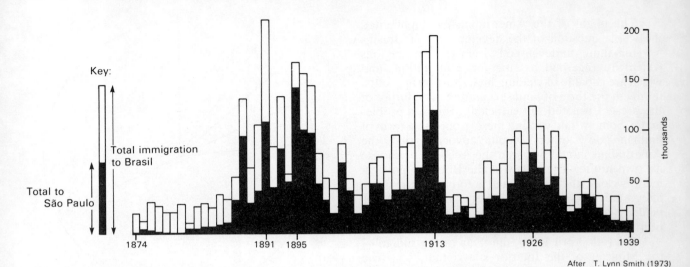

After   T. Lynn Smith (1973)

3.7. Immigration to Brasil as a whole and São Paulo in particular, 1874–1939.

numbers of internal migrants. Its success, and the concern of the Italian government as to the treatment of Italians in São Paulo, caused Italy to prohibit subsidised emigration in 1902. This loss was countered by agreements with Japanese companies, and over 200 000 Japanese entered the state after 1902. Today, São Paulo contains nearly a million people of Japanese descent.

The First World War caused a marked decline in immigration and, though there was a temporary recovery, only in 1926 did the annual total again exceed 100 000. In 1934 the federal government established an immigration quota system which limited the total to a maximum 77 000 per annum, and the contribution of each nation to two per cent of its contribution from 1884 to 1933. In 1938 further legislation ensured that a minimum of 80 per cent of immigrants were farmers and their families. The quota system

was established to reduce immigration and to ensure the growth of a skilled rural labour force.

Throughout this period, miscegenation continued so that the distinction between the three main racial elements of the colonial period became progressively more blurred. The population also became 'bleached' as most later immigrants were of Caucasian race. The Caucasian immigrants (predominantly Europeans) tended to form a higher social stratum, with considerably lower infant mortality rates. Whilst there is today no marked 'colour bar' or racial

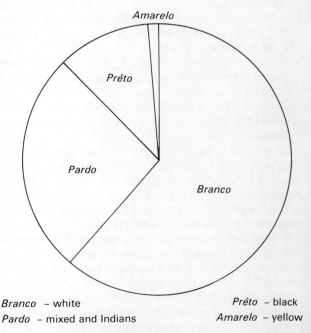

Branco – white
Pardo – mixed and Indians

Prêto – black
Amarelo – yellow

3.9. Ethnic Composition, 1950.

3.8. The Relationship between Colour and Social Status.

After   Thales de Azevedo

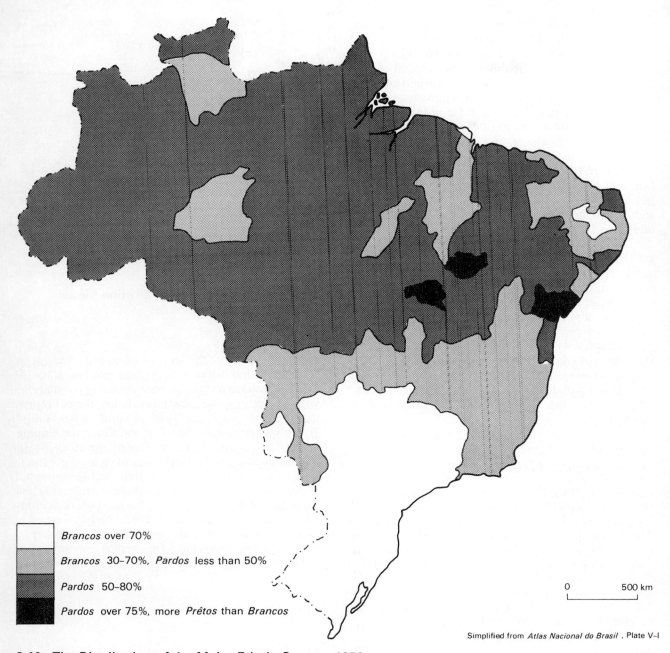

Brancos over 70%

Brancos 30–70%, *Pardos* less than 50%

Pardos 50–80%

Pardos over 75%, more *Prêtos* than *Brancos*

0   500 km

Simplified from *Atlas Nacional do Brasil* , Plate V–I

3.10. The Distribution of the Major Ethnic Groups, 1950.

discrimination in Brasil, there is a correlation between colour and social status, as shown by **3.8**. Neither colour nor race are now recorded by official censuses. The most recent data available is for 1950 (see **3.9**), but this does not give an accurate anthropological picture as in reality there are few 'pure' whites, and the census returns suggested that most respondents regarded themselves a 'shade whiter'. In contrast with most other ethnic groups, the Japanese avoided mixing with other Brasilians to any large extent. This 'racial cyst' has caused concern in a country where racial mixing is considered of paramount importance in the development of a distinctive Brasilian culture. However, in recent years, middle-class Japanese males have increasingly intermarried with other ethnic groups, producing a *nisei* strain.

The marked spatial contrasts in development and immigration have produced regional contrasts in ethnic composition. Map **3.10** shows that the greater part of the South-east and South regions, and the *agreste* of Pernambuco, contain over 70 per cent *brancos*; that there is a peripheral zone consisting of the southern part of the plateau, the central coastal area, the 'shoulder' of the North-east and outlying areas of Amazonia, which has a relatively even mix of the three main elements; and that in only three areas do the *prêto* and *pardo* groups dominate, to the virtual exclusion of *brancos* (see also **9.11** on page 132).

Recent foreign immigrants are relatively insignificant in terms of their numbers, averaging 11 500 per annum in the mid 1970s. They are economically significant, however, in that they are mostly skilled and over 18 years of age, and therefore contribute directly to economic development, without having made demands on the education and social welfare services. São Paulo, Paraná and Rio de Janeiro states are the major beneficiaries, attracting 45 per cent, 25 per cent and 16 per cent respectively.

The most significant population movements of the 1970s were those associated with urbanisation (see Chapter 4). Peripheral rural areas are losing thousands of migrants to urban core regions. In some cases this loss is greater than natural increase, so that the rural population is in absolute decline. In contrast, new frontier regions are experiencing absolute increases.

Demographic Growth

It was not until 1872 that Brasil's population exceeded ten million, and this was in part the result of immigration. The high rates of natural increase within the immigrant population also contributed greatly to future demographic growth. By 1905, over a period of 33 years, the population had doubled. By 1939, it had doubled again to 40 million; however, it took only another 26 years to reach 80 million in 1965. The estimated population for 1980 was 123 million. From the 1940s to the present, therefore, Brasil has experienced increasingly rapid rates of natural increase.

The major elements of this 'demographic explosion' are shown by **3.11**. The 'demographic transition model' illustrates the four demographic regimes or stages which economically advanced countries have experienced. In these countries, the change from high fluctuating birth and death rates in stage 1 to the high rate of natural increase in stage 2 was caused by a sharp decline in the death rate. This coincided with the Industrial Revolution. Very rapid population growth persisted for 150 years, until a gradual rise in average living strandards had the effect of reducing the birth rate and rates of natural

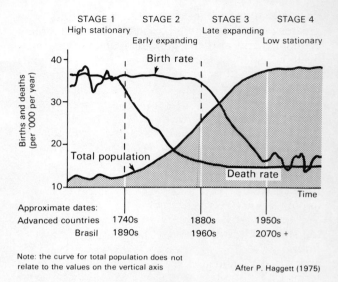

Note: the curve for total population does not relate to the values on the vertical axis

After P. Haggett (1975)

3.11. The Demographic Transition Model.

increase. By 1950, many advanced European countries (and some others) had entered stage 4. Some now have a static or even declining population, with a demographic growth rate below the net reproduction rate of an average of 2.2 children per family. Brasil's experience, like that of many developing countries, is quite different. During the 1950s Brasil experienced annual growth rates of up to 35 per thousand. The major difference is that the 'demographic transition' of stages 2 and 3 is taking considerably less time than it did in Europe—about 70 years as compared with 150 years. Since 1962, the birth rate has begun to fall so that the growth rate has fallen to below 28 per thousand. This reflects major socio-economic changes, such as those resulting from in-

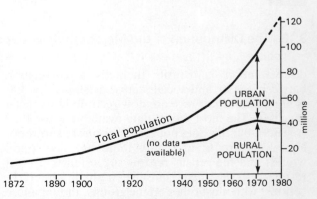

3.12. Brasil's Demographic Growth, 1872–1980.

dustrialisation, urbanisation, the absorption of a greater proportion of the population into the money economy, and also the greater availability of artificial methods of birth control. Urbanisation has undermined the extended family, and has stressed the material advantages accruing from limiting family size. These advantages become even greater as real incomes rise.

It is important to realise that it is not simply the rates of natural increase that are significant, but also the size of the population base to which these are related. Thus, even though the rate of natural increase has declined since 1962, the absolute growth in population continues.

Brasil's rapid population growth has necessitated short-term estimates and long-term forecasts of future population, as these are needed for economic and social planning at many levels. In very crude terms Brasil is not an overpopulated country, but as shown in the introduction, its present population is above the optimum level in terms of the provision of social services, the current level of resource exploitation and the level of economic development. Since economic development is highly localised in urban core regions, the processes of rapid rural depopulation and urban growth are considered by the federal government to be advantageous, as a greater proportion of the population is being brought within the sphere of influence of the metropolitan regions. Though already faced with great population pressure, the metropolitan regions will be better equipped to solve problems of ill-health, poverty, education and unemployment in the future.

The National Housing Bank (1973) has outlined three simple linear hypotheses for Brasil's future demographic growth:

a) If Brasil's population continues to double at decreasing time intervals—which has been the case until the 1970s—then a total of over 220 million will have been reached by the year 2000, and 460 million by the year 2026. This hypothesis is extremely unlikely as the rate of natural increase is already declining, and is now well below the rate of economic growth.

b) There is at present no national population policy, but if a massive family planning programme was initiated in the early 1980s, then population would continue to grow until the 2060s when it would stabilise at about 273 million.

c) If Brasil's rapid demographic transition continues to follow the general trends already experienced by the advanced countries, then a net reproduction rate would result by the 2070s, and the population would stabilise at about 520 million.

Whilst all three hypotheses make several major and unproven assumptions, it is probable that the third will be proved to be the most accurate. If so, then a fourfold increase in population, within such a short period of time, would necessitate even higher annual economic growth rates than that experienced in the so-called 'Golden Age'.

Demography and Social Development

Before the 1930s, social development was retarded by an essentially 'colonial' economy which perpetuated a vast subsistence sector with very low standards of living, health and education. Whilst there have been improvements resulting from economic growth and from attempts to provide adequate social services, rapid demographic growth continues to undermine current programmes by continuously increasing the pressure on already inadequate services. It also has a dramatic effect on the age structure of the population. In 1980 an estimated 42 per cent of the population was under 15 years of age—a proportion which is almost double that of advanced countries. This not only has repercussions in terms of the provision of education and medical care, but also limits the proportion of the population which is economically active (see **3.13**).

There is evidence to suggest that the age structure of the population has even greater ramifications than was previously thought to be the case. It has been estimated that a one per cent increase in population, with its consequent effects on the increased proportion of children, necessitates a capital increment of about four per cent just to maintain the status quo.

An increase in the average standard of living results from an increase in real per capita income through economic growth and increased productivity; but the latter can only be achieved by a general rise in the skills and training of the labour force. The existence of a large illiterate population, involved in subsistence or semi-subsistence activities, increases the problems of diffusing innovation, knowledge, skills and new technology. However, economic growth and increased average living standards do not in themselves necessarily result in a more equitable distribution of wealth and personal incomes. Major inequalities in the distribution of wealth persist, which have their root in the legacy of the colonial social and economic structures. From 1960 to 1970, the top 5 per cent income group increased its share of the GDP from 27 per cent to 36 per cent, whilst the share of the lowest 40 per cent income group fell from 11 per cent to 9 per cent. Over that decade, in fact, the poor suffered an absolute decline in real

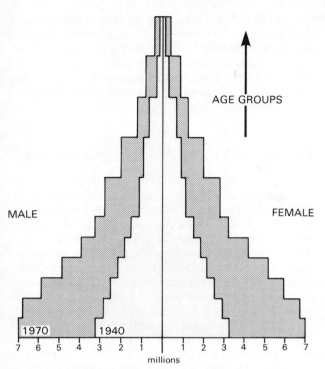

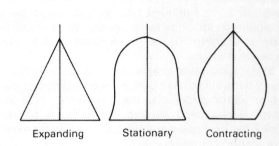

Note: the pyramids for Brasil are clearly expanding.
Note also that the three idealised pyramids give a good indication as to the population structure at various stages during the 'demographic transition.'

3.13. The Age and Sex Structure of Brasil's Population, 1940 and 1970, and a comparison with other idealised pyramids.

income, and the 'poverty gap' widened considerably. During the 1970s, government activity has been more successful in highlighting the fundamental problems and in adopting major development programmes with a substantial social content. The 'social budget' already absorbs about a third of total government expenditure, with social security, education, health, housing and sanitation accounting for two-thirds of this. However, 'social readjustment' is a relatively long-term process.

Poverty in Brasil is widespread, but it also shows marked spatial variations. It is most chronic in the North-east which in 1970 had a mere 14 per cent share of the national income—less than half the national per capita average. Within the region, the most severe poverty is amongst the *favelados* (shanty dwellers). Their plight has been widely publicised by Dom Helder Camara, the Archbishop of Recife, who has converted the Episcopal Palace into the offices of 'Operation Hope'. This organisation attempts to feed and educate the poor. In a BBC television interview in 1977 he recounted his first visit to a Recife *favela*:

'The first time I came here I asked, "Why don't you get out of this rubbish?". "Why should we?" they said, "It is our wealth!". You see, they don't just hunt for rags and paper in the garbage; no, they also hunt for food!'.

Whilst there has been considerable recent progress in the cities of the North-east, malnutrition and dietary deficiencies are still common. In some cases this can cause irreversible mental retardation, thus damaging the most precious of Brasil's resources—the human resource.

Medical services and improved health are a major priority. The average life expectancy has increased from 43 years in 1940 to over 60 years at present, but the continuing problem of high rates of infant mortality is serious. Mortality rates for children up to the age of five are greater than 100 per thousand. Many tropical diseases are no longer endemic, but are still responsible for about 40 per cent of deaths. The most dangerous diseases are tuberculosis, pneumonia, measles and diphtheria; the incidence of meningitis, tetanus, whooping cough and poliomyelitis is also still significantly high. Some predominantly rural diseases have recently reappeared in urban areas as a result of rural-urban migration. But mass inoculation programmes have had considerable success, especially in the near-eradication of yellow fever, malaria and smallpox. Some 3 million children are now inoculated each year, and this has saved an estimated 14 000 lives already.

It is claimed that about 80 per cent of Brasilians now have access to some form of medical care, but doctors, hospital beds and other medical services are heavily concentrated in the South-eastern cities. Many remote rural areas have no medical services whatsoever, and most rural areas are very badly served. The urban areas are now beginning to experience new health hazards such as cancer and cardiac diseases, which tend to be associated with more affluent societies.

The generally low standards of public health are exacerbated by malnutrition and dietary deficiencies which lower resistance to disease. As shown in **3.14**, malnutrition and ill-health lower the productivity of the labour force, and the poverty cycle continues unless affected by external influences. Brasil is not short of food—annual production of foodstuffs is sufficient to provide an average daily consumption of about 3 000 calories per capita—but, as with personal incomes, there is a gross imbalance. There are major problems even in the commercial sector, as an estimated 20 per cent of the gross agricultural product is lost through inadequate transport, storage and marketing facilities. Food distribution is now being rationalised and entrusted to a developing network of large state-run food distribution centres—CEASA's—of which 22 had been completed by 1980.

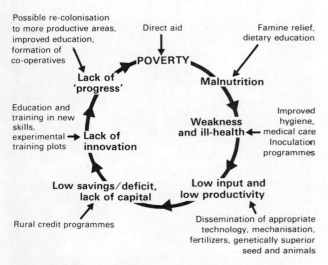

3.14. The Poverty Cycle in Rural Areas, and Possible External Remedial Measures.

Major successes have been achieved in pharmaceuticals production since a government organisation (CEME) was established in 1972. The main difficulty in the mass production of essential medicines is that at present Brasil has to import over 75 per cent of the raw materials, and thus they are expensive. Public health would also be considerably improved by pro-

viding adequate sanitation which would help to control the vectors which transmit disease. At present only 30 per cent of dwellings are served by adequate sewers, and only 55 per cent by a mains water supply. The national sanitation plan is making significant progress, but this is also mainly confined to large urban areas because the spatial concentration of dwellings enables a more efficient and effective use of the limited finances available.

In developing countries, spatial contrasts in social development are usually considerable. This phenomenon is very marked in Brasil because the recent dramatic economic growth has been largely confined to the cities of the South-east, and to peripheral 'poles' in the South and (to a lesser extent) the North-east. It is in these areas that the employment structure, and the provision of educational, medical and other social amenities, are most highly developed. Thus, there is a strong correlation between urban development and economic and social development.

Compulsory education from the ages of seven to fifteen was introduced as recently as 1961, but only about ten per cent of pupils complete secondary education. This proportion has risen considerably in recent years, especially since the provision of free school meals for some eleven million children. However, the opportunities for higher education are extremely limited. The South-east contains about 75 per cent of all higher education institutions. However, even this region has its problems, as recent economic growth has been mainly in the form of high technology manufacturing industries. These are capital- rather than labour-intensive, and therefore require a relatively small but highly trained labour force. The problems of peripheral areas are very different, as they are still dominated by the colonial legacy of subsistence and primary activities. In many rural areas there is a marked lack of educational and employment opportunities, food production is still regarded as the responsibility of the individual, and there is little incentive or opportunity to achieve significant advances in living standards.

However, some attempts have been made to remedy these problems. Apart from the regional development programmes, which are discussed elsewhere, three social projects are noteworthy. The MOBRAL adult literacy programme has had considerable success, and has reduced the number of illiterates by 3 million despite demographic growth; this is an essential programme, as only adult literates are allowed to vote. The 'Minerva' radio education project now serves some 15 000 schools, and 'Project Rondon', launched in 1967, uses volunteer students to help rural communities to develop improved hygiene, medical care and educational standards.

Plate 9. A pedestrian precinct in 'down-town' Belo Horizonte. This purpose-built state captial of Minas Gerais was planned along similar lines to Washington D.C. (U.S.A.), and is now a major industrial centre. *J. Allan Cash Ltd.*

Brasil's employment structure is still dominated by a large primary sector, and is characterised by low wages and productivity, and by high rates of unemployment and underemployment. The proportion of economically active persons (51 per cent of the population over 10 years-of-age in the mid 1970s) has fallen steadily in recent decades because of the high birth rate. It has been affected by improved educational opportunities and by earlier retirement, made possible through the introduction of pension schemes. Underemployment is largely a rural phenomenon and is most significant in the Northeast, whereas unemployment is predominantly urban. The latter results mainly from the massive influx of rural migrants. Only in São Paulo city is there an absolute labour shortage; this reflects its dominant industrial position, and the increasingly commercialised farming activities within its large sphere of influence.

Since over two-thirds of Brasilians are now urban dwellers the problems of social development cannot be divorced from those of urban development. These problems are considered in Chapter 4.

Plate 10. A *favelado* (shanty dweller) begs in the street. Even in Belo Horizonte many poor Brasilians have benefited little from the 'economic miracle'. *J. Allan Cash Ltd.*

4 Urbanisation, Urban Problems and Urban Planning

The term 'urbanisation' refers not only to the increasing proportion of people who live in cities, but also to the various social and economic causes and effects of this.

Brasil's contemporary urban and rural settlement patterns developed at different times and were affected by very different factors. The plantation system dominated the rural colonial economy and, as shown in Chapter 2, the early towns were pre-industrial ports. Apart from the planned centre around the *praça*, the general form of the towns was unplanned and was greatly affected by site restrictions. There are many excellent examples of this which still survive. Salvador is divided by a scarp into an *alta* (high) section and a *baixa* (low) coastal section; Recife, as its name implies, was built upon a discontinuous reef; and Rio fits into every nook and cranny between the granite sugar-loaves on the western shores of Guanabara Bay.

The interior towns began to develop in the eighteenth and nineteenth centuries either as market centres or fairs, such as Campina Grande in the North-east, or as mining centres, such as Ouro Prêto. However, during the colonial period there was virtually no development of rural villages, because the rural labour force was tied to the plantation. It was only during the late-nineteenth century that true rural settlements emerged, following the emancipation of the slaves and the need to provide food crops to supply the rapidly expanding ports and mining towns.

An interesting feature of post-colonial urban development was the careful planning and establishment of a number of new towns. These included Teresina in 1852, Belo Horizonte—the 'City of Minas'—in 1894, and Goiânia in 1937. The major factor was the need to create new administrative and, in some cases, industrial capitals because the colonial capitals were unsuitable. This process was eventually to culminate in the establishment of the new federal capital of Brasília in 1960. However, most cities still grew in an unplanned and indeed haphazard manner, so that their structures were unsuited to the needs of twentieth century Brasil. Thus, many cities have been unable to cope with the rapid influx of rural migrants, the demands of commercial and industrial development, and the need for greater intra-urban mobility. Many industrial plants therefore, have a peripheral location, and major industrial developments have taken place in well defined sectors outside the former built-up area.

Brasil's Urban Transformation

Rapid urbanisation is probably the most significant process in contemporary Brasil, as the city has become the focus of major economic and social changes. The rapidity of Brasil's transformation from a predominantly rural to a predominantly urban society is such that it can be regarded as premature. The rate of urban population growth exceeds the rate of urban economic growth, and the provision of services and amenities has been unable to keep pace.

Table **4.1** illustrates this rapid transformation. From 1940 to 1970 Brasil's population as a whole increased by 129 per cent, whereas the urban com-

4.1. Brasil's Urban Transformation, 1940–80.

Year	Urban Population (in '000s)	% Urban	Rural Population (in '000s)	% Rural	Total Population (in '000s)
1940	12 880	31.2	28 356	68.8	41 236
1950	18 783	36.1	33 162	63.9	51 945
1960	32 005	45.1	38 988	54.9	70 993
1970	52 905	55.8	41 604	44.2	94 509
1980 (est.)	80 000	66.7	40 000	33.3	120 000

Source: Brasilian Housing Bank

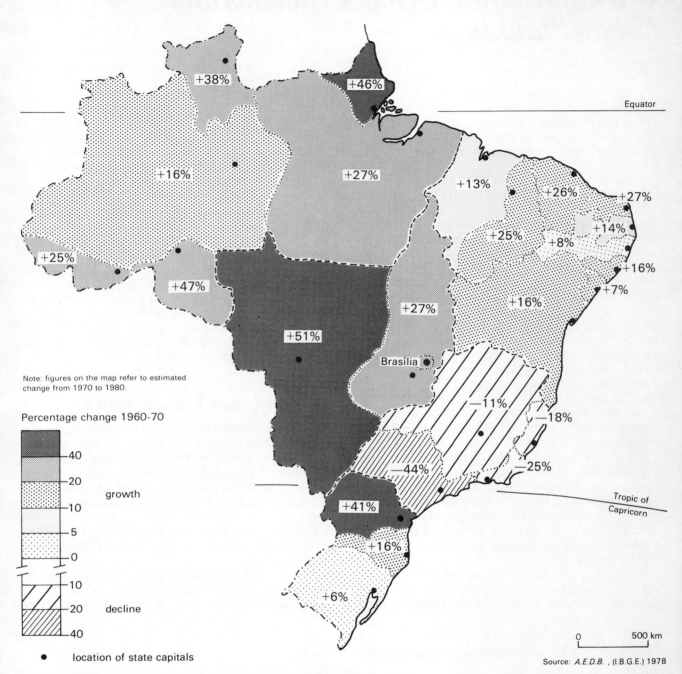

Note: figures on the map refer to estimated change from 1970 to 1980.

Percentage change 1960-70

growth

decline

●   location of state capitals

Source: *A.E.D.B.* , (I.B.G.E.) 1978

4.2. Rural Population Change 1960–70, and 1970–80. By states.

ponent of population increased by 311 per cent. Since 1940 the rate of growth in the rural population has declined steadily, so that by 1972 it had ceased to grow. It has since declined further. Maps **4.2** and **4.3** illustrate the regional patterns in rural and urban population change from 1960 to 1970. By 1970, only four states had experienced an absolute decline in their rural populations—the four states of the South-east region. This broad regional pattern was similar in 1980. However, the increase in rural population in

some other states was also essentially urban in character, as it occurred in regions of high population density in close proximity to large urban settlements.

The rate of urban growth is high in all regions, but is far from being homogeneous. In 1970, only seven states were predominantly urban—Minas Gerais, Rio de Janeiro (including Guanabara) and São Paulo in the South-east; Rio Grande do Sul in the South; Pernambuco in the North-east; and Rondônia and Amapá in Amazonia. By 1980, it was

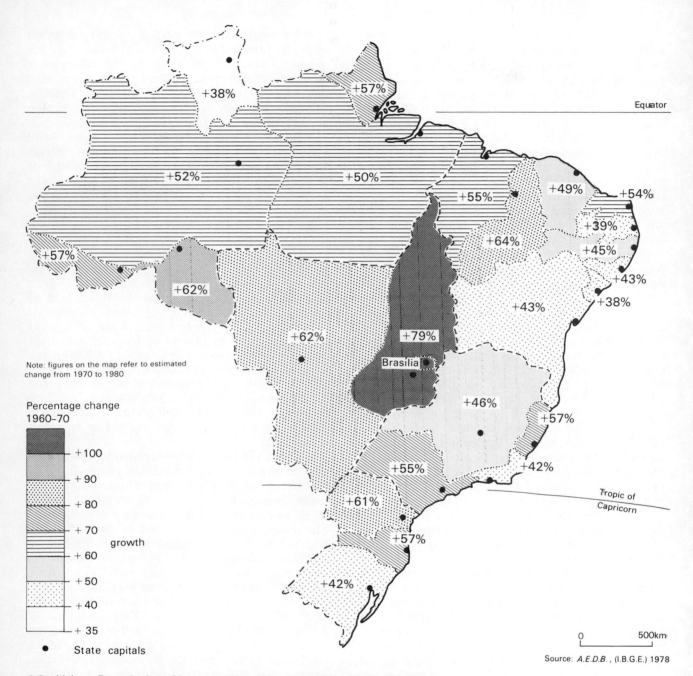

Note: figures on the map refer to estimated change from 1970 to 1980

Percentage change 1960–70

+100
+90
+80
+70
growth
+60
+50
+40
+35

● State capitals

Source: *A.E.D.B.*, (I.B.G.E.) 1978

4.3. Urban Population Change 1960–70, and 1970–80. By States.

estimated that six others were also predominantly urban—Pará, Rio Grande do Norte, Sergipe, Espírito Santo, Santa Catarina and Goiás. Whilst the greatest absolute increase in urban population is taking place in the largest cities, the greatest rates of increase (of over 60 per cent!) are being experienced in the Central-west region and in the states of Paraná and Maranhão—all areas of rapid recent colonisation.

Brazilian censuses classify all nucleated settle-

ments as being urban, so that a more detailed analysis is necessary to determine the relative growth of towns and cities of different sizes. In 1950, towns of under 5 000 inhabitants accounted for 26 per cent of the total urban population, but by 1970 their share had fallen to 14 per cent. It is clear, therefore, that the most recent rapid urban population growth is taking place in the large cities. In 1970, cities with over 20 000 inhabitants accounted for 65 per cent of the total urban population.

In Brasil the rapid urban transformation is considered to be, on balance, an advantageous process as, by concentrating population, it increases the potential for integrating the rural population within the wage economy, and thus provides a means of reducing both sectoral and regional imbalances. Countries with a highly dispersed rural population are generally characterised by chronic underdevelopment and widespread poverty. The importance of the city reflects the advantages of polarised development in 'central places', the economies of spatial concentration, and the strong centripetal forces which cities exert on peripheral areas. The experience of advanced countries shows that urban growth and industrialisation are mutually supportive, as the city is the major market, the centre of investment, and also promotes increased agricultural productivity within its sphere of influence. Brasil's cities already contribute 87 per cent of the GDP.

The causes of Brasil's rapid urban transformation are complex, involving interrelated environmental, historical, economic, social, political and psychological factors. Essentially, the fundamental cause can be expressed in terms of the positive advantages of the urban 'core' and the negative disadvantages of the rural 'periphery' (See Chapter 5). During the 1960s only 13 per cent of new employment opportunities were rural-based. In the South-east in particular, increased agricultural production and productivity have both been achieved by greater mechanisation and by the application of new technologies at the expense of the rural labour force. The consequence has been massive rural depopulation.

Ever since the abolition of slavery in 1888, and the shift of the economic centre of gravity from the North-east to the South-east, the rural population has been mobile; as early as 1900, many cities contained large numbers of rural migrants. However, apart from the forced migrations caused by droughts in the North-east, the motivation to migrate was minimised by isolation, poor transport and a lack of knowledge. The more recent improvements in interregional transport, and the advent of now widespread mass-communications systems, such as the radio and television, have increased the rural population's awareness of the opportunities provided by urban life, and has widened what T. Lynn Smith (1973) refers to as the 'zone of exasperation'. The city epitomises the Brasil of the twentieth century, and reflects both personal and national aspirations for material advance.

However, the reality of urban opportunities is often quite different from preconceived mental images. The unskilled rural migrant has to compete with thousands in the same predicament for unskilled work. This usually means employment in the rapidly growing construction industry. Those rural migrants who were involved in commercial agriculture are frequently worse off, as wages in the construction industry are on average less than those in commercial farming—the latter also receive 'in natura' benefits. But the subsistence farmer who finds urban employment can achieve a higher standard of living.

Rural depopulation is the single most important factor in Brasil's rapid urban transformation, though high rates of natural increase in cities also contribute to overall urban growth. The cities have also been most successful in attracting recent foreign immigrants.

Internal Migration

The 1970 demographic census recorded over 13 million Brasilians who were not residing in their state of birth. This represented over 14 per cent of the total population in that year. Map **4.4** shows the major inter-state movements up to 1970. The patterns broadly follow those of the previous censuses in 1950 and 1960, but the number of recorded migrants has increased greatly, from 5 million and 8.6 million in 1950 to 1960, to 13.2 million in 1970. Maps **4.2**, **4.3**, and **4.4** together reveal the major migratory movements.

By far the largest inter-regional movement was the net loss of nearly 3.5 million people from the North-east region. Eight out of the nine states in that region recorded a net loss, the major movements being to São Paulo state. The only exception was Maranhão, which was selected by SUDENE (the regional development agency for the North-east) as an area of colonisation. The project was funded by a loan from the World Bank, and has attracted numerous colonists mainly from Piauí and Ceará.

The state with the largest loss was Minas Gerais (2.8 million), mainly to São Paulo and Rio de Janeiro, but also to the now well established and rapidly developing regions of northern Paraná, south-east Goiás, and the federal district. Paraná experienced the greatest net gain—2.1 million—reflecting its now dominant role in coffee and soya cultivation, and the planned growth of a number of urban centres such as Londrina, related to the development of commercial agriculture.

Rural depopulation within the states of the South-east region has also been massive. It is not only the result of urbanisation, but also of movements to the developing frontier regions. It is significant that whilst São Paulo state recorded a net gain of nearly 2 million, it also lost nearly 1.3 million, mainly to Paraná state.

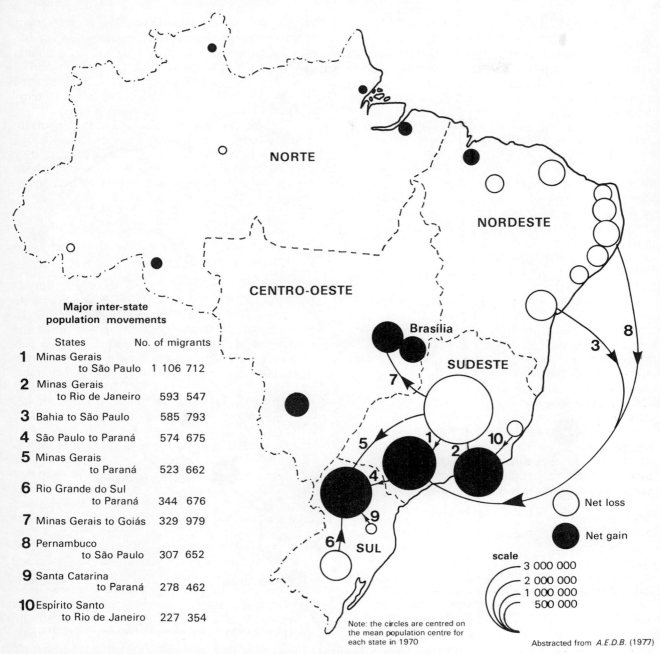

Major inter-state population movements

	States	No. of migrants
1	Minas Gerais to São Paulo	1 106 712
2	Minas Gerais to Rio de Janeiro	593 547
3	Bahia to São Paulo	585 793
4	São Paulo to Paraná	574 675
5	Minas Gerais to Paraná	523 662
6	Rio Grande do Sul to Paraná	344 676
7	Minas Gerais to Goiás	329 979
8	Pernambuco to São Paulo	307 652
9	Santa Catarina to Paraná	278 462
10	Espírito Santo to Rio de Janeiro	227 354

Net loss

Net gain

scale
3 000 000
2 000 000
1 000 000
500 000

Note: the circles are centred on the mean population centre for each state in 1970

Abstracted from *A.E.D.B.* (1977)

4.4. Internal Migration: Net Migration by States up to 1970.

It is significant that Mato Grosso also recorded a net gain of 400 000, reflecting its gradual integration into the national economy through improved road linkages. However, the entire North/Amazonia region recorded a net gain of only about 100 000 people; about 80 per cent of this was to two states only, Rondônia and Pará. It is likely that the results of the 1980 census will confirm an increase in migration into Amazonia and the Central-west, resulting from the effects of the regional development programmes and associated colonisation projects.

Before discussing other migratory movements, it is useful to analyse migration into the nation's major urban and industrial core region, Greater São Paulo. In 1970, 53 per cent of its population had been born outside the metropolitan region. Map **4.9** on page 53 shows the proportion of migrants to the total population for each of the region's eight sub-regions,

The Urban Hierachy

- ⬤ (with white square) **1a** Major National Metropolis
- ⬤ (shaded) **1b** National Metropolis
- ⬤ **1c** Metropolitan Regional Centre
- ⬤ **1d** Major Regional Centre
- • **2a**
- ○ **2b** Regional Centres

Note: the full hierarchy also includes class 3 sub-region centres and class 4 local centres, and their spheres of influence. Brasília has the status of a second order regional centre (2b)

0   500 km

Source: *Divisão do Brasil em Regioès Funcionais Urbanas* , (I.B.G.E.), 1972

4.5. The Urban Hierarchy and Major Urban Regions.

and the origin of the migrants. The great majority (70 per cent) have settled in the 'city' itself, but migrants form a much greater proportion of the populations of the outer sub-regions. The relatively large population, and proportion of migrants, in the south-east sub-region results from the comparatively recent major industrial developments in the 'ABC' industrial complex—the municipalities of Santo Andre, São Bernardo and São Caetano—which lies between the 'city' and the coastal industrial region

around the port of Santos and the town of Cubatão. (See also **4.10**, on page 55). Two-thirds of the migrants were from within the South-east region, a significant number from the North-east, and nearly 10 per cent from abroad.

Rural depopulation is not a simple process of direct rural-urban migration. In fact the 1970 census shows that this accounted for only about 20 per cent of total migration. Most movements (nearly 50 per cent) were urban-urban; this shows that many migratory movements occur in stages. Many migrants have a history of movement from small urban centres in predominantly rural areas to larger cities; in some cases individual migrants have moved from rural area to small town, and then to the city, whilst in other cases the movement may have taken several generations. This type of migratory flow is common, and is related to later migrants occupying the spaces in zones closer to large cities which earlier migrants had vacated.

Many Brasilians are also involved in other relatively short-term and/or short distance movements. In rural areas, seasonal movements associated with farming are common. These include shifting cultivation, the seasonal movement of pastoralists in areas with a marked dry season such as the *cerrado* (referred to as transhumance), and migrant farm labour. In urban areas also, improved public transport is increasing urban mobility so that commuting is now much more common than in the past. Air shuttle services also allow the movement of administrators, industrialists and businessmen between major cities, and in particular to and from Brasília.

The Urban Hierarchy

The urban hierarchy is dominated by the two primate metropolitan regions of São Paulo and Rio de Janeiro, which are both considerably larger than the 'rank-size rule' would suggest (see **4.6**). Their economic status is even greater, as they are the centres of highly urbanised and industrialised regions which contain a number of regional sub-centres. In 1975, Brasil's nine metropolitan regions contained 45 per cent of Brasil's total urban population. With the exception of São Paulo, Belo Horizonte and Curitiba, they all developed as ports. Even these inland centres are coupled with major ports—São Paulo with Santos; Belo Horizonte with Vitória and Rio; and Curitiba with Paranaguá. R. P. Momsen (1963) regards this development of 'coupled nuclei' as being common where natural barriers such as the Serra do Mar curtailed the development of ports as route foci. In all three cases mentioned above, the cities became either route foci or centres of agricultural or mineral production. Momsen also suggests that as intranational trade developed, the inland route focus became the dominant commercial centre and surpassed its port. This was certainly the case with São Paulo and Curitiba, and more recently Governador Valdares has surpassed its port of Vitória.

In 1972 the *Instituto Brasileiro de Geografia* produced a hierarchy of Brasil's 718 urban settlements, and defined ten major regional centres and their spheres of influence (see **4.5**). This was based on a

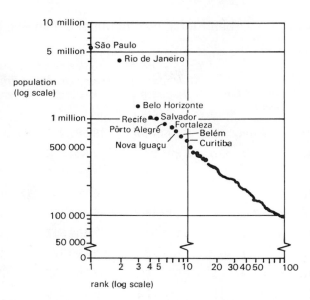

Note: the anomalous positions of Rio and Belo Horizonte in particular.

Theoretically, the line should be perfectly straight obeying the

formula $Pn = \frac{Pl}{n}$ where Pn is the population of the town ranked n

and Pl is the population of the largest town.

Source: Abstracted from *Anuario Estatistico* (1974)

4.6. The Rank-Size of Brasil's 100 most Populous Urban Municipalities in 1970.

number of criteria such as freight and passenger movements, transport linkages, the flow of services, and the location of markets and distribution centres. Table **4.7** summarises the major characteristics of these regions. The general pattern and hierarchy is predictable, but it is clear from the map (**4.5**) that Belo Horizonte's status is greater than the rank-size rule suggests. The city is now an important urban and industrial 'core' and has captured a part of Rio's former sphere of influence. São Paulo's sphere includes much of Mato Grosso state, as the latter has no dominant major urban centre. The hierarchy indicates a broad tiering of central places, with each metropolitan region being served by an average of seven regional centres, 19 sub-centres and 52 local centres.

The graph (**4.8**) shows the growth of Brasil's five largest cities. It illustrates the correlation between the growth of urban population and the urban economy. The three largest cities are those which are the most industrialised and have experienced the most rapid rates of population growth. In contrast, both Recife and Salvador are situated in the Northeast and, although they are the major industrial centres within that region, their economic status is far below the cities of the South-east.

4.7. The Urban Hierarchy and Major Urban Regions, Selected Data.

Metropolitan Regions	Population of Metropolitan Regions (1970)	Population of Major Urban Regions (1970)	Average Population Density /km² (1970)	Population of Metropolitan Regions (1975)	Number of urban centres in each category			Total
					(2)	(3)	(4)	
1a São Paulo	8 139 730	19 581 288	14.6*	10 041 132	17	61	86	164
1b Rio de Janeiro	6 891 521	7 684 319	63.3	8 112 202	5	13	34	52
1c Belo Horizonte	1 645 519	7 096 275	15.4	2 069 784	4	19	57	80
1c Recife	1 729 126	10 399 731	24.1	2 085 185	8	19	68	95
1c Pôrto Alegre	1 548 140	6 654 132	23.1	1 854 584	12	11	53	76
1c Salvador	1 194 578	7 150 317	13.3	1 460 153	6	9	48	63
1d Curitiba	821 233	4 596 322	23.0	1 013 279	7	11	41	59
1d Fortaleza	1 036 799	7 506 537	18.1	1 317 496	4	10	38	52
1d Belém	669 768	3 740 619	0.86	818 622	1	11	14	26
1d Goiânia**	—	3 226 501	3.5	—	2	8	31	41

* With that part of São Paulo's sphere in Mato Grosso excluded, the average density is 40 /km².
** Goiânia is not designated as a Metropolitan region.

Source: *Divisão do Brasil em Regiões Funcionais Urbanas, I.B.G. 1972.*

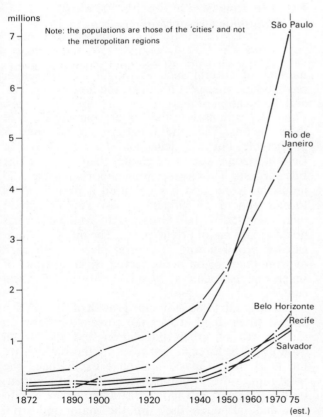

4.8. The Growth of Brasil's Five Largest Cities, 1872–1975.

Urban Structure

The internal structure of Brasilian cities varies considerably. The major causes of this are related to the economic forces which were operative during the early stages of their urban expansion, and their degree of industrialisation.

Many of Brasil's pre-industrial cities, such as the ports which developed to serve hinterlands with predominantly agricultural economies, have a reversed structure as compared with typically 'western' industrial cities. In the latter there is a broad concentric zonation of urban land-use, with increasingly higher-class residential areas further from the central business district. In the pre-industrial city, the élite land-owners built their luxurious town houses close to the commercial centre alongside those of the merchant classes and administrators. Consequently, the lower class zones are reversed, with the lowest in the outer suburbs. In colonial cities this zonation was reinforced by rural depopulation, especially in the North-east, because the immigrants settled in shanty towns around the periphery of the built-up area. There were exceptions to this, as shown in the next section.

Few essentially colonial cities had room for the development of industrial plants within the existing urban fabric, so that in most cases new industrial sectors emerged. But not all cities shared in Brasil's industrial growth, so that many colonial cities still retain the structure outlined above. In contrast, planned cities (such as Belo Horizonte) have planned industrial sectors, with their own residential sectors. Industrial giants (such as São Paulo) have also experienced major structural changes. These are discussed in detail later in this chapter.

In 'western' cities, there is a steep population density gradient away from the centre, but as the commercial core expands and the inner city area is redeveloped this creates a 'density crater'. Thus the zone of highest density gradually migrates outwards through time. This does not appear to happen on so large a scale in Brasil. In São Paulo, for example, chronic congestion of the core—even greater than in the largest 'western' cities—is causing the development of new high-class residential areas, with their own commercial cores at peripheral locations not affected by shanty development.

Since many 'western' cities (especially in the 'old world') have undergone a pre-industrial phase in the past, it is likely that many more industrial cities in Brasil will eventually follow the 'western' pattern. This is likely to be reinforced by planning policies.

The Problems Resulting from Rapid Urbanisation

Brasil's premature urbanisation can be demonstrated by the lag in the provision of basic services, utilities and amenities referred to in Brasil as *urbanizacão*. These include housing, sanitation, mains water supply, and educational and medical services. Many smaller cities, with little industrial or commercial development, have outgrown their ability to solve their own problems. The increased concentration of the urban population in huge cities such as São Paulo and Rio is also creating new problems, which are beginning to threaten their future development. Some of these problems have now reached crisis proportions, and necessitate urgent and comprehensive planning. However, only recently has the planning of future urban growth in these cities been subject to detailed studies, and been adequately financed.

Massive rural depopulation and migration to cities is causing severe social problems, both for the source areas and the cities. Migration itself is a selective process, as usually young males form the major element. This denudes the rural periphery of its most innovative and energetic human resource. Migration results in a break-up of the traditional, self-sufficient and socially integrated extended family. It also leads to increased social stratification, and increased frustration. Frustration results from an inability to escape from the 'poverty trap' and leads to a growth

in crime, the breakdown of married life, high suicide rates, and the abandonment of children. For the urban poor, life is a fight for survival, and only the fittest survive.

The extreme problems are illustrated by the life of the *favelado* (shanty dweller). *Favelas* are characteristic of nearly all of Brasil's major cities. The *favela* is usually situated at the periphery of the built-up area, but also on any land that is unsuitable for property speculation and construction. In Rio, the *favelas* flank the *morros* (hills) which are too steep for normal housing; in Salvador, they are built precariously on stilts in tidal mud flats; and in São Paulo, they have been pushed from the floodplains of the River Tietê and its southern tributaries to a peripheral location, by the construction of urban parks. As the suburbs grow outwards, the *favelados* are pushed even further from the centre, so that those fortunate in having a job are forced to live far from their place of work. Low wages and generally poor public transport services place a further burden on these fortunate few.

The precise number of *favelados* is unknown—various estimates give a figure of between 400 000 and 1 100 000 for Rio alone, whilst in other large cities *favelados* are estimated to account for over 10 per cent of the urban population.

The *favela* is a collection of ram-shackle huts constructed of any available materials, and in many cases lacking virtually all essential amenities, even water and sanitation. The inhabitants of Escondidinho *favela*, for instance, have to negotiate 352 steps to reach the nearest fresh water supply—a roadside tap 1 km away. The *favelado* is frequently destined to a life of squalor, and destitute parents are often forced to abandon unwanted children. In a recent (1979) ITV television programme on São Paulo, it was stated that in that city alone there were 600 000 abandoned children, and about 15 million in Brasil as a whole. Many are forced to beg or steal for a living. Young girls have fewer opportunities than boys, and they frequently become maids, earning about £7 for an 80-hour week. Some take to the streets as prostitutes—a job which can offer much higher rewards, as teenage prostitutes can earn considerably more than the élite motor-vehicle workers. The most conspicuous of Rio's *favelas* are those on the flanks of the *morros*; their inhabitants have the best views of one of the world's most beautiful cities, but this hardly compensates for such a precarious existence. In 1966 and 1967, for example, torrential rainfall and subsequent landslips caused the destruction of many shanties and great loss of life.

A survey in 1967 found that *favelas* function as complete neighbourhood units, and that there was considerable social and economic variation between

Plate 11. A *favela* in Rio de Janeiro. This ramshackle collection of shanties has sprawled over the flanks of one of the many granite *morros* in the city. (See also Plate 29, page 147). ***J. Allan Cash Ltd.***

them. Many *favelados* were recent migrants, but others had a long family history in the same *favela*. Despite the fact that all *favelados* are illegal squatters, some shanties are quite sophisticated, with brick walls, two storeys, and even power supplies and television sets.

Several attempts have been made to rehabilitate selected *favelas*, although some projects have failed because of inadequate funds, a lack of consultation with the community leaders, and site problems. During the mid-1960s, a housing programme was initiated by COHAB (*Companhia de Habitacão Popular*). Within three years over 10 000 government-designed low-cost houses were built, each with water, sanitation, gas and electricity supplies. The new owners were allowed to extend them, and could purchase building materials at cost price. In order to take part in this self-help project, the potential purchaser had to pay a deposit of 10 per cent, had to be in employment and had to have a clean criminal record. There were ten applicants for each new house, but the purchase of private housing is beyond the reach of the vast majority. In recent years property speculation has increased land prices by over 2 000 per cent, and in 1979 even a two-room house could cost as much as £7 000, an astronomical figure when compared with the average wage.

Rio's *favelados* have a strong African strain and many still cling to ancestral traditions such as the *macumba* (white magic) form of voodoo, which is a complex mix of Amerindian mythology, African voodoo and Christian ethics. The voodoo priestess enjoys a considerable social as well as religious status. Rio's *favelados* make a major contribution to the ninety-six hours non-stop carnival in early February each year. They organise themselves into seven 'official', elaborately costumed *escolas de samba* (samba schools) which compete for the accolade of champions of the year. The carnival is still a major tourist attraction in Rio and also occurs in other cities.

Whilst the *favelas* illustrate the extreme case of urban deprivation, most Brasilian cities still have a large poor population and a small wealthy élite. In 1970, only 55 per cent of urban dwellings were served by a general water supply, whilst 24 per cent used springs and wells which were frequently polluted. Pollution is reaching chronic levels. Copacabana beach—a major tourist attraction—is frequently defiled by untreated sewage, and industrial effluent has made the River Tietê and the lower Billings reservoir in São Paulo anaerobic. Atmospheric pollution is greatest in São Paulo city where, until recently, it frequently reached levels three times as high as the recommended maximum.

Sanitation is also grossly inadequate. In 1970, 30 per cent of urban dwellings were linked to public sewers, but 15 per cent were served by cesspools, and a further 41 per cent by only rudimentary pits and similar methods. Many, therefore, had no sanitary facilities whatsoever. Without these basic facilities disease spreads rapidly. Refuse collection and disposal are also grossly inadequate.

Increased population pressure on already inadequate amenities and services has widespread effects. Over the last decade the infant mortality rate has increased by 40 per cent, to a level of 95 per thousand for children under 4 years of age. The crime rate is increasing by over 8 per cent per annum, and the education service which in 1960 catered for an estimated 90 per cent of school-aged children now caters for less than 80 per cent. Even the affluent have their

Plate 12. A *favela* in São Luis (Maranhão). The environment of the *favelas* is intimate, but squalid. Less than a half of urban dwellings have mains water, and less than a third are served by sewers. *Hoa-Qui.*

problems, including a two-year wait for telephone connections.

The circulation of people and goods is of vital importance in the metropolitan regions, yet urban mobility is severely limited by inadequate public transport, traffic congested streets and increasingly longer journeys to work. In 1974 there were 105 000 traffic accidents involving 6 000 fatalities—one of the highest rates in the world—and the rate is increasing by 20 per cent per annum. An analysis of São Paulo's public transport system illustrates the problems associated with increasing urban mobility. The city has the world's largest bus fleet, but this slows to an average speed of 3 km/hour at peak rush-hour periods. In all, seventy separate bus companies carry 7 000 000 passengers per day on 1 300 different routes (London has a mere 300 routes). Schedules have to be continuously revised to prevent traffic jams. However, they still occur with monotonous regularity. Some commuters have become so frustrated that they have been known to 'hi-jack' buses and

Plate 13. A vertical aerial view of Recife's floating district. The city has a reef site, so that space is limited. Numerous bridges link up the reefs and connect them with the mainland where most new urban and industrial development is taking place. *Hoa-Qui.*

their drivers and to force them to take different routes.

A project which started in 1974 has redesigned the surface transport system. It uses standardised colour coding for buses, routes and street furniture. District route maps, similar to that of the London underground, are displayed prominently. The cartography was a major problem in itself, as at several road foci more than forty different routes intersect. However, the communication of information to the public remains a major problem.

The inadequacy of surface transport systems has been apparent in São Paulo and Rio for over 30 years, but it was not until the fiscal reforms of 1965 that plans were outlined for the development of underground 'metro' systems in these cities. The first

phase of São Paulo's metro was opened in 1975, and now carries 600 000 passengers per day. By 1990, it is hoped that a system of five lines will be completed. It will form the backbone of an integrated surface and metro system. The metro itself will be capable of handling 50 per cent of projected passenger movements. The construction of the metro has also created 7 000 new jobs for low-skilled workers, and a further 2 400 are employed in the planning, administration and operation of 'Line 1', which is 17 km long and runs from Santana through the business district (the *Triangulo*) to Jabaquara (see **4.10** on page 55).

Work on Rio's metro began in 1970. Its slow progress and the construction of an ultra-modern station before the line itself, has attracted the scorn of the *Cariocas* (inhabitants of Rio). But the 'world's most expensive hole' will be part of a three-line system, which will in the 1990s be capable of handling 80 000 passengers during the rush-hour. The system will be linked to a 'pre-metro' surface system, which will serve the outer suburbs and therefore provide improved employment opportunities there. It is possible that this could also affect the location of new industries in other urban nuclei such as Nova Iguaçu. Another major reason for the development of metro systems in both cities is their potential for saving petroleum. The new electrified system could reduce the present energy consumption of public transport systems by as much as 75 per cent, and atmospheric pollution could also be very significantly reduced.

There is no doubt that planning in the metropolitan regions is beginning to have an effect. Within a decade of the formation of the National Housing Bank in 1964, 800 000 new houses had been built. The bank is now heavily committed to financing and building improved housing and urban services; and it is involved in general aspects of urban planning. It estimated that demographic growth in the 1970s in itself necessitated the provision of six million new homes, in addition to those which would be required to rehouse the *favelados*. Clearly this requires massive investment, but housing already absorbs about 20 per cent of total capital investment, corresponding to 4 per cent of the GDP.

It is clear from the discussion above that Brasil's urban problems are great. Significant improvements in the future can only be achieved by a commitment to social development, and to the redistribution of wealth. These goals can only be achieved within a rapidly expanding national economy.

In the following sections the particular characteristics, problems and planning strategies of two contrasting cities, São Paulo and Brasília, are examined in more detail. Brasil's other major cities are discussed in Chapter 10, along with their industries.

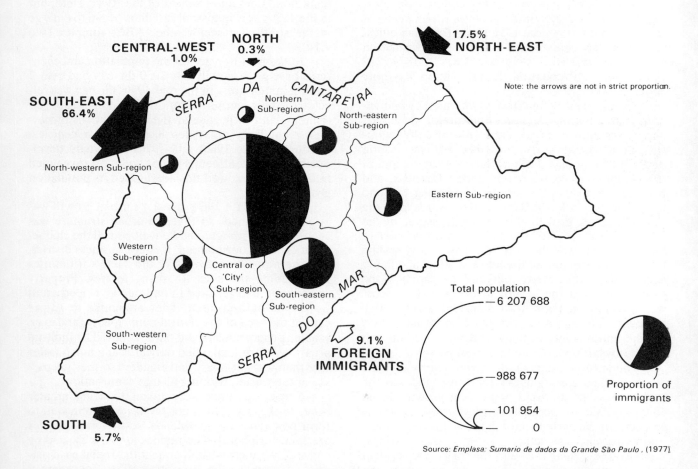

4.9. Immigrants Residing in Greater São Paulo in 1970: Their Origin and Contribution to the Total Population, by Sub-regions.

Greater São Paulo: A Case Study of Urban Growth and Planning in Brasil's 'Megalopolis'

The São Paulo Metropolitan Region, established in 1973, is an urban agglomeration of vast proportions. Its built-up area is over 1 000 km^2 and growing by over 60 km^2 per annum, and its population is already 10.5 million and growing by over 600 000 per annum. If growth continues at present rates it could well be the world's second largest city by the year 2000, with a population of over 25 million.

Greater São Paulo is also the continent's leading industrial region, accounting for about 40 per cent of Brasil's industrial output and GDP (see Chapter 10).

São Paulo de Piratininga was founded by the Jesuits in 1554 near the confluence of the Rio Tietê and it southern tributary the Tamanduatei, the site being at an altitude of 760 m. It became one of several *bandeirante* bases located at defensive sites, which were to develop into the major urban nuclei of the metropolitan region. Like many Brasilian cities, until the late nineteenth century its population growth was relatively slow (see **4.8**). In 1874, 320 years after its foundation, its population was only about 25 000.

The city's early wealth was generated by *bandeirante* expeditions, but the first major economic impact resulted from the expansion of coffee cultivation onto the *terra roxa* soils of the plateau. It soon displaced Campinas, both as the state capital and as the commercial centre of the coffee *fazendas*, and became the focus of a rapidly developing rail and later road network which radiated outwards from the city. The future growth of the city was assured by the completion in 1867 of the rail link with its port of Santos, as this was the only major routeway scaling the great escarpment of the Serra do Mar. São Paulo became the 'coffee metropolis' and the 'capital of the *fazendeiro*', and the wealth of the 'nouveau riche' was lavished on their town mansions and prestige buildings. The city also became an important centre for the nation's intellectuals, and this together with its great wealth guaranteed political power.

The massive influx of 'new' immigrants gave the city a marked cosmopolitan character, and was the major cause of its rapid population growth. From 1875 to 1920 its population grew from 25 000 to 580 000. In the early twentieth century the city had a 'mono-nuclear' structure around the business district—the *Triangulo*—and the high class residential zone which fringed it. The street pattern consisted of radial highways connected by a concentric sub-system, the latter tending to segregate high and low class residential districts. Unlike the typical 'western city', the residential zones were progressively poorer outwards from the centre, reflecting the limited economic base of the city and the low degree of intra-urban mobility.

Industrial growth was stimulated by a number of factors: the completion of the Cubatão Hydro-electric plant in 1901; the city's success in attracting a considerable share of domestic and foreign investment (including coffee export revenues); compensation from the federal government for the high transport costs incurred in scaling the escarpment; and the availability of the nation's most highly developed infrastructure. The period from 1915 to 1940 was characterised by the 'metropolitanisation' of the city, related to rapid industrial and population growth. By 1940 its population had reached 1.3 million as a result of immigration from rural areas and high rates of natural increase. Industrial growth introduced marked sectors into the urban fabric: the first industrial districts were located on the south bank floodplain and terraces of the River Tietê, but in the 1930s new industrial satellites began to emerge in the south-east sector—the 'ABC' complex (see **4.10**).

In the post war period the population and economic base grew rapidly. By 1950 the city had over 2 million inhabitants. In the mid-1950s the city was selected by the government for priority industrial development, and in particular the development of new high technology industries such as motor vehicles. Throughout the 1960s and 1970s São Paulo developed into the continent's major and most diversified industrial centre, and this accelerated its population growth.

Until the late-1960s the city's urban growth was largely unplanned, so that the urban structure was chaotic. The *Triangulo* had developed all the characteristics of a 'transplanted' western business district, and the numerous ravines of the Tietê's tributaries had become the sites for many *favelas*. Property speculation had resulted in large undeveloped areas within the built-up area. They amounted to 13 per cent of the area of the central municipality, and even greater proportions of the outer zones. The built-up area, therefore, expanded outwards at a much faster rate than was necessary and engulfed formerly separate urban nuclei, forming a large conurbation.

Some measures were taken to bring greater order to the city. The inner *favelas* were removed to form new inner city parklands, so that most *favelas* are now peripheral. The ravines are now crossed by some 20 viaducts which connect the radial road arteries. However, the first attempts to formulate a comprehensive and integrated planning strategy for the conurbation were made only in 1968, and these

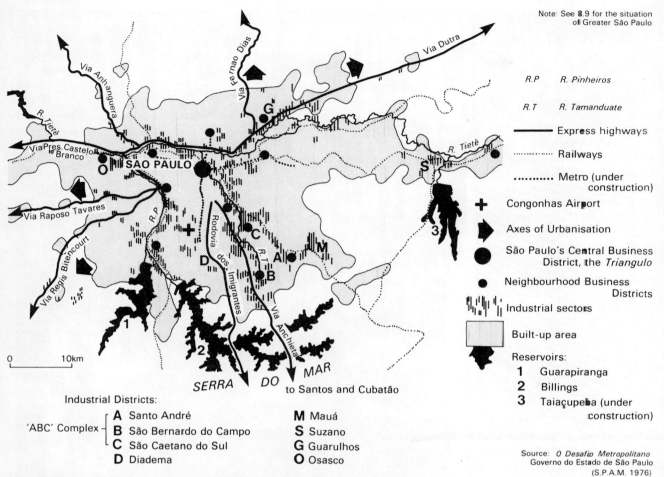

Note: See 8.9 for the situation of Greater São Paulo

R.P   R. Pinheiros

R.T   R. Tamanduate

——— Express highways

············ Railways

·········· Metro (under construction)

+ Congonhas Airport

◄ Axes of Urbanisation

● São Paulo's Central Business District, the *Triangulo*

• Neighbourhood Business Districts

Industrial sectors

Built-up area

Reservoirs:
1 Guarapiranga
2 Billings
3 Taiaçupeba (under construction)

Source: *O Desafio Metropolitano* Governo do Estado de São Paulo (S.P.A.M. 1976)

Industrial Districts:

'ABC' Complex —
A Santo André
B São Bernardo do Campo
C São Caetano do Sul
D Diadema

M Mauá
S Suzano
G Guarulhos
O Osasco

4.10. Greater São Paulo: Major Urban and Industrial Characteristics.

led to the establishment of the metropolitan region in 1973. The fundamental need was to coordinate federal, state, civic and municipal administration, and to indentify the common problems faced by the region's 37 municipalities.

In 1974 the Metropolitan Planning and Administration System (SPAM) began to develop the operational tools necessary for planning. These included the first detailed mapping of the region, the collection and processing of demographic, economic, transport and social data, and the definition of the problems. A pilot 'geo-codification' project in São Bernardo do Campo yielded some surprising results, the most significant being an 883 per cent increase in property taxes resulting from the first accurate assessment of property and housing, and the establishment of municipal files. The increased revenues are vital for the implementation of future projects. The pilot project is now being extended to cover 85 per cent of the region's population.

In recent decades the mono-nuclear structure of

the city has been breaking down. This is not only because of problems of intra-urban mobility, which have forced the spontaneous development of suburban business districts and semi-autonomous centres such as Santo Amaro, but also because the emerging middle-class has increasingly sought low-density housing away from the congested inner city. This has been made possible by greatly increased motor car ownership.

The Metropolitan Planning Corporation (EMPLASA) has developed a comprehensive structure plan for the region, based on the continuing development of a 'poly-nuclear' conurbation. The built-up area has been divided into 30 sections by a grid, each section centred on an existing or projected urban commercial nucleus. The aim is to make each section as autonomous and self-contained as possible, with a full range of services and amenities. Transport planning is vital to the success of the plan; the sections are to be flanked by arterial roads, but the local networks are to be 'dead ends' thus prevent-

Plate 14. São Paulo's business district, the *Triangulo*. São Paulo is the largest and fastest growing conurbation and industrial centre in the continent. Note the church dwarfed by the Hilton, office blocks and department stores. ***Hoa-Qui.***

ing through traffic. It is hoped that through the 1980s and 1990s the expanding metro system will develop as the main form of public transport, especially to and from the *Triangulo*.

A major element of the plan was initiated in 1975 with the Water Resources Protection Law, which effectively stopped the further expansion of the built-up area into the forested water catchments of the Serra da Cantareira in the north and Serra do Mar in the south. Thus, future growth is to be along the east-west axis parallel to the River Tietê. The western sections are to remain predominantly resi-

dential, whilst in the east new industrial, commercial and related residential development will follow the Dutra Highway. The industrial growth of the 'ABC' complex in the south-east will continue, along the transport links with Santos.

The present planning of the conurbation is taking place in a climate of increasing population pressure, which results in deteriorating services. Greater São Paulo cannot be planned in isolation. EMPLASA is entrusted with enforcing a policy of controlled future growth and containment. If population is to be diverted to satellite cities, then these must develop as major industrial centres. Thus, industrial decentralisation is a key component in urban planning (see Chapter 10, page 145). São Paulo's industrial dominance has now reached a level where further concentration of economic activity will lead to 'diseconomies of scale'. In contrast many of Brasil's other major cities still have a narrow and underdeveloped economic base.

Brasília: 'An Act of Faith'

New towns have been used as a key component in regional development programmes in many countries. They have been established for a number of reasons, such as to redirect urban and industrial growth, to act as a focal point in the development of underdeveloped regions, and to relieve congestion in large conurbations. However, some countries such as the United States of America, Australia and Brasil have created new capital cities. In the cases of Canberra and Washington D.C., the primary factor was a need to create a new capital to, 'sidestep political rivalry between several large cities or regions of the country' (P. Merlin, 1973). This was also a major factor in the establishment of Brasília, but it was also intended to accelerate the economic development of the underdeveloped regions.

The emergence of a new independent Brasil, freed from colonial rule, and later also from the monarchy, stimulated a search for a symbol of new national aspirations and the great potential of the country. The idea of a new capital, separated in time and space from Brasil's colonial past, was discussed as early as the 1870s. In 1891 it was written into the first constitution, and its general location was also decided. The new capital was to be located in the interior, away from the major cities. As previously stated, Belo Horizonte was the first major new town to be established. It replaced the former state capital of Ouro Prêto because the latter had a very restricted site and no room for further industrial and urban

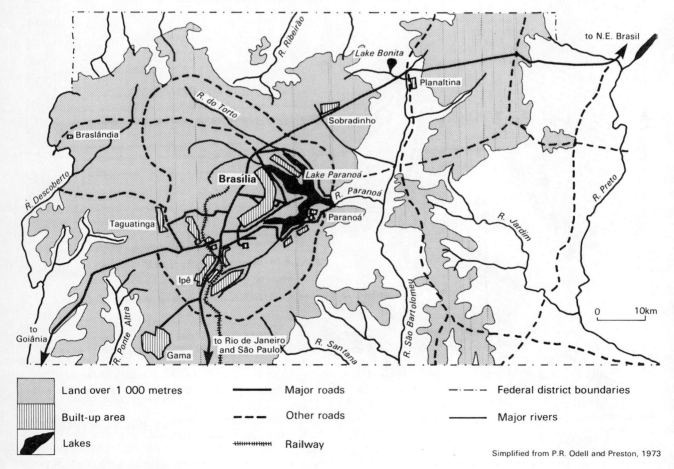

Land over 1 000 metres	——— Major roads	—·—·— Federal district boundaries
Built-up area	– – – Other roads	——— Major rivers
Lakes	+++++++ Railway	

Simplified from P.R. Odell and Preston, 1973

4.11. The Federal District.

expansion. Belo Horizonte was planned along similar lines to Washington D.C. However, the construction of Brasília did not start for another sixty years after the inauguration of Belo Horizonte.

The location of the capital was to be in the *sertão,* near the junction of the watersheds of the rivers São Francisco, Tocantins and Paraná, where the boundaries of the regions of the North-east, Central-west and South-east met; a symbolic linking of the 'Brasils'. However, the selection of site was more problematic, and two commissions were established to report on this. The first, a team of geographers, concluded that the new capital should be sited in the *Triangulo Mineiro*, part of north-west Minas Gerais. This proved politically unacceptable. The second commission was made up of political representatives of each state, and their findings were accepted. Preston E. James (1959) explains the decision in terms of the greater number of state representatives from the North-east. This region had nine votes, as compared with only four votes from the South-east and South. Detailed photogrammetric surveys were used to pin-point the site. It was at an altitude of

910 m, in an area of undulating terrain drained by the Rio Paranoá, a tributary of the Paraná, and 960 km from the coast. It was close to sources of most construction materials, and the river could be dammed to form a large lake (see **4.11**).

It is interesting to note that the site is near to the mean centre of the state capitals, and approximately halfway between the mean population centre and the 'geodetic' or territorial centre of the country (see **3.1**.). Thus it is an optimum location in terms of access by air from the state capitals.

However, if the new capital was to succeed in economic terms, then it would also have to develop as a focal point for the opening up of the interior. The site is outside the spheres of influence of both Rio de Janeiro and São Paulo, but not so remote from them that it could not add momentum to the *Marcha Para O Oeste* (The March to the West). Earlier colonisation of the interior had been on a very limited scale, and had done little to develop the underdeveloped regions. The *sertão* had long been regarded as being capable of supporting only limited colonisation, and providing only short-term gains.

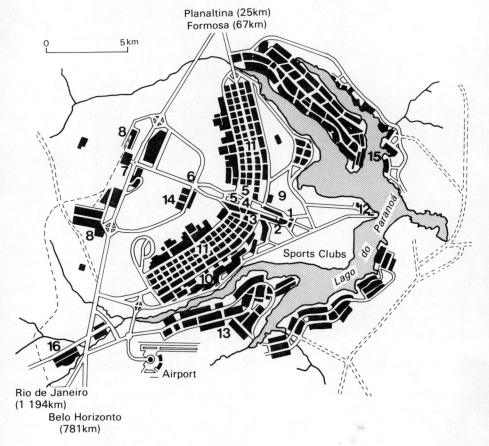

1 Square of the Three Powers
2 Government buildings
3 Cathedral
4 Cultural Sector
5 Central Business and Commercial Centres
6 Municipal Square
7 Railway Station
8 Warehouses and small industries
9 University
10 Embassies and Legations
11 Residential Sectors
12 Palace of the President
13 South sector of individual houses
14 Graphic and design industries
15 North sector of individual houses
16 Suburb 'Parkway Mansions'.

4.12. Brasília: The Plan of the Capital.

Plate 15. Brasília, Brasil's purpose-built capital. This view shows the *'Superquadras'*, the self-contained residential apartment blocks. **Aerofilms Ltd.**

The new capital was also to be symbolic in other ways. It had to be a national and international symbol of Brasil's progress and potential. Thus it was an 'act of faith' in Brasil as a developing country, and especially in its underdeveloped regions.

It was during the presidency of Juscelino Kubitschek de Oliveira (1955–61) that the dream became reality. Oscar Niemeyer, an internationally famous Brasilian architect, was selected to design the now famous futuristic buildings which have been described as a 'concrete revolution'. But the major problem was to find an equally futuristic plan for the city. This was made the subject of a national competition. The entrants were given only six months—sufficient time to create the 'grand design', but insufficient time for detailed studies. The competition was won by Lucio Costa whose design was conceived in a restaurant on the back of a menu card. It was based on a cruciform outline, resembling the shape of an aeroplane, and adapted to the curved shores of the lake (see **4.12**).

The construction of the city was entrusted to a special government sponsored company, aptly named NOVACAP, under the management of Israel Pinheiro. Kubitschek was also closely involved, spending much of his time in the small wooden site

headquarters; he was determined that the capital would be constructed and inaugurated within his presidency. Consequently the forty-five thousand construction workers, mainly from the North-east and Minas Gerais, worked in shifts so that construction continued twenty-four hours each day for three years. The workers were housed in the 'Cidade Livre' (Free City), so-called because accommodation was free, and they were also given tax-free permits for four years. There were problems, such as the need to fly in many materials (including the runway asphalt!) but generally this, the greatest feat of civil engineering in Brasil, was very successful. The major highways and buildings were completed in three years, and on its inauguration as national capital on the 21st April 1960, Brasília was hailed as a 'triumph of administration' and in itself responsible for creating a new national spirit of determination.

The city plan is symmetrical about a central raised 'monumental axis'; this runs from the municipal buildings through the central banking, commercial and shopping centre, and along the Esplanade of Ministries to the Plaza of the Three Powers, which contains the Congress, Supreme Court and Executive buildings. The curved, wing-shaped lateral axis consists of over a hundred neighbourhood 'superblocks', each of which are self-contained with open landscaped areas, upwards of ten six-storey apartment blocks, a primary school and a shopping centre. Fronting this residential axis are the foreign embassies and, to the north of the central axis, the university. The lake shores are dotted with recreation clubs. The lake peninsulas were developed as suburbs with detached houses, but more recent suburban growth has been less well planned. It was not foreseen that the *candangos* (construction workers) would become so caught up in the spirit of the new capital that they would not wish to leave it. Consequently the satellite towns, originally planned along the lines of Ebenezer Howard's 'Garden Cities', were flooded by this overspill from the capital. They are now much larger than intended and are relatively poorly served with medical, educational and other urban amenities and services. They are dormitory settlements rather than the self-sufficient communities that were envisaged. However, Brasília does not have the *favelas* characteristic of the large coastal cities.

From the beginning, the city was a planned route focus for the new roads which were to radiate outwards into the Central-west and Amazonia. Costa regarded it as, '—the capital of the airplane and the highway, city and park'. Since its inauguration on the 21st April 1960, it has been the planned focus of the national highway network. It is linked to Belo Horizonte (781 km) and Rio (1 194 km) by the BR7 'Jaguar Highway'; to São Paulo (1 140 km); and to Belém (2 227 km) by the BR14, which links with the 'Trans-Amazonica' highway. Near the capital, the improved transport links with Ceres, Anápolis and Goiânia have stimulated the development of flourishing agricultural colonies. In 1968 the city was also linked by rail to the South-east.

It is difficult to assess the success of Brasília, as this has to be assessed on the basis of several criteria. There is no doubt that it has succeeded in its primary function as national capital. Also, it has already grown beyond its planned population of 500 000. By 1970, the city itself had a population of over 270 000, and the federal district totalled 537 500. By 1975, this had reached an estimated 760 000. It has attracted little industry apart from printing and publishing, both related to its administrative function, but it was not part of the 'grand design' that Brasília should be a large industrial city to rival those of the South-east. It has certainly contributed to the phenomenal growth of Belo Horizonte, and has become a new 'geo-economic growth pole'. The total cost of the capital will never be known, but it certainly contributed to the stagnation of the economy in the early 1960s, a situation which prompted the military coup in 1964. A former finance minister is reputed to have

described the phenomenal cost of Brasilia as, 'a crime against the country's economy'.

It is clear that Brasília's long-term success is largely dependent on the growth of the national economy, and on the future development of Brasil as a whole. It is indeed 'an act of faith'. Its long-term prospects as the route focus for the national road network have been affected by the continuing energy crisis and, from this point of view, it is probably one of the most vulnerable of Brasil's cities. Yet it is now an international city, served by international airlines as well as the daily air-shuttles to and from Rio and São Paulo.

The role and development of Brasilia is discussed further in the later sections on regional development, transport, and the Central-west region.

Brasil's Urban Development Strategy

The Second National Development Plan (II PND) included an urban development strategy which reflects the regional imbalances in economic and urban development. It recognised that rapid urban growth in the 1980s will accentuate the imbalance in the urban hierarchy by, 'an excessive proliferation of small cities, and an insufficient number of medium-sized cities to provide a reasonable balance'. The imbalance between urban and economic growth is most chronic in the North-east. The three metropolitan regions—Fortaleza, Recife and Salvador—account for about 7 per cent of Brasil's urban population, but only about 3 per cent of industrial employment; this in spite of regional development programmes which have achieved increased industrial growth in these cities in recent years.

The major elements of the urban development strategy are summarised below and mapped in **4.13**.

(a) The implantation of the nine metropolitan regions.

(b) The promotion of an efficient functional division between the national metropolitan regions, regional centres and secondary nuclei.

(c) The planned decentralisation of economic activity to secondary nuclei with over 50 000 inhabitants, and the revitalisation of commercial agriculture and associated industries in smaller urban centres.

(d) The control of the excessive urban growth of Greater São Paulo and Greater Rio, and of the spontaneous industrialisation of the Rio–São Paulo–Campinas axis. The planned growth of Belo Horizonte, and the industrialisation of Vitória.

(e) The expansion of the regional centres of the South region, and the control of the growth of

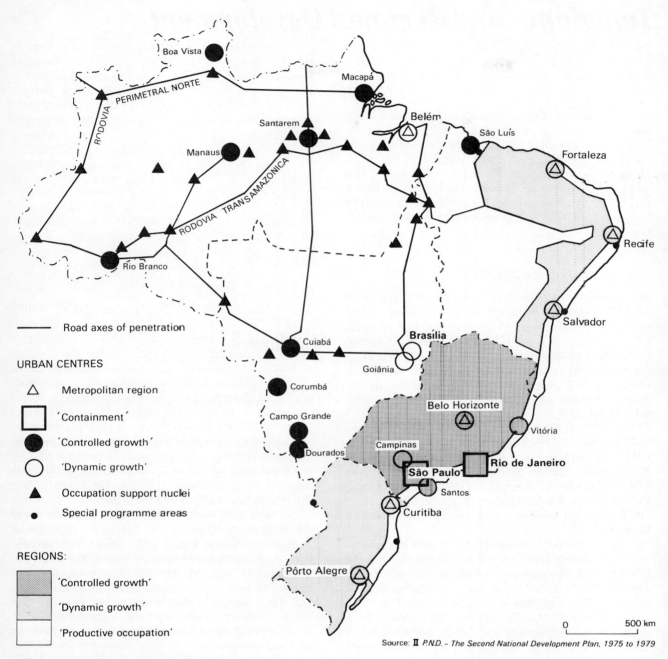

Road axes of penetration

URBAN CENTRES

△ Metropolitan region

☐ 'Containment'

⬤ 'Controlled growth'

○ 'Dynamic growth'

▲ Occupation support nuclei

• Special programme areas

REGIONS:

'Controlled growth'

'Dynamic growth'

'Productive occupation'

Source: II *P.N.D. – The Second National Development Plan, 1975 to 1979*

4.13. Urban Development Strategy.

Curitiba and Pôrto Alegre. Also, the promotion of the new urban nucleus associated with the Itaipu hydro-electricity project.

(f) The development of Brasília, Belém, Manaus and Santarem, and the urban nuclei along the new highways of the Central-west and Amazonia. This is intended to support the process of occupation of the underdeveloped regions.

(g) The revitalisation of the North-east by sup-

porting 'growth poles' at Salvador, Recife, Fortaleza and São Luis.

(h) The controlled and rigorously planned occupation of the coastal region, with a view to preserving its natural beauty and historic cities, and promoting the domestic and international tourist industry.

It is clear that these are long-term objectives, and are closely related to both continued national economic development and regional development.

5 Economic Development, Regional Imbalance and Regional Development

It is appropriate at this stage to analyse Brasil's economic development in structural and spatial terms. The general principles and characteristics of development are also discussed here, in order to provide a framework and perspective, and to emphasise the links and relationships between the systematic topics and themes in later chapters. The role of transport in national and regional development is also considered.

Stages in Development

The problem of identifying well defined stages in Brasil's economic development is made more difficult by the lack of a generally accepted and comprehensive conceptual model, and the relatively recent emergence of diversified agricultural and manufacturing sectors. As has been previously shown in Chapters 2, 3 and 4, massive immigration, demographic growth and urbanisation have all had profound effects on economic development.

Brasil's political transformation from a colony to a modern independent nation state was a relatively long process, but 'economic independence' is much more recent. Brasil's economy now ranks eighth in the world in terms of GNP (Gross National Product) but the development process has yet to achieve a high level of social, spatial and structural balance.

Here, Rostow's model (1955) is used as a framework. It suffers from an over-simplification of the many complex processes involved in economic development, but it does offer a means of placing Brasil's economic development in a wider context.

The 'Traditional Society' is characterised by a primitive technology and a self-sufficient subsistence economy. It corresponds to the indigenous Amerindian culture. At this level, both economy and society are highly adapted to the environment, and the basic necessities are provided initially by hunting and gathering, and later by the development of shifting or sedentary subsistence agriculture. Agricultural systems evolve as a direct result of technological progress, and the methods depend largely on the possibilities offered by the environment and the degree of population pressure on the biosphere. In pre-Columbian Brasil, the Amerindian population was probably not greater than four million, giving an average density of only about 0.5/km². Population

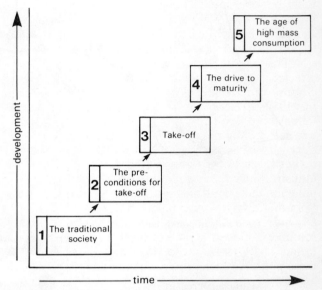

5.1. Rostow's Development Stage Model.

pressure was therefore very slight. The cultivators practised shifting cultivation within the rain-forests, using the *roça* system of forest clearings; these were abandoned at intervals of two-to-three years once the fragile latosols had lost their fertility.

The second stage in Brasil is not an extension of the indigenous economy, but marks the intrusion of European colonial values and culture. The 'colony' was regarded as a means of increasing the wealth of the 'mother' country, through the production and export of primary products including exotic crops and, later, precious metals and gemstones. The colonial economy was therefore 'export-based'; so much so that the colonists adopted the *roça* system of food production. As has been previously discussed, throughout the colonial period and during the nineteenth century there was little diversification of the primary sector, and virtually no development of manufacturing. The economy grew as a result of massive immigration. At first slave labour was the major producer of wealth, but later voluntary immigrants played a major role in the development of mining and export-based commercial agriculture, especially in the South-east region.

The 'preconditions for take-off' were largely a phenomenon of the late nineteenth century and early twentieth century. Development was delayed by the existence of a semi-feudal society and a narrow economic base. Coffee export revenues were largely responsible for providing the capital investment necessary during the early stages of industrial growth, but industrialisation did not gain momentum until the 1920s. It was not at first based on fossil fuels, but on charcoal, and then hydro-electricity. As in the colonial period, biological and mineral resources provided the basis for growth. Only later did imported petroleum make a major contribution.

The development of manufacturing was greatly affected by government activity and political decisions, notably President Kubitschek's decision in the 1950s to adopt A. O. Hirschman's concept of 'unbalanced growth'. The motor vehicles industry was selected by the government as a target for priority investment by foreign corporations and domestic investors. This was because it is a key industry which uses a great variety of different components, and its success would therefore result in a 'spin-off' effects, encouraging the growth of other key industries. This would in turn mobilise national resources. Government policies also included the formation of state corporations and industries. It was these policies which provided the initial stimulus for a phase of rapid industrial growth, and resulted in Brasil's 'take-off', which is defined by Rostow in terms of 'a rise in the rate of productive investment' and 'the emergence of a political, social and institutional framework' capable of supporting further development. Brasil's 'take-off' dates from the late 1950s and early 1960s. The economy has matured so that there has been increasing diversification of economic activity. However, the stage of 'high mass-consumption' has yet to be reached, and there are still great spatial inequalities in economic development. It must be stressed that advanced countries still exhibit marked regional contrasts, but they do not suffer from the gross inequalities in personal incomes that characterise developing countries such as Brasil. Neither do they suffer from rapid population growth and its effects on the age structure of the population. In Brasil the relatively low proportion of working people, compounded by high unemployment and underemployment, retards high mass-consumption. Thus, lower rates of natural increase and a wider distribution of wealth must accompany economic growth, if this stage is to be reached.

Structural Change

Economic development can also be viewed in terms of the relative development and changing contribution of sectors within the economy. Three main sectors can be defined: the 'primary' sector which includes agriculture and extractive activities; the 'secondary' sector which includes manufacturing, power and construction; and the 'tertiary' sector which includes the services such as commerce, transport and communications. Some classify research activities into a fourth or 'quaternary' sector.

The major characteristics of the model are illustrated by **5.2** and **5.3**. Both diagrams illustrate the same essential features, the former by means of a compound line graph, the latter by a comparative line graph. Note however that **5.2** refers to the total population, whilst **5.3** refers only to the percentage employed.

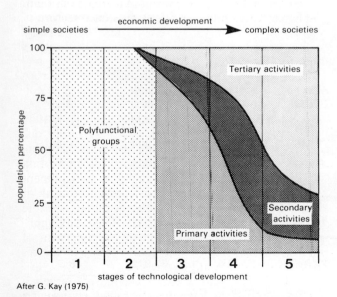

After G. Kay (1975)

5.2. The Sector Model; Compound Line Graph.

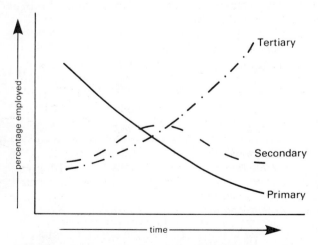

5.3. The Sector Model: Comparative Line Graph.

As both diagrams show, in the early stages of economic and technological development primary activities dominate, though **5.2** also recognises an earlier stage which is dominated by subsistence activities—the stage of 'polyfunctional groups'. Throughout the development process the proportions of the three main sectors vary, so that eventually the secondary and tertiary sectors develop and absorb those in the primary sector. Most advanced countries have reached a stage where the tertiary sector begins to dominate. It is difficult to place Brasil's economy within a narrowly defined stage because the model is highly generalised, and relatively rapid structural changes are taking place within the Brasilian economy.

The pattern of employment is shown by **5.4**. Note the high proportion of the population which is not 'economically active', and the great contrasts between male and female employment. A closer analysis of table **5.4** shows that primary activities still dominate male employment and total employment, but these figures also include subsistence activities. The secondary sector still employs a relatively small proportion of the labour force, whilst the tertiary sector is very strong. This would at first sight appear to be anomalous. However, the nature of the tertiary sector contrasts greatly with that of advanced countries. The figures for Brasil are boosted by a large number, especially females, employed in menial occupations.

The structure of the economy can also be viewed in terms of the value of production. In 1976 the primary, secondary and tertiary sectors contributed 12 per cent, 38 per cent and 50 per cent of the net domestic product respectively. This places the primary sector in true perspective, but also emphasises the comparative strength of the secondary and tertiary sectors which are both predominantly urban-based. The strength of the tertiary sector is in large measure a result of commercial activities.

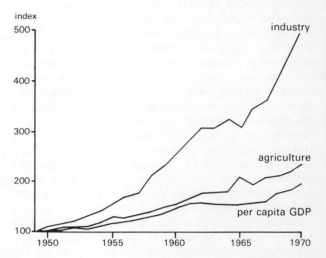

5.5. The Relative Growth of Industry, Agriculture and Per Capita Gross Domestic Product, 1949–70.

This analysis illustrates the structural weaknesses in the economy, whilst **5.5** shows the rapid development of industry. The low rate of growth in per capita GDP results from rapid population growth.

Brasil's economic status is still that of a developing country, but it is to be expected that continued rapid economic growth will absorb increasingly greater proportions of the labour force into higher level activities. This will result in a greater structural balance, and a much smaller subsistence sector.

5.4.   The Employment Structure of the Brasilian Economy, 1976

Sector	Men ('000s)	% *	Women ('000s)	% *	Total ('000s)	% *
Primary	11 394	29.7	3 201	8.0	14 595	18.7
Secondary	7 775	20.3	1 549	3.9	9 324	11.9
Tertiary	7 964	20.6	6 439	16.3	14 403	18.4
Others	1 347	3.5	569	1.4	1 916	2.5
Economically Active Population	28 480	74.1	11 757	29.6	40 237	51.5
Non Economically Active Population	9 928	25.9	27 982	70.4	37 910	48.5

* Note that the percentages are of the total population over 10 years of age.

Source: *Anuario Estatistico do Brasil, 1977.*

Regional Imbalance

The great imbalance between the developing and underdeveloped regions is the most important characteristic of Brasil's economic development and present economy. To some extent, regional contrasts in development are unavoidable because the natural environment is not homogeneous. The natural endowment of topography, climate, vegetation and soils, and of biological and mineral resources, is unequal. However, the environment does not determine economic activity, but presents man with a variety of possibilities. Few environments do not have a 'comparative advantage' in some form or other.

The root cause of Brasil's regional inequalities lies in its history of development. C. Prado (1970) has interpreted Brasil's development as a series of 'cycles', each being characterised by a single export commodity, and each commodity being produced in a different part of the country. Each commodity gave rise to a distinctive regional economy and culture. The 'cycles' can be differentiated as follows:

(a) *'Pau brasil'*, in the sixteenth century, at isolated coastal locations.

(b) Sugar, from 1550 to 1700, in the coastal rain-forest zone of the North-east.

(c) *'Mineracão'* gold mining and diamond prospecting, in Minas Gerais in the eighteenth century.

(d) The coffee, cocoa and rubber cycles of the nineteenth and early twentieth centuries, in São Paulo, Bahia and Amazonia respectively.

Whilst some 'boom and bust cycles' were ephemeral, such as the gold-rush and rubber boom, other commodities (though suffering a relative decline) were absorbed into a more diversified national economy. Also, some of the cycles were not mutually exclusive; coffee for example was cultivated in many parts of Brasil. However, five distinct regions emerged from this speculative response to world markets:

(a) The North-east: an overpopulated coastal region which stagnated with the decline in sugar; with a large African population and an aristocratic agrarian society; and a semi-arid interior plateau stricken with drought.

(b) The South-east: a dynamic region which attracted a large European immigrant population and which became dominant with the success of coffee. Industry developed as a direct result of invested coffee revenue, the raw materials of Minas Gerais, and hydro-electric power.

(c) The South: a region of more recent European immigration with a diverse agricultural base.

(d) The Central-west interior: a remote plateau region with small mining towns and large cattle ranches.

(e) Amazonia: a backwater; the realm of rivers, forest, and the Amerindian.

The regions retain much of their historical distinctiveness to the present, as shown by Diegues' classification of culture regions (**5.6**).

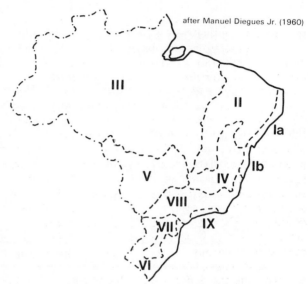

after Manuel Diegues Jr. (1960)

I The Agrarian North-east a) sugar
                                              b) cocoa

II The Pastoral North-east

III Amazonia

IV Eastern Highlands Mining region
                                    (Mineracão)

V The Central-west

VI The Pastoral South   **VIII** 'Coffee'

VII The 'European' South   **IX** The Industrial Belt

5.6. Culture Regions of Brasil.

J. R. P. Friedmann (1963) has developed a conceptual model related to Latin American countries, which provides an useful base for a deeper analysis of regional development. He identified four major phases of development:

(a) Initial coastal development.

(b) The development of semi-autonomous, externally-orientated regions.

(c) Industrialisation and the development of a centre-periphery structure.

(d) The final integration of the national space economy through the spread of metropolitan regions

Brasil has certainly passed through the first three stages, but the South-east has a geo-economic status far above that of any other region. The process of spatial integration is in its infancy. The metropolitan regions of São Paulo and Rio de Janeiro form a strong bi-nuclear core region, which has virtually monopolised development to the detriment of the other regions as shown by the following table:

5.7. Selected Indicators of Regional Inequality: Percentage Share, 1970.

Indicator	South-east	South	North-east	Central-west	North
Area	11	7	18	22	42
Population	43	18	30	5	4
National Income	63	17	14	3	2
Industrial Production	55	22	16	5	2
Industrial Employment	70	17	10	2	1
%Urban	73	44	42	48	45

Source: After *I.B.G.E.*

The 'Core-Periphery' phenomenon has been explained by Gunnar M. Myrdal (1957) in terms of a process of 'cumulative causation': 'the play of forces in the market normally tends to increase, rather than decrease, the inequalities between regions'. The 'core' is the centre of economic growth, and as such denudes the periphery by 'backwash' effects. These include the selective migration of young males, and the attraction of most domestic and foreign investment. The 'core' absorbs the human and physical resources of the periphery, and as a result of the 'multiplier effect' enters a stage of rapid growth. This results from the advantages of a vastly superior infrastructure, a large labour force and market, and the economies of agglomeration. Once a dominant manufacturing centre develops it becomes the best location for new industries.

Rio was Brasil's first core; its function as federal capital and the major port resulted in administrative, commercial and industrial superiority. However, its site was congested, and it lay outside the developing coffee lands. Rio is still a major core, but was overtaken by São Paulo which developed as the commercial centre of coffee production. As a result of the investment of coffee revenue, political influence, and its site and location advantages, São Paulo secured the major share of industrial growth. This was boosted further by the development of the motor vehicle industry in the 1950s. Thus, the core also developed as a result of government involvement. The 'backwash' effects were not confined to the outer periphery, but also to the inner periphery within the South-east region. Small-scale, inefficient, and low technology rural industries atrophied as a result of a flood of new goods and services from the core. It is significant that all states of the South-east region are experiencing rapid urbanisation and rapid rural depopulation as shown by table **5.8**.

The table shows that the 'backwash' effect of rural depopulation in the South-east continues. The mechanisms are shown by diagram **5.9**. This is likely to prove an irreversible trend because, as the core develops and 'spread' effects predominate, investment in the core stimulates capital-intensive

5.8. Urban Growth and Rural Depopulation in the South-east (in '000s)

	1960		1970		1980 (est.)	
	Urban	Rural	Urban	Rural	Urban	Rural
Minas Gerais	3 825	5 833	6 060	5 427	8 839	4 850
Espírito Santo	368	803	722	877	1 137	723
Rio de Janeiro*	5 215	1 396	7 906	1 089	11 202	820
São Paulo	8 020	4 790	14 276	3 496	22 052	1 952
South-east	17 461	13 170	28 965	10 889	43 229	8 346

*Rio de Janeiro and Guanabara data combined for 1960 and 1970.

Source: *A.E.D.B.* various years.

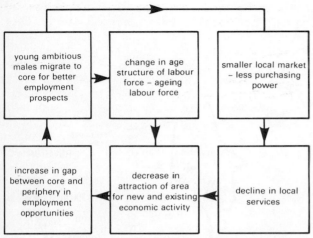

After M.G. Bradford and W.A. Kent, 1977   adapted from Myrdal

5.9. Rural Depopulation resulting from 'Backwash' Effects.

industries in the larger settlements in the periphery. At the same time rural economic activity, such as commercial farming, is stimulated by the diffusion of new techniques, mechanisation and a higher level of organisation. Both processes perpetuate depopulation, as each requires a smaller but more highly trained labour force.

Until 1946 there had been no planned attempt to develop the peripheral regions. Many believed—and still believe—that regional development is a luxury, as it encourages less efficient production in high cost locations. However, the increasing dominance of the core became increasingly unacceptable in social and political terms. The core had resulted in some benefits to the peripheral areas—referred to as 'spread' effects by Myrdal and 'trickling down' effects by Hirschman. These included improved agricultural technology, innovation, and some small-scale industrial developments, but even these were largely concentrated in the inner periphery of the South-east.

Ultimately the rapid urbanisation and industrialisation of the core leads to internal 'diseconomies of scale' such as congestion, pollution, the growth of shanties, a decline in the quality of life, and population pressure on urban services and amenities.

Regional Development

The inauguration of Brasília as the federal capital in 1960 marked the first major step towards regional development, though regional development agencies had been established for Amazonia (SPVEA) and the North-east (SUDENE) in the 1950s.

Brasília has had two major effects:
(a) The development of a new 'growth-pole' in the interior, which has stimulated colonisation.
(b) Its development as the planned focus of a number of new roads which link the underdeveloped regions with the South-east, as part of the 'Programme for National Integration' (PIN).

It may also have contributed to the recent phenomenal growth of Belo Horizonte, which is now part of a new 'multi-nuclear' core region together with São Paulo and Rio, and the towns along their linkages.

The regional development agencies proved unsuccessful during the 1960s because of the stagnation of the national economy, inadequate government support, and some political opposition. In 1966, SPVEA (Superintendency for the Economic Evaluation of Amazonia) was replaced by SUDAM (Superintendency for the Development of Amazonia). This was structured along similar lines to SUDENE (Superintendency for the Development of the North-east). Both SUDENE and SUDAM have been criticised; the former is regarded by some as merely a clearing house for new projects, whilst others argue that it should be responsible for supervising the overall development of the overpopulated and chronically poor North-east region. SUDAM has been criticised for approving a number of ranching projects which are in danger of causing irreversible damage to the rain-forest ecosystem.

Following the economic recovery of the late 1960s, new regional development agencies were established under the PIN programme—SUDECO for the Central-west, and SUDESUL for the South (see **5.10**). The Second National Development Plan (1975–79) proposed an investment equivalent to £10 billion in the North, Central-west and North-east. This was claimed by the federal government to be equivalent to, 'two and a half times the aid disbursed by the developed world (OECD members) to the developing nations of Africa, Asia and Latin America during 1973'. Investment in 'National Integration' was to represent about 10 per cent of total domestic investment.

The plan also marked a change in the development strategy. Three sub-programmes were established to promote selected 'growth-poles' or 'integrated areas'—POLAMAZONIA, POLOCENTRO and POLONORDESTE. Many of the 'growth poles' selected for agricultural development are based on labour-intensive rather than capital-intensive methods of production, whilst large-scale capital investment is still concentrated in the mining

5.10. Brasil's Regional Development Agencies.

and manufacturing sectors. The plan gave priority to the development of the Carajás iron ores and Trombetas bauxite ores, the development of the petro-chemicals complex at Camaçari near Salvador, and the industrial district within the free-trade zone of Manaus (SUFRAMA).

It is as yet still too early to assess the success of these programmes. It is clear, however, that continued investment relies heavily on rapid economic growth, the success of the energy policy in reducing Brasil's dependence on imported petroleum, and the increased diversification of exports.

The problems of Brasil's regions differ markedly, as do the aims of the various regional development programmes. The problems of the North-east are the antithesis of those of Amazonia and the Central-west. SUDENE has yet to make significant progress in alleviating the chronic poverty of the North-east, and the South-east continues to absorb the major share of domestic and foreign investment.

From 1950 to 1964, São Paulo increased its share of industrial production from 48 per cent to 62 per cent.

The regional development programmes are discussed in some detail in later chapters, particularly chapters 9 and 10.

The Role of Transport in Development

Transport networks and systems affect the circulation and flow of people, resources and products, and the diffusion of innovations and new technologies. Efficient and well integrated transport systems encourage the spatial integration of the national economy, and thus have a vital role in both national and regional development. They allow regions to specialise in those forms of economic activity in which they have a comparative advantage, and this in turn improves productivity and accelerates economic growth.

Brasil does not suffer from many of the severe environmental constraints that affect transport in the neighbouring mountainous Andean states. The single major problem is that of scaling the great escarpment in the South-east. However, this is more than offset by problems of scale—Brasil's extreme territorial limits are over 4 300 km apart.

The effects of distance on movement is illustrated by the simple 'gravity model' (see **5.11**). It is based on Newton's Law of Universal Gravitation which states that, 'bodies are attracted to each other in proportion to the product of their masses and inversely as the square of their distance'. When applied to transport movements it illustrates the frictional effect of distance which results in 'distance

decay'. Two typical distance decay curves are shown by **5.11**, curve Y illustrating a rapid decay function, and curve Z a less rapid decay function. The model also explains the greater transport movements between the largest urban and industrial cores in the South-east, and the net flow of migrants discussed in Chapter 3.

Before analysing the development of transport in Brasil, it is worth contrasting the cost-efficiency of various modes of transport, especially in terms of distance. Generally transport costs increase with increasing distance, but as **5.12** shows, different modes of transport have different cost-distance curves. The result is that for short movements road transport is most cost-efficient, whilst for longer distance movements rail and then water are best. The letters X, Y and Z on the diagram show the distances over which road, rail and water are most cost-efficient.

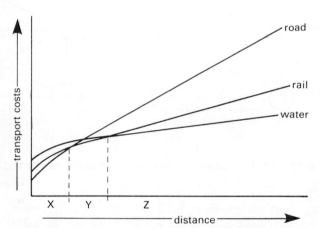

5.12. The Cost Structure of Three Modes of Transport.

During the sixteenth and seventeenth centuries, economic activity in Brasil was confined to parts of the eastern seaboard. The North-east region developed first because it was closest to the mother country, whilst the South was too remote, and the potential of the Amazon river system was virtually ignored. The level of technology was low, so that draught animals were the main mode of transport. Few major rivers flow directly to the Atlantic, and those that do are not navigable for any great distance inland (see **7.12** on page 103). Thus, economic activity was confined to the small hinterlands of a number of ports which were isolated from each other and unconnected by land routes.

Taaffe, Morrill and Gould (1963) have developed an evolutionary transport model based on West African countries, which closely parallels the devel-

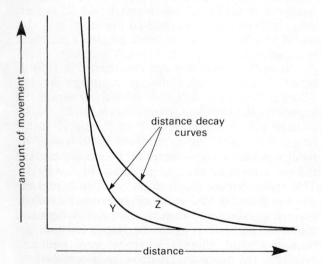

5.11. The Interaction between Movement and Distance.

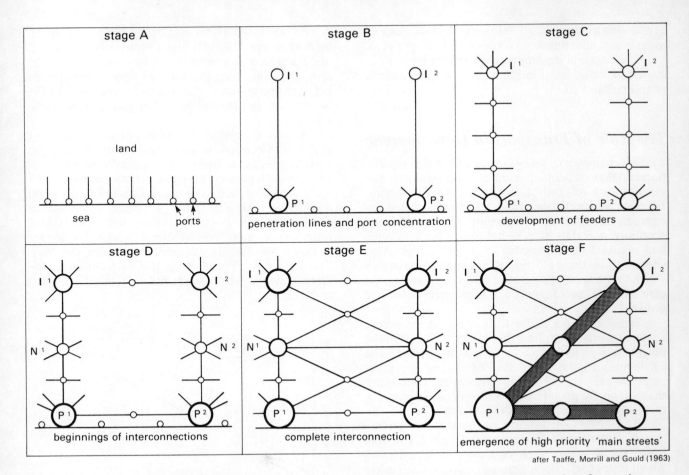

after Taaffe, Morrill and Gould (1963)

5.13. An Evolutionary Model for the Development of Transport Networks in Developing Countries.

opment of transport in Brasil. It not only shows stages of development but, because of the differences in the levels of transport development in Brasil's major regions, it also illustrates contemporary regional imbalances. As **5.13** shows, Stage A corresponds to the pattern outlined above. By Stage B, dominant ports develop and these are linked with inland centres of production such as mines or plantations. Through Stages C, D and E, new settlements develop along the main transport routes; these develop and encourage 'feeders'. Eventually the connectivity of the transport network improves as the level of economic integration between the settlements increases. By Stage E, all major settlements are directly connected. Stage F illustrates an advanced network serving a hierarchy of urban settlements. The main movements between the major cities—a characteristic explained by the gravity model—stimulate the development of improved transport arteries or 'main streets'. Reference to **5.14** and an atlas showing Brasil's road and rail networks will confirm the usefulness of the

model, and in particular will reveal the striking resemblance between the network of Stage F and the transport networks of South-east Brasil. However, only the South-east has reached this level. It is also useful to refer back to the urban hierarchy discussed in Chapter 4 and illustrated by **4.5**.

Brasil's first railway was constructed in 1854. It resulted from a fourteen-year campaign by Dr. Thomas Cochrane, a British subject, to secure the support of the Brasilian government in linking Rio de Janeiro with its summer resort at Petrópolis in the mountains above the escarpment. British involvement was also a major factor in the development of the rail system on the coffee plateau of São Paulo. This radial system focussed on São Paulo, and the city was linked in 1867 to its port of Santos by a single line using cables and cogs to scale the escarpment. However, the radial system developed few linkages because several different rail guages were used.

The rail system expanded considerably but, despite partial electrification and the continuing importance of coffee exports, this progress was slowed

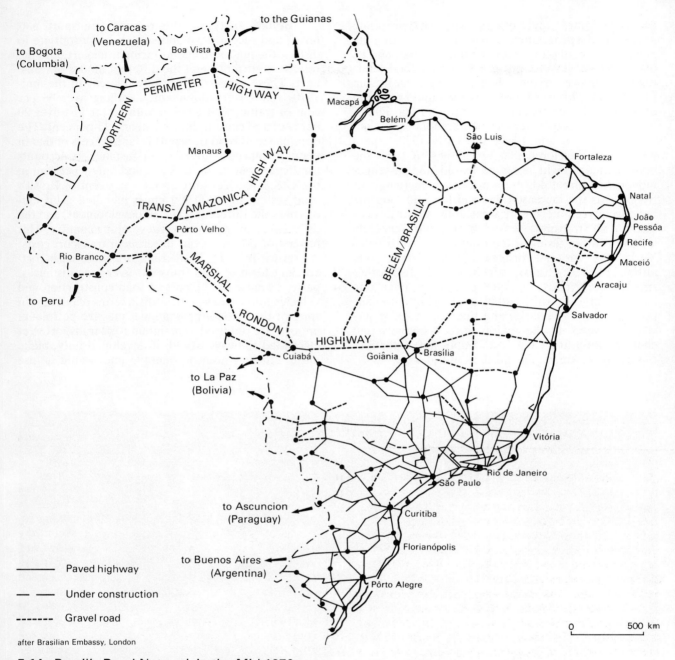

5.14. Brasil's Road Network in the Mid 1970s.

by Brasil's enforced economic isolation, as world trade was affected by the world wars and inter-war world depression. As the relative importance of rail declined, so that of roads increased. At this time air transport was the only means of access to many remote areas, and over 1 450 airports and simple landing strips were developed. By the early 1950s, the underdeveloped and badly connected surface transport systems were placing major constraints on economic and regional development.

Major changes in transport policy and improvements in the transport system date from the late 1950s and early 1960s. In 1957, the federal government acquired eighteen of the twenty-two private railway companies, and began a major rationalisation programme. This involved the closure of uneconomic lines and others with inappropriate gauges, and a programme aimed at standardising the gauge. The inauguration of Brasília in 1960, and its planned focal position in a new national and inter-regional highway system, changed the emphasis from rail to road. This was boosted by the rapid expansion of motor vehicles production in Greater São Paulo, and the increased ownership of automobiles.

During the late 1960s and early 1970s, there were other developments. From 1964 to 1974, the volume of air freight increased sixfold, and passenger movements threefold. A major cause of increased air freight was the increased demand for beef, and the need to tap remote supply areas in the Central-west. Today, air transport is significant, but relatively unimportant in terms of the total volume of freight. Varig (the national airline) and Vasp (the state airline of São Paulo), together with two other smaller companies, operate a fleet of over one hundred large aircraft. Today, over one hundred airports are used regularly, and there are regular services between all the major cities. Company and charter aircraft have an important function, especially in Amazonia and the Central-west.

Before analysing the regional transport patterns, and recent developments, it is appropriate to discuss the major problems facing transport, and the relative contribution of the different modes of transport. These aspects are closely related. In the mid-1970s roads were dominant, handling over 68 per cent of traffic, whilst rail accounted for just over 20 per cent and coastal shipping nearly 11 per cent. The dominance of road transport is far in excess of that in many advanced countries; for instance, it accounts for 25 per cent in the U.S.A., and only 7 per cent in the U.S.S.R.. Yet only about 6 per cent of Brasil's road system of 1 300 000 km is metalled. This emphasises the different levels of development, and the different requirements of a developing country. This has major repercussions in terms of transport costs. As shown by **5.12**, road transport is the least cost-efficient form of land transport over long distances, partly because of the cost of road construction and vehicles, but more significantly in terms of energy. In spite of the alcohol programme, massive petroleum imports are required to maintain road transport. Yet electrified railways would, if developed fully, make more efficient use of energy, and would utilise

Plate 16. *Rodovia dos Imigrantes.* This now completed highway scales the Serra do Mar, and links São Paulo with its port of Santos. The ninety-six kilometre long highway has twenty viaducts and nearly four kilometres of tunnel. ***Camera Press Ltd.***

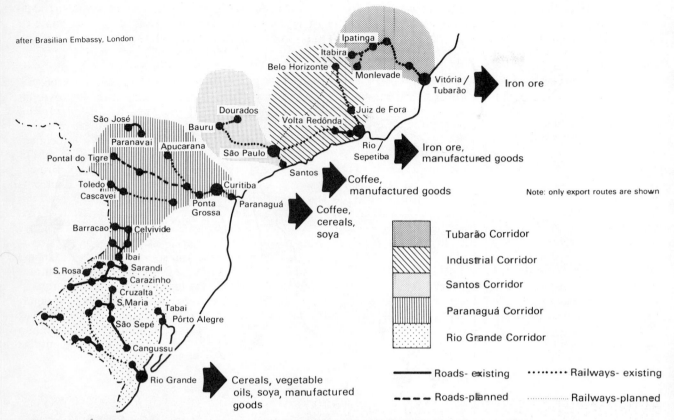

after Brasilian Embassy, London

Note: only export routes are shown

	Tubarão Corridor
	Industrial Corridor
	Santos Corridor
	Paranaguá Corridor
	Rio Grande Corridor

Roads- existing   ⋯⋯ Railways- existing

- - - Roads-planned   ⋯⋯ Railways-planned

5.15. Brasil's Major 'Export Corridors', Export Ports, and Associated Hinterlands.

Brasil's major domestic energy resource. Hydro-electricity already contributes over 25 per cent of Brasil's gross energy supplies, and much of the potential is still unrealised (see Chapter 7). Efforts are now being made as part of the five-year development plans to transfer freight from road to rail and water. As previously stated, coastal shipping accounts for nearly 11 per cent of total movements. This reflects the need for coastal trade to serve ports in the underdeveloped North-east, and the transport of some raw materials to the South-east. It also emphasises the highly localised nature of new industries such as petrochemicals, and the need to distribute the products of these industries. Inland waterways are locally important, but contribute considerably less than on per cent of total movements.

Regional imbalances in transport networks are considerable. This reflects the economic status of the regions and the priority given to developing export routes.

The regions of the South-east and South—the most highly developed in terms of energy production, commercial agriculture and manufacturing—contain about three-quarters of Brasil's railway trackage and a similarly high proportion of paved roads (see **5.14**). These regions supply most of Brasil's exports, as shown by **5.15** and **5.16**. Nearly all the major transport improvements, including the up-grading of existing routes and the construction of new ones, are related to major export routes within well defined 'export corridors' (as shown by **5.15**).

These ports handle over 75 per cent of Brasil's imports, and about 66 per cent of exports by value. The most significant routes are those from the 'iron quadrilateral' in Minas Gerais to the new ocean terminals at Tubarão near Vitória and Sepetiba near Rio; and the routes converging on São Paulo-Santos and Curitiba-Paranaguá. São Sebastião, in São Paulo state, has also been developed as the major petroleum import terminal. All of these ports have been improved during the 1970s, special emphasis being given to improved warehouse storage, improved handling facilities, and containerisation facilities. In the state of Rio Grande do Sul, Pôrto Alegre (despite its name) is no longer a major port because of the silting up of already shallow channels in the estuary at the head of Lagôa dos Patos. Rio Grande, therefore, is being developed as the major port of the temperate grassland region.

In the North-east, port improvements and

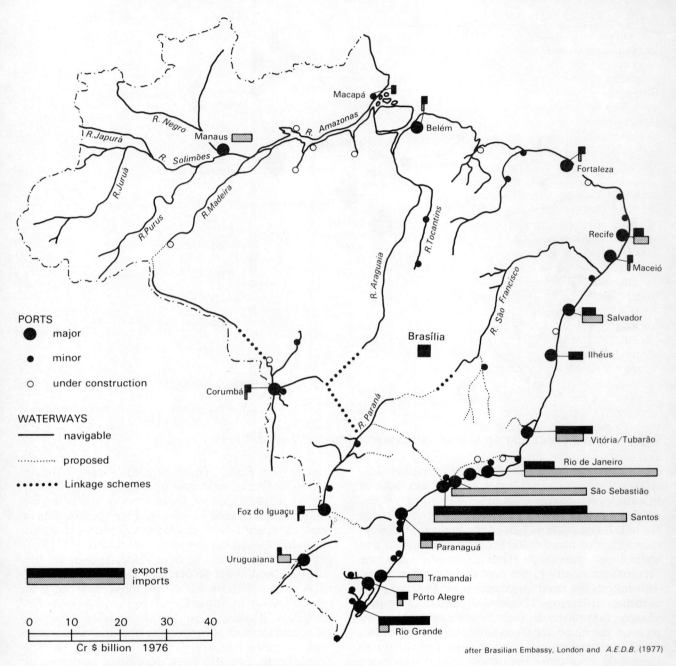

PORTS

● major

• minor

○ under construction

WATERWAYS

—— navigable

·········· proposed

•••••• Linkage schemes

exports
imports

0   10   20   30   40

Cr $ billion   1976

after Brasilian Embassy, London and *A.E.D.B.* (1977)

5.16. The Major Ports and Navigable Waterways.

related transport improvements have been on a smaller scale, and are more localised. New port developments are related to the development of industrial 'growth poles', at Salvador and Recife in particular. The intra-regional road network is still relatively underdeveloped, and is similar to that of Stage D in the development model discussed previously. However, efforts are being made to improve links with the South-east and Amazonia. A new road now links with the Trans-Amazonica highway system, and Salvador is linked to Vitória and Rio. Further roads are being constructed to link Salvador and Ilhéus with Brasília (see **5.14**).

The transport network of the South-east and South developed with the growth of commercial farming and exports, and to link urban areas; those of the North-east were primarily export routes. The roads of the Central-west and Amazonia, however, have developed for very different reasons. Many of the roads built in the 1960s linked the regions to the federal capital, and thus the motivation at this stage was as much political as economic. The expansion of the road system was designed to promote 'national integration'.

The first major project of this type was the Belém-Brasília highway, a 2 230 km paved road which crosses open *cerrado* and cuts through dense *selva*. This was a very ambitious project. Construction costs were great, and so are maintenance costs because flash-floods can destroy sections of the road and bridges overnight. The bus journey from one end to the other takes a minimum of four days, even without mishap. This road was also planned to accelerate colonisation by acting as a 'growth corridor'. It has been successful in this aim, but it cannot hope in itself to solve the problems of overpopulation in the North-east. Goodland and Irwin (1975) point out that, 'The Northeasterners represented by only one year's (population) growth would scarcely have room to lie down head-to-toe on the entire Belém-Brasília highway'. This comment is perhaps over-critical, because over 500,000 colonists have settled along the highway, and are now making a major contribution to the regional economy. Particularly important are the colonies near Brasília, which provide the capital with much of its food requirements.

Cuiabá, in the state of Mato Grosso do Norte, has also developed as an important focus for two new gravel roads. The Marshall Rondon highway links Brasília via Cuiabá to the mining regions of Rondônia, and the Cuiabá-Santarém highway links the Central-west region to the new Trans-Amazonica highway.

The controversial Trans-Amazonica highway is a gravel road about 6 400 km long, running from the North-east coast to the Peruvian border in the west. Its route was not planned to link urban centres, but to link the heads of navigation of the Amazon's southern tributaries. The entire project was more or less completed during the 1970s. The primary objective of the road was to promote the 'productive occupation' of Amazonia; however, to date it has not attracted very large numbers of colonists. This is partly because colonisation is being highly planned (see Chapter 9) and concentrated in growth poles. Many of these new colonies are still remote even though they are on the highway.

Many of the new roads to Amazonia and the Central-west have an important political and strategic function. This is not a new function in Brasil, as many of the long established roads in Rio Grande do Sul were constructed to reinforce Brasil's territorial claims to the area near the Uruguayan border. Many of the new highways connect with roads in neigh-

Plate 17. The Trans-Amazonica Highway. This gravel road now links the North-east coast with the Peruvian border. It is a key element in the future development of Amazonia. ***Camera Press Ltd.***

bouring countries to form part of the 'Pan-American' highway system. Along that part of the border with Paraguay which follows the Paraná river, the road links serve to improve relationships with Paraguay. This is very important because of the bi-national venture to build the world's largest hydro-electric plant at Itaipú.

In 1973, construction began on the *Rodovia Perimetral Norte* (northern perimeter highway). It is planned to skirt Brasil's northern and north-west frontiers, and to join the Trans-Amazonica highway at Cruzeiro do Sul. The military are highly involved in its construction, as they were with many of the other new roads. The importance of this new road is undoubtedly its strategic value. It connects very few settlements or productive areas, and is unlikely to attract large numbers of colonists in the foreseeable future.

It is clear that Brasil's transport infrastructure is developing rapidly, and that developments in different regions contrast markedly in both their purpose and characteristics.

Brasil's Foreign Trade

Coffee export revenues, heavy borrowing from the World Bank, and investment by foreign corporations, have all made major contributions to Brasil's economic growth. In the early 1970s, Brasil's net foreign debt and current account trade deficit both declined, but the 1973/74 oil crisis transformed a current account deficit equivalent to about only 2 per cent of the GDP in 1973, to a figure approaching 8 per cent in 1974. Whilst this has since declined, the net foreign debt now stands at about 17 per cent of the GDP—a very high figure.

Since 1945, import substitution policies have protected industrial growth and diversification, so that by the mid 1960s Brasil was virtually self-sufficient in manufactured goods. But further industrialisation has necessitated the import of certain raw materials and capital goods. The preoccupation with industrialisation also led to a neglect of exports. This, and monetary problems, resulted in several balance of payments crises.

Since the introduction of an exports incentive scheme in 1968, which used fiscal measures to encourage the export of manufactured and semi-manufactured goods, these have now become dominant as shown by **5.17**. This transformation has also been achieved by a major shift in the pattern of trade. Whilst Brasilian exports to North America and Western Europe increased from 1968 to 1978, their shares of the Brasilian market have fallen from 35 per cent to 24 per cent and from 39 per cent to 36 per cent respectively. Brasil's economic status, rapid economic growth, and expertise in tropical technology has enabled it to make major inroads into 'Third World' markets, especially in exports of motor vehicles, and in construction projects such as roads, railways and hydro-electric plants.

In the face of international and domestic criticism against Brasil's export subsidies and import restrictions, these measures are to be phased out in the early 1980s. The planned depreciation of the *cruzeiro*—Brasil's unit of currency—will stimulate exports and discourage imports, but it is also likely to cause increased inflation which is still running at

5.17.   The Transformation in Brasil's Exports, 1968 and 1978.

	1968		1978	
	Value in Us $ million	*% of Total*	*Value in US $ million*	*% of Total*
Primary Products	1 495	79.5	5 970	47.2
Coffee beans	775	41.2	1 940	15.3
Sugar	102	5.4	196	1.6
Cocoa beans	46	2.5	454	3.6
Iron ore	105	5.6	1 027	8.1
Soya beans	25	1.3	1 219	9.6
Other primary products	442	23.5	1 134	9.0
Industrial Products	377	20.0	6 500	51.4
Semi manufactures	178	9.4	1 416	11.2
Manufactured items	199	10.6	5 084	40.2
Other	9	0.5	181	1.4
Total	1 881	100.0	12 651	100.0

Source: *Boletim do Banco Central do Brasil*

5.18.   The Pattern of Brasil's Foreign Trade, 1968 and 1978.

	1968		1978	
	Exports	*Imports*	*Exports*	*Imports*
	% of Total	*% of Total*	*% of Total*	*% of Total*
United States	33.3	32.2	22.8	21.1
Canada	1.4	1.7	1.2	2.6
Western Europe	38.8	33.6	36.0	22.9
Latin American Free Trade Association	10.3	13.0	12.5	10.4
Central American Common Market	–	–	0.5	–
Comecon	6.4	4.3	5.8	1.4
Middle East	1.1	6.2	2.8	26.9
Africa	1.5	1.9	5.0	3.6
Asia and Oceania	4.4	3.9	9.6	9.9
Other	2.8	3.2	3.8	1.2
Total	100.0	100.0	100.0	100.0

Source: *Boletim do Banco Central do Brasil.*

5.19.   The Brasilian Economy in 1980, Basic Data.

Industrial Production

Steel ingots (1 000 t)	15 333
Rolled steel (1 000 t)	12 970
Pig iron (1 000 t)	12 695
Coke (1 000 t)	4 088
Crude oil (1 000 m³)	10 563
Natural gas (10^6m³)	2 133
'A' gasoline (1 000 m³)	10 856
Diesel oil (1 000 m³)	19 373
Fuel oil (1 000 m³)	17 124
Vehicles (units)	1 164 993
Tractors (units)	69 991
Cement (1 000 t)	27 193
Electricity (consumption, 10^6 KWh)	112 137

Exports (US$ million)

Total (FOB)	20 132
Green coffee	2 486
Industrialized products	11 384
Soy flour and cake	1 449
Soybeans	394
Raw sugar	625
Iron ore	1 557
Transport equipment	1 512

Imports (US$ million)   21 133

Exchange (Cr$/US$)   65.50

Source: *Brasilian Ministry of External Relations.*

above 50 per cent per annum. The increasing foreign debt has to be paid for by increased export earnings at a time when the world recession is reducing the demand of the advanced countries for raw materials. Brasil's new policies will, however, give a much needed boost to the neglected agricultural sector, and it is likely to recover a part of the share in imports which it lost in the 1970s.

Throughout the 1970s, Brasil's large import bill has been dominated by petroleum (averaging over 40 per cent by value), a wide range of capital goods, copper, and wheat. Wheat is the only staple food in which Brasil is not self-sufficient. It is clear that world economic recession of the 1970s and early 1980s is such that great efforts must be made to reduce dependence on imported energy. This problem is discussed in detail in the later section on energy resources.

6 Agricultural Development

The agricultural sector employs about 36 per cent of the labour force, accounts for about 10 per cent of the GDP, and contributes about 58 per cent of export revenue if processed commodities are included. Yet only about 15 per cent of national territory is actively farmed, and only a quarter of this is cultivated. Brasil's colonial legacy of a large subsistence sector and a commercial sector preoccupied with cultivating plantation crops for export, and more recent pre-occupation with industrialisation, has had a marked effect on the neglect of agriculture, on rural land-use patterns and on land tenure. It has also contributed to the marked spatial patterns in agricultural methods and productivity.

Whilst the self-sufficient subsistence farmer cultivated his plot intensively to meet the needs of his family, the plantation owner was more concerned with maximising profits. The increased production of plantation crops was achieved by clearing new land rather than increasing the productivity of existing land. This reflected the belief that land was an 'infinite resource', and that the environment could be sacrificed in the interests of monetary gain. Brasilian agriculture still reflects the dichotomy between small-scale intensive farming, referred to as 'minifundio', and large-scale extensive farming, referred to as 'latifundio'. However, the planned and spontaneous colonisation of southern Brasil by Europeans has diversified agriculture considerably during the twentieth century, and has produced a dynamic commercial farmscape. This is especially true in São Paulo and parts of the South, where the competition for land is intense, and farmers produce for large domestic urban markets as well as for export.

The marked spatial patterns produced by the agricultural 'booms' still persist in the relatively underdeveloped regions, particularly in the sugar and cocoa lands of the *zona da mata* in the Northeast, and in the more remote cattle pastures of the *cerrado* in the Central-west. Rural land-use in the South-east core region is, however, considerably more complex. It is also more responsive to changes in both domestic and world markets. This is helped by the nation's most complete infrastructure, increasing technological diffusion from the cities, and by the advance of the frontier of cultivation which allows diversification in the former traditional areas.

Whilst drought, frost and generally poor soils impose physical constraints in various regions, the tropical and sub-tropical environments offer a wide range of possibilities for future agricultural development. Economic forces and political policies are becoming increasingly important. The stagnating agricultural sector of the 1960s is now being replaced by a so-called 'green revolution', involving increased mechanisation, technological improvement and government support. This is a major component of the Third National Development Plan (III PND).

Subsistence Farming

Amerindian agriculture had developed well before the European colonisation of Brasil, and was typically based on the cultivation of manioc which provided the carbohydrate-rich staple. The site for the forest clearing was carefully selected, *padroes* (tree guides) indicating land of superior fertility. The clearing (*roça*) was made by felling the larger trees, cutting down the undergrowth, and then allowing the branches to dry before burning. This 'slash and burn' system, which is still used, enriches the soil with ashes, but also destroys much organic matter and beneficial bacteria. The fire also destroys weeds and seeds, and makes the soil friable. Manioc can be easily planted by using a dibber, without the need for tilling. The *roça* is dotted with large tree stumps, as the larger trees with buttress roots have to be cut well above ground level; uprooting would be far too arduous. Manioc is interspersed with variety of other crops such as the stimulants coca (cocaine) and tobacco. It matures after about eight months, but as there are no marked seasons in the rain-forest, harvesting is continuous once the clearing is well established. Whilst the manioc root consists mostly of water, starch and sugars, it also contains poisonous prussic acid which has to be rinsed and squeezed out before the manioc is ground to flour which is used to make a tough, leathery unleaven bread. Its major advantage lies in its very high yield and its simple method of cultivation.

The *roça* is capable of continuous cropping for only two to three years, as the latosols become quickly exhausted of nutrients, and leached, resulting in declining yields. The gradual regeneration of the forest makes maintenance increasingly arduous. This method of 'shifting cultivation', whereby new forest clearings are required at frequent intervals, had little environmental impact in rain-forest areas with very low average population densities, because the forest had ample time to regenerate. The clearings were small and were soon re-colonised by the surrounding forest. However, the preoccupation of the early colonists with cultivating export crops led them to adopt the *roça* system for food production. It was used both within the plantation boundaries and by the few smallholders. But increased population pressure resulted in increased deforestation, and large clearings coalesced leaving isolated forest remnants. The result was that the forest degenerated to a scrub, soil exhaustion led to an incomplete plant cover, and large areas, especially on sloping land, were stripped of their soil by sheet-wash and gully erosion.

The *roça* system was also used by plantation owners as a means of clearing land for cultivation and cattle rearing. The peasant farmer—the *caboclo*—was allowed to cultivate a *roça* in return for his family's labour. As a result of this clearance, and the large-scale deforestation to produce firewood and

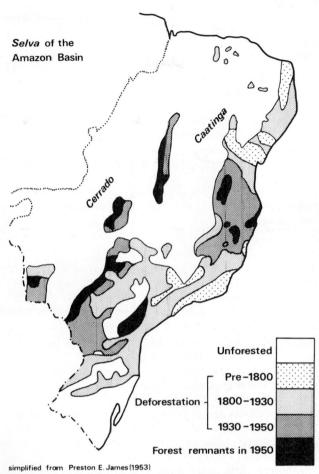

Selva of the Amazon Basin

Caatinga

Cerrado

	Unforested
	Pre–1800
Deforestation	1800–1930
	1930–1950
Forest remnants in 1950	

simplified from Preston E. James (1953)

6.1. The Clearing of Brasil's Eastern Forests.

Plate 18. A farmstead in northern Paraná. *Roça* (forest clearing) subsistence farming is still very common even in areas of predominantly commercial farming. Note the Paraná pine which is typical of Brasil's southern plateau. **Barnaby Picture Library.**

charcoal, much of Brasil's eastern forests had been cleared by the mid-twentieth century, as shown by **6.1**.

The *roça* system is today widespread throughout the cultivated areas, and manioc is second only to sugar-cane as the major crop by weight. Brasil is the major world producer of manioc but exports very little. This reflects its role as a staple, its use as a fodder crop, and more recently its use as a raw material for alcohol production.

The effects on agriculture of widespread *roça* cultivation and associated deforestation are illustrated by **6.2**. The destruction of the forest canopy causes a leaching of nutrients in the forest litter, and thus breaks the nutrient cycle.

The subsistence sector has attracted little interest or attention from the federal government. The *caboclo* has been offered virtually no incentives to improve his methods or his land. Indeed, many *caboclos* are squatters, farming unregistered land. As a result the rural population has a long history of

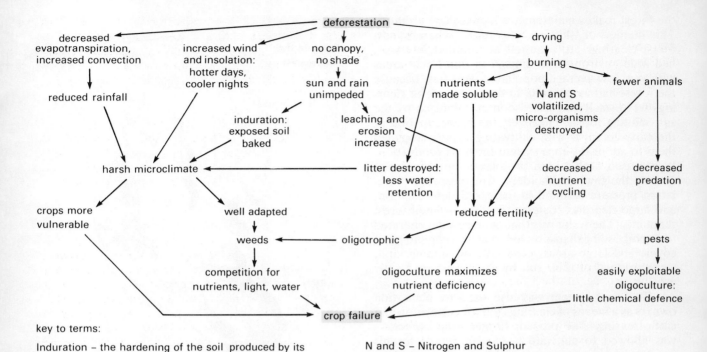

key to terms:

Induration – the hardening of the soil produced by its
      exposure to direct sunlight

Leaching – the washing out of soil nutrients as a result
      of exposure to torrential rainfall

N and S – Nitrogen and Sulphur

Oligotrophic – (soil) with few nutrients

Oligoculture – the over-cultivation of only a few crops

after Goodland and Irwin, fig.5, (1975)

6.2. The Relationship between Deforestation and Crop Failure.

mobility, moving from one 'boom' area to another. Rural poverty, and the belief that the city holds the only opportunities for material improvement, have led to massive rural depopulation in many areas, especially in the rural periphery around the urban core regions of the South-east.

It should be emphasised at this stage that many *caboclos* living at or near subsistence level have been attracted by the many colonisation and resettlement projects which have been developed in the 1970s; but most still have to fend for themselves.

Coffee: Its Development and Role in the Economy

Brasil's success in the cultivation and marketing of coffee has had a profound effect on the rural land-use, settlement, and the regional economy of the South-east and northern Paraná, as well as on the growth and development of the national economy. From the 1850s to the early 1960s its contribution to export revenue averaged over 60 per cent per annum. Coffee export revenues provided the finance for commercial and industrial development, and led

directly to the development of the continent's second largest railway network. Its success also attracted thousands of new immigrants and nationals to São Paulo and Paraná states, contributed to the development of the highly commercialised agriculture of the region, and to the development of a wage economy.

Coffee was first introduced into Brasil in 1727, having been smuggled from French Guiana, but it did not become the major export until 1825. It was not until the late-nineteenth century that production was significant in absolute terms. It was at first cultivated as a garden crop on the lowlands around Rio de Janeiro, known as the Baixada Fluminense. It then spread to the Paraíba valley which became the first major producing area. Its early cultivation was by no means successful. The valley slopes were deforested and overcultivated, resulting in soil exhaustion and severe gully erosion. It is unlikely that this could have been avoided because most *fazendeiros* (estate owners) were illiterate and others used manuals which were, 'empirically unsound and theoretically dubious' (J.A. Rios, 1973). The first *fazendas* (estates) relied heavily on cheap slave labour; even in the decade following the abolition of the slave trade, 40 000 slaves entered Rio state alone, having been transferred from the North-east. Before 1822, the year when government land grants were stopped, estate owners and squatters both contributed to production; but later the large *fazenda* became dominant.

The development of the *latifundio* (large estate) system of land tenure resulted from the need to buy sufficient land to offset the effects of soil exhaustion. Considerable capital was required for such land purchases, as well as to build the *casa grande* (mansion), to clear the land, and to provide labour. Conditions therefore favoured the large land-owner. Labour was a major factor, because only those land-owners whose estates were well stocked with slaves before 1852 flourished, as slave prices subsequently increased rapidly. Later, immigrant labourers—*colonos*—were used, especially in São Paulo. The *colono* was instrumental in the success of São Paulo and the decline of the Paraíba valley which had relied entirely on slave labour, and thus collapsed after the gradual liberation of the slaves from 1850 to 1888. The large estate persisted because of a heavy land sales tax, but an ineffective land-ownership tax.

From 1825 to 1835, cultivation spread onto the plateau. Here climatic conditions were near optimum, with mean monthly temperatures from 18°–23°C, and an annual soil mosture deficit of less than 200 mm rainfall equivalent. However, few areas of the *planalto* are climatically unsuited for coffee cultivation. The major controlling physical factor proved to be the *terra roxa* (red earth) soils, derived from the weathering of the plateau volcanics. They are porous and free-draining, deep, well textured, and rich in humus and iron.

At first the coffee economy was precarious. The 'robusta' bush, though having a productive life of about 30 years, was prone to fluctuating yields and was vulnerable to climatic hazards such as frost, strong winds, drought and torrential rainfall. The monocultural farming methods and primitive technology also made it vulnerable to insect pests such as the *Broca* (borer) and *Elachista Coffela* (coffee plague), and to *Ferrugem*, the coffee-rust disease.

In the mid-nineteenth century, Campinas became the commercial centre, and cultivation spread northwards to Ribeirão Prêto and westwards to Botucatu (see **6.3**). From 1857 to 1906, three 'cycles' can be identified:

(a) 1857–68: Coffee prices rose because of the increasing shortage of slave labour, and the effects of the coffee plague which limited supply. In São Paulo, resources were switched from sugar to coffee and cultivation spread further over the *terra roxas*. The substitution of exports of 'green coffee' by packaged roasted coffee marked a major technological

advance, and allowed the maintenance of high export revenues during the European recession of 1866. In 1867, the railway scaling the great escarpment linking Santos with São Paulo was completed, and São Paulo became the route focus and commercial centre.

(b) 1869–85: A drastic rise in coffee prices resulted from frost damage in São Paulo in 1870 but, because of favourable currency exchange rates, coffee maintained its 60 per cent contribution to exports. São Paulo became the major producer as greater productivity made cultivation more profitable.

(c) 1886–1906: Fluctuations in the coffee harvest were compensated by high prices following the end of the American recession in 1884. Coffee became more profitable as market price and the currency exchange rate diverged. From 1890 to 1900, new plantings trebled and production doubled. In 1902, São Paulo state prohibited further planting, but in 1906 production reached a massive 20 million bags. This was the equivalent of the entire world demand for coffee and consequently prices fell to half their former level.

Up until 1906, Brasil had been fortunate in that the effects of climatic hazards, pests, and favourable currency exchange rates had regulated supply and had maintained profits; but in 1906 the government had to intervene. The congress authorised the first 'valorisation' scheme. This involved the government purchasing the surplus, and thus helping to stabilise prices. In 1907 about a third of the crop was purchased by means of a £15 million foreign loan. This was so successful that the loan was repaid by 1914. The disruption of world trade, caused by the First World War and continued inflation, led to a second scheme from 1917 to 1920. However, small harvests resulting from frost damage in 1918 resulted in higher prices, and this regulated the coffee economy. By 1921 the bushes had recovered, forcing a third scheme from 1921 to 1924. Again, two successive low harvests reduced the need for major government intervention. The three valorisation schemes had been successful in protecting the coffee producer, but in 1924 a permanent control scheme was established.

To some extent the coffee bush itself contributed to market stability, because an abnormally high yield weakened the bush, resulting in lower yields in the following years. But over-production continued. Four massive harvests coincided with the world depression from 1929 to 1933. By then, cultivation had spread over the entire *terra roxa* region and onto marginal soil types. From 1931 to 1944 the equivalent

Plate 19. Coffee bushes on the Fazenda Jacarecatinga. This *fazenda* situated near Aracatuba in western São Paulo has 800 000 coffee bushes, but these occupy less than four per cent of its area. Most of the 30 000 ha estate is used for rearing and fattening 40 000 beef cattle. ***J. Allan Cash Ltd.***

of three years' world consumption (78 million sixty-kilogramme bags) had to be destroyed. Coffee was burned, dumped at sea, and even used to fuel loco-motives. From this period onwards, Brasil lost its comparative advantage as Colombian and African producers increased their share of the world market.

Increased competition had a direct effect on farm size, and on the extension of cultivation into northern Paraná state. The large *fazenda* proved unable to solve the technological problems of pro-ducing higher quality coffee, and in São Paulo especially there was a dramatic increase in the medium-sized estate with less than 10,000 bushes. The spread of coffee cultivation into northern Paraná was encouraged by declining yields in São Paulo, and by planned and highly organised colonis-ation. It was initiated in 1927 by the British managed company 'Parana Plantations Ltd.'. The company planned the farmscape as a series of rectangular plots, each bounded by an access road following the river divide, and by a river. Thus each plot had a cross section of relief and soil types. Railways and

new urban centres such as Londrina and Maringa were also planned, and Paranaguá became the region's port. The company was taken over by *Pau-lista* businessmen in 1944 and re-named '*Companhia de Melhoramentos do Norte do Paraná*' (Company for the Improvement of Northern Paraná). From 1940 to 1960, Paraná increased its share of produc-tion from 7 per cent to 52 per cent, and thus became the major producing state, despite the greater risk of frost damage.

Following the Second World War, Brasil organ-ised its coffee policies so as to maximise foreign exchange receipts. The investment of export revenue was one of the best means of achieving rapid econ-omic development. Industrialisation had by now become the major priority for such investment. Brasil could control market price by regulating exports; although in 1954 exports were 38 per cent lower than in 1948, exchange receipts were 93 per cent higher. However, whilst Brasil was able to control prices because of her massive share of the world market, the U.S.A. was able to establish ceiling prices, as it was the major importer. During the mid-1950s, production costs were reduced as a result of the higher productivity of the new plantations of northern Paraná, so that the revenue from coffee reached record levels. This was achieved despite increased competition from other producers, which enabled them to capture 20 per cent of the world market for the first time.

From 1954/55 the valorisation policies were reversed, and a new support system was established. Bonuses were granted to exporters, and producers received higher profits. This enabled producers to overcome the frost damage in 1956. In 1957 Brasil secured agreement with other Latin American producers to limit exports and so maintain prices. In 1959 the 'International Coffee Agreement' fixed annual export quotas at a level equivalent to 90 per cent of the best year in the period 1949–58, and a maximum of 88 per cent of real exportable production. The quota system allowed the rationalisation of coffee cultivation for the first time. From 1961 there was a massive eradication scheme resulting in the destruction of nearly half the coffee bushes. The scheme had major effects. It eliminated production in marginal areas and concentrated production in the most productive areas, and it also led to diversification because former coffee growers were compensated and given considerable support. A further effect was to reduce the rural labour force, as the surviving areas had a higher degree of mechanisation and technology.

During the early 1960s, production was greatly affected by climatic hazards. In 1963, a severe drought and fire affected the entire producing region, and frost also damaged many of the surviving bushes of Paraná. In order to secure future export revenues, Brasil decided to build up a massive stock of 50 million bags. This policy contributed directly to inflation. In the late 1960s and early 1970s, coffee cultivation was once more affected by climatic hazards and disease. In 1970 production was threatened by coffee-rust, and this necessitated costly spraying with fungicides, with a resulting increase in production costs. The same disease had completely destroyed the coffee bushes of Ceylon (now Sri Lanka) in the late nineteenth century, at a time when it was the world's major producer. The introduction of new strains such as '*Novo Mundo*' (New World) proved beneficial but also very expensive.

During the 1970s there were dramatic fluctuations in annual coffee output as a result of severe killing frosts. Two low harvests in 1969/70 and 1972/73 resulted in a three-year plan to plant 600 million new bushes. Whilst the dominance of the 'new' coffee lands of northern Paraná has led to a dramatic increase in productivity, and has encouraged considerable agricultural diversification in São Paulo, it also made coffee production more vulnerable to killing frosts, as shown by **6.4** and **6.5**. In 1975 the most severe frost for 30 years, following a very large harvest, devastated the plantations of Paraná and São Paulo, and reduced production in 1976 by

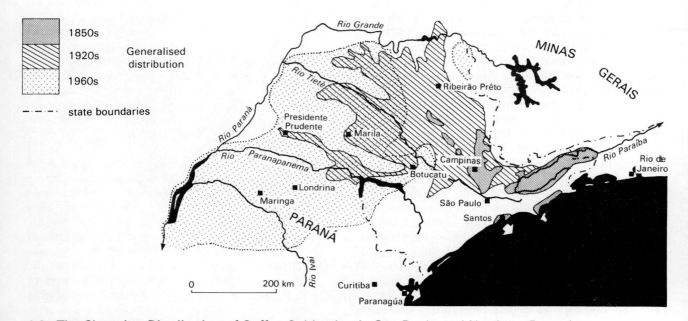

6.3. The Changing Distribution of Coffee Cultivation in São Paulo and Northern Paraná.

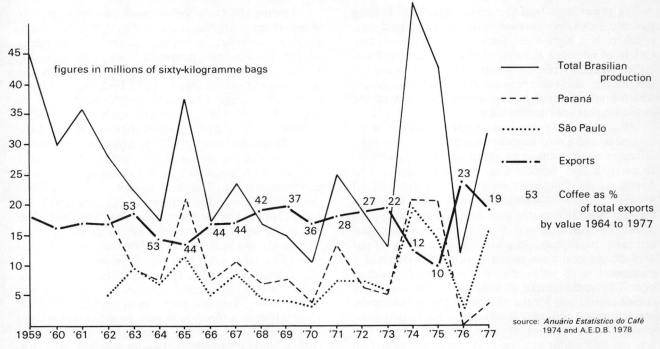

figures in millions of sixty-kilogramme bags

Legend:
Total Brasilian production
Paraná
São Paulo
Exports
53 — Coffee as % of total exports by value 1964 to 1977

53 53 44 44 44 42 37 36 28 27 22 12 10 23 19

1959 '60 '61 '62 '63 '64 '65 '66 '67 '68 '69 '70 '71 '72 '73 '74 '75 '76 '77

source: *Anuário Estatístico do Café* 1974 and A.E.D.B. 1978

6.4. Brasilian Coffee Production and Exports, 1959–77.

over 75 per cent! Production was so low that African coffee was imported and then exported to satisfy the demands of Brasil's trading partners. Europe now imports more Brasilian coffee than the U.S.A.

Coffee production has now recovered from this major catastrophe, and in future is likely to be far less susceptible to killing frost. Paraná, the former leading state, now has a more diversified agriculture, and Minas Gerais has responded by planting over a billion bushes. From 1976 Minas Gerais became the leading state, accounting for 38 per cent of Brasilian production in that year. Significantly these new plantations are also giving the highest yields per hectare, and the state continues to maintain its leading position closely followed by São Paulo. Thus Brasil's problem is no longer related to production, but once again to maximising export revenue.

It is remarkable that the dynamic South-east region can respond so quickly to both climatic hazard and changes in the world market. This is true not only of coffee cultivation, but also of other types of commercial agriculture. Even in the agricultural sector, coffee is no longer Brasil's single largest source of export revenue. In the mid 1970s, for example, both soya and sugar temporarily gained this position. But even more significant than this is the fact that exports of manufactured goods now exceed those of the entire agricultural sector.

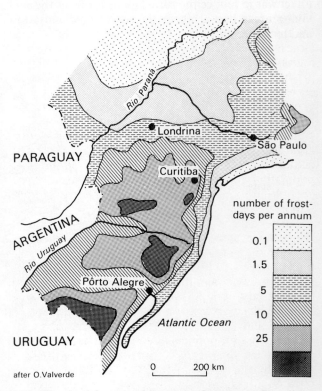

PARAGUAY

Londrina

São Paulo

Curitiba

ARGENTINA

Rio Uruguay

number of frost-days per annum

0.1
1.5
5
10
25

Pôrto Alegre

Atlantic Ocean

URUGUAY

after O.Valverde

0   200 km

6.5. The Incidence of Frost in Southern Brasil.

In order to maximise coffee export revenue it was also important to change the character of coffee exports, from unprocessed beans to processed beans and 'instant' coffee. The first 'instant' coffee processing plant was established by Nestlé as early as 1953, but major developments only came about after the creation of the *Instituto Brasileiro do Café* in 1965. There are now seven 'spray-dry' and four 'freeze-dry' factories, and a liquid extract plant. They are all located in São Paulo and Paraná. Exports of instant coffee are increasing rapidly, in line with 'western' tastes. Thus, the value added by processing is maximising export revenues.

The future for Brasilian coffee is assured as the organisation, planning, research and implementation of the Institute's policies is resulting in increased quality, and greater productivity. Foreign competition is intense, but Brasil has the advantages of economies of large-scale production, of technological progress resulting from dramatic economic growth, and of 'spin-off' from manufacturing industries into commercial agriculture.

Contemporary Agriculture: Problems, Trends and Progress

Contemporary agriculture in Brasil is paradoxical. On the one hand, Brasil is the 'free world's' second largest exporter of foodstuffs; yet the relative contribution of the agricultural sector to the gross domestic product has fallen from 41 per cent in 1939 to a current level of about 10 per cent. This is in part explained by the rapid development of manufacturing, but also by the relatively small investment in agriculture. Industrial growth has until recently been regarded as the economic panacea. However, agricultural production has expanded at a faster rate than population growth, and thus Brasil provides 95 per cent of her food requirements. The only major food import is wheat.

The fundamental problems facing agriculture are related to the gross imbalances in landownership, generally low productivity, and the continuing large subsistence sector. A major reason for low productivity and the large subsistence sector has been the lack of opportunity for smallholders to own sufficient land to provide a reasonable standard of living. Land ownership is still a measure of social status, a base for political power, and a hedge against inflation for the wealthy. Even as late as 1967, a survey by the Brasilian Institute for Land Reform (IBRA) found that 0.1 per cent of land-owners owned 25 per cent of all agricultural land. In fact 100

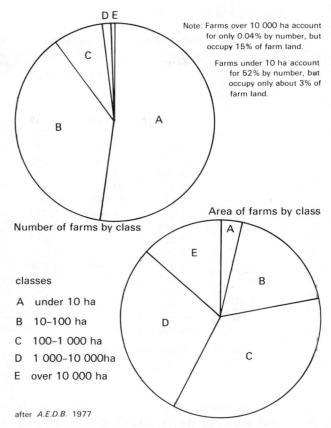

Note: Farms over 10 000 ha account for only 0.04% by number, but occupy 15% of farm land.

Farms under 10 ha account for 52% by number, but occupy only about 3% of farm land.

Number of farms by class

Area of farms by class

classes

A   under 10 ha

B   10–100 ha

C   100–1 000 ha

D   1 000–10 000ha

E   over 10 000 ha

after *A.E.D.B.* 1977

6.6. The Number and Size of Farms by Classes, 1975.

latifundio contained 5 per cent of all agricultural land. The dominance of the *latifundio* encourages large numbers of share-croppers, seasonal labour and tenant farmers. The continuing dominance of large farms is shown by **6.6**. In 1971, IBRA was replaced by INCRA (National Institute for Land Reform). A rural territorial tax was introduced to tax unused land, and powers were granted to expropriate land in extreme cases. INCRA has already distributed over 50 000 new titles. However, 10 per cent of land-holdings are still not farmed, whilst on very large farms as much as 55 per cent of their area is under pasture. In some areas, land ownership is also a problem because many farm boundaries are not mapped or clearly defined in deeds.

Agriculture is also subject to frost in the south, and drought in the North-east, so that production fluctuates wildly from year to year. Table **6.7** illustrates the fluctuating yields in coffee and wheat as a result of frost, and in tree cotton in the North-east as a result of drought. Although it is impossible to select a 'typical' year, the dramatic increases in soya, sugar, wheat and oranges are clear. The table also

6.7. Brasil's Major Crops.

Major Crops	Value in 1973 (Cr$ million).	Production '000 tonnes		Cultivated Area '000 ha, in 1975	Average Yield Kg/ha		Major Producing State, percentage in 1975	
		1965	1975		1973	1975		
Soya	5 565	523	9 893	5 825	1 386	1 698	R.G. do S.	47
Maize	5 123	12 112	16 335	10 855	1 430	1 504	Paraná	23
Rice	4 410	7 520	7 782	5 306	1 493	1 466	R.G. do S.	23
Kidney Bean	4 317	2 290	2 283	4 146	585	550	Paraná	27
Coffee	3 988	3 664	2 545	2 217	839	1 148	Paraná	48
Manioc	3 465	24 993	26 118	2 042	12 609	12 793	Bahia	20
Sugar	3 177	75 853	91 525	1 969	46 965	46 477	São Paulo	39
Herbaceous Cotton	2 567	1 986†	1 330	1 547	849	859	São Paulo	37
Wheat	1 495	585	1 788	2 932	1 104	610	R.G. do S.	69
Tree Cotton	1 321	—	418	2 330	240	179	Ceará	45
Oranges*	1 296	11 428	31 566	403	54 871	78 289	São Paulo	67
Potato (Irish)	1 088	1 246	1 655	191	7 087	8 653	Paraná	26
Potato (sweet)	353	1 721	1 600	153	11 487	10 428	R.G. do S.	24
Cocoa	1 005	161	282	451	471	624	Bahia	96
Banana**	937	349	364	314	1 141	1 159	Ceará	18

*million fruits.   **million bunches.   †1965 includes tree cotton.

Source: After *A.E.D.B. 1966, 1974, 1977.*

illustrates the marked regional crop variations. In 1973 São Paulo, Paraná and Rio Grande do Sul contributed over 55 per cent of the value of Brasil's ten major crops.

Productivity in agriculture is generally low and crop yields are still well below those in many other major agricultural countries. However, there have been significant improvements in the 1960s and 1970s. These have been the result of several factors: the shift from traditional staples to high value commercial crops; an increase in the cultivated area; a lower rate of increase in the growth of the agricultural labour force; greater productivity; the cultivation of traditional crops in new areas; increased mechanisation; improved land-management; and the increased use of fertilizers. Many of these factors are inter-related, especially in São Paulo and Paraná states where the levels of innovation and technology are at their highest.

Since 1960, the degree of mechanisation has increased dramatically. In that year only 1 per cent of farms were mechanised; today over 60 per cent of farms producing wheat and soya are mechanised. In 1959, over 140 different types of tractors were in use, so that this lack of standardisation hindered their further adoption. Domestic production is now in the order of 60 000 per annum. The distribution of tractors is a good index of mechanisation, as shown by **6.9** and **6.10**.

A further problem is the relatively low use of fertilizers. It has been estimated that of the nutrients being taken from the soil by cultivation, only 12 per cent were being returned. This is a major factor in the declining yields of traditional agricultural areas. Since the early 1950s, the use of fertilizers has increased dramatically. From 1953 to 1968 consumption increased over fourfold, in spite of the fact that a very large proportion had to be imported. A massive injection of capital would be necessary to achieve self-sufficiency, as current consumption has reached a level of about 1 million tonnes per annum. The exploitation of the recently discovered phosphate reserves at Patos de Minas, estimated at between 16 and 20 million tonnes, could have dramatic results in the 1980s. Development is urgent because from 1973 to 1975 the price of phosphate on the world market increased over sixfold.

Livestock rearing is extremely important, contributing over half the value of production in the agricultural sector. Brasil is now self-sufficient in beef, and also produces a small surplus for export. Pigs, sheep and goats are also reared. A major problem with livestock rearing is the low nutritional value of tropical grassland. This is gradually being rectified by the addition of lime and by the introduction of new scientifically bred grasses. The development of livestock rearing is discussed further in Chapter 9.

A fundamental requirement in developing

Brasil's agricultural sector is that of achieving the rapid diffusion of new ideas and techniques, and a number of inputs which are as yet little used. The term 'diffusion' refers to the process of dissemination (the spread of new ideas and methods), and to the process of adoption (the use of these ideas and methods). The sources of new ideas and methods in Brasil are the agricultural research centres, based mainly in the cities of the South-east. Because of the 'neighbourhood effect', successive zones with different degrees of diffusion can be recognised in the areas of commercial agriculture in the South-east, the innermost zones having the highest degree of adoption. The adoption of innovations also varies over time as shown by **6.8**. The theoretical curve of adoption is a 'logistic function', the equivalent of a 'normal distribution' but with a cumulative scale along the vertical axis. The graph shows that any innovation will at first be adopted by a small number of 'leaders', but then the rate of adoption increases rapidly, eventually tailing off sharply as the few remaining farmers, the 'laggards', also adopt the innovation. Clearly, the rate of dissemination is of vital importance. This has increased considerably in Brasil within the last decade, because of vastly improved telecommunications, and a number of government sponsored programmes designed for this purpose.

Diffusion is well illustrated by **6.9**. As is shown, in 1950 the relatively few tractors in Brasil were concentrated in São Paulo and Rio Grande do Sul; but by 1960, numbers had increased dramatically, and whilst these two states still dominated, the use of tractors had spread to many new areas, notably those adjacent to São Paulo.

However, there are many barriers which slow the rate of diffusion. These can include cultural, social, economic and political factors. It is ironic that it is the most successful farmers, in economic terms, that can best afford to innovate. High profits reduce the risks involved in introducing new methods and ideas. The subsistence farmer, on the other hand, is in a much more difficult position. He frequently uses traditional methods which have proved themselves through years of experience. Any change in methods involves a major risk to his livelihood.

In Brasil, although the subsistence sector has progressed slowly, many projects have been established to improve the lot of the subsistence farmer. The major programmes involve new agricultural colonies, which receive support from the regional development agencies and other organisations such as EMBRAPA and EMBRATER, mentioned below.

The new military government of 1964 recognised that the agricultural sector was a brake on economic development, and outlined a series of objectives to remedy this. These included the provision of adequate food supplies and industrial raw materials, diversifying agricultural exports, increasing productivity, and expanding the frontier of cultivation. It also attempted to encourage more owner-farmers, as 14 per cent of farms were manned by tenants or sharecroppers. From 1964 to 1970 the annual agricultural growth rate doubled. In 1971 the annual rate was over 11 per cent, but frost caused this to decline to less than 4 per cent in 1973.

The Second National Development Plan reinforced these policies by guaranteeing the producer a greater share of the sector's income, by extending labour and social security benefits, and by increasing the provision of resources to the regional development agencies. The 'integration' of the Central-west and Amazonia, and the planned irrigation of a further 100 000 ha in the North-east, would enable greater regional specialisation in the agricultural sector and would increase productivity by stimulating areas with a comparative advantage. This would also have the effect of increasing productivity in the developed South-east, as it would release land producing economically marginal crops for the cultivation of more viable crops.

EMBRAPA (Brasilian Agricultural Research Company) is now co-ordinating formerly disjointed research, and has had major successes in improving the genetic strain of a number of crops, notably, cotton, soya, wheat, beans, potatoes, maize, rice and peanuts. EMBRATER (Brasilian Technical Assistance and Rural Extension Company) is making considerable attempts to improve organisation between

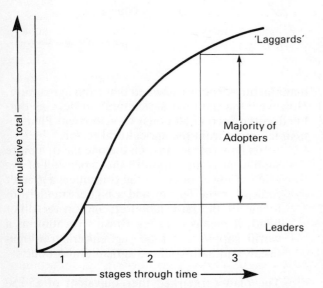

6.8. The Curve of the Adoption of Innovations over Time.

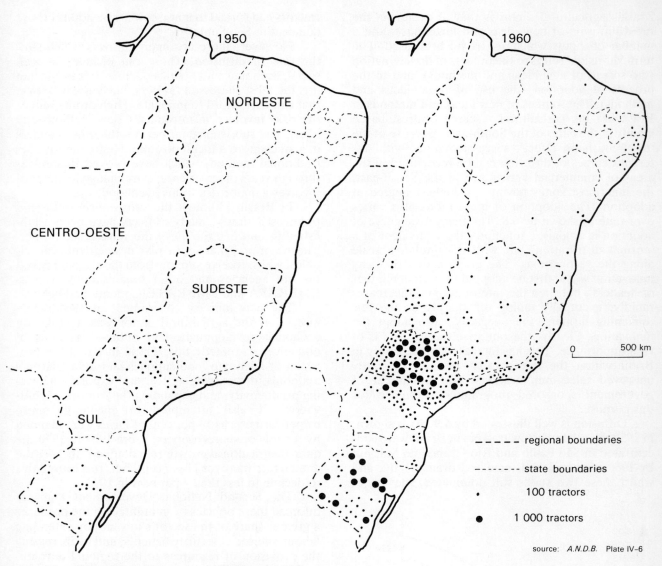

6.9. The Diffusion of Tractors, 1950 and 1960.

farmers, especially through the formation of co-operatives.

A further problem—perhaps the most important in national terms—is the loss of an estimated 30 per cent of agricultural production because of pests and diseases, together with inadequacies in transport, storage and distribution. In 1975, only 820 farms in the entire country were equipped with silos, but in that year a national storage programme was initiated to develop a network of silos, mainly in the South. Twelve state food distribution centres (CEASAs) had also been constructed by 1975 and a further ten have since been added.

Brasil is no longer a predominantly agricultural country. In 1980 only 36 per cent of the population were classed as rural, and exports of minerals and manufactured goods exceeded that from agriculture. However, the national agricultural strategy as outlined in the Second National Development Plan demanded more from the agricultural sector:

'Its new role means, on the one hand, a more significant contribution to the expansion of the GDP at lower prices to the consumer, a greater return for the farmer and a higher standard of living for the farm labourer; and on the other hand, it means realising Brasil's vocation as a world supplier of food, agricultural raw materials and industrialised agricultural products.'

The plan earmarked the equivalent of £5 250 million for agricultural development, of which over half was to be invested by the Bank of Brasil.

Since 1979, as part of the Third National Development Plan (III PND), the government has attempted to launch a new agricultural programme. Its aims were to stimulate the small and medium sized farms by providing cheap credit, to speed up funds to priority areas, expand the crop buying system, and to raise guaranteed prices for the major crops, but chronic inflation has curtailed these plans. In 1979 about three-quarters of the wheat consumed had to be imported, costing about £1 400 000 000. There have also been problems in beef production, and in 1978 beef had to be imported for the first time.

As with all other types of economic activity there are enormous regional contrasts in agricultural methods, land-use, productivity and technological development. These contrasts, and the regional development programmes will be discussed at length in Chapter 9. The following table (**6.10**) illustrates some of the major contrasts between the *Grandes Regiões* and states.

6.10. Selected Indicators of Regional Contrasts in the Agricultural Sector   Source *A.E.D.B.*

Key: *1*—Total area of farmland in '000 ha, 1975.   *2*—Number of farms in '000s, 1975.
3—Average size of farms in ha, 1975.   *4*—Total Cultivated area in '000 ha, 1975.
5—Number of Tractors, 1970.   *6*—Persons employed in '000s, 1975.
7—Number of Beef Cattle in '000s, 1974.

Grandes Regiões and States	1	2	3	4	5	6	7
NORTE	29 768	338	88	1 017	1 035	1 445	2 211
Rondônia	3 092	26	119	193	40	107	41
Acre	3 717	25	149	35	11	81	100
Amazonas	4 500	93	48	189	60	418	318
Roraima	1 633	3	544	20	4	19	286
Pará	16 088	187	86	558	885	801	1 378
Amapá	739	4	185	22	35	19	88
NORDESTE	79 781	2 361	34	10 615	6 177	9 009	16 244
Maranhão	12 992	497	26	1 021	136	1 488	1 722
Piauí	10 560	217	49	672	172	617	1 468
Ceará	11 062	253	44	2 072	580	1 047	2 042
Rio Grande do N.	4 397	106	42	822	488	397	731
Paraíba	4 770	201	24	1 114	734	826	1 036
Perambuco	6 312	318	20	1 524	1 387	1 201	1 439
Alagoas	2 308	116	20	698	876	521	596
Sergipe	1 806	103	18	228	385	308	727
Bahia	25 571	552	46	2 466	1 418	2 606	6 482
SUDESTE	72 856	881	83	10 172	79 852	4 415	30 386
Minas Gerais	44 754	465	96	3 851	9 332	2 337	17 077
Espírito Santo	3 881	61	64	646	1 001	322	1 684
Rio de Janeiro	3 459	77	45	602	3 718	228	1 433
São Paulo	20 762	279	74	5 073	65 801	1 468	10 192
SUL	46 541	1 158	40	12 868	60 684	4 922	20 763
Paraná	15 754	479	33	5 545	17 258	2 141	5 641
Santa Catarina	6 970	207	34	1 426	5 068	866	2 161
Rio Grande do S.	23 817	472	51	5 897	38 358	1 915	12 961
CENTRO-OESTE	93 676	270	347	4 131	9 598	1 263	22 892
Mato Grosso	50 182	114	440	1 711	4 044	540	11 874
Goiás	43 310	154	281	2 409	5 294	714	10 977
Distrito Federal	185	2	93	12	260	9	42
BRASIL (total)	322 621	5 007	64	38 803	157 346	21 054	92 495

7 The Resource Base: 'Exploitation' and 'Development'

Brasil's lithosphere and biosphere contain a massive aggregate stock of mineral and biological resources. In the past some biological resources such as the red dye wood *pau-brasil,* the rubber tree *Hevea brasiliensis,* and timber used for construction and charcoal, have been exploited for only short-term benefit. In many cases, over-exploitation of potentially renewable resources has resulted in ecological damage and a consequent reduction in the stock. The maintenance of these resources requires scientifically planned development, at a level which allows regeneration—a 'conservationist strategy'.

Mineral resources are finite and therefore non-renewable. Their exploitation is related mainly to economic factors such as the need for export revenue, the demands of domestic industry, and the stage of technological development. Brasil is fortunate that in the past the pre-industrial economy made relatively small demands on minerals. However, increasing population pressure and political aspirations in an increasingly industrialised society have increased the demand for minerals and energy considerably in recent decades. Brasil has significant problems in terms of the lack of certain minerals and energy sources, so that exports of abundant minerals, especially iron ore, will have to be increased to pay for imports.

There is a significant difference between resource 'exploitation' and 'development', even when applied to finite resources. Finite stocks can be 'exploited' for short-term gain, but this can result in the loss of a resource which may have much greater value in the future. Planned resource 'development' is vital for continuing economic growth, especially as the world stock of all types of finite resources is declining at a rapid rate.

Biological Resources

Brasil's forests cover an area of over 3.5 million km^2, representing nearly 18 per cent of the world total. The largest reserves occur in the Amazon basin, which is the world's largest virtually untapped region of rain-forest. The *selva* contains over 400 marketable hardwood species. However, in spite of the over-exploitation of some species, notably rosewood, the region contributes only 6 per cent of Brasil's timber production by value. Its major products are special hardwoods, Brasil nuts, coagulated rubber and Balata Gum (see **7.2**).

The forestry industry is heavily concentrated in the South-east and South regions as shown in Table **7.1**. The most exploited region is the accessible *Pinheiras* Paraná pine forest close to the industrial centres of southern Brasil and major ports. The soft-woods provide timber for the construction industry and pulp for paper manufacture. About 20 per cent of total output is exported, mainly high quality pine for furniture. Some thirty producers in the South have combined to form Madebras, S.A. (The Brasilian Lumber Exporters Corporation). They have reserves of about 51 million m^3, of which about 300 000 m^3 are exported annually. The corporation controls over ninety lumber yards, saw-mills and processing factories, and also produces a wide range of products such as cellulose, cardboard and pre-fabricated houses and sheds. The benefits of co-ordinated large-scale production have enabled improved port facilities at Rio Grande, São Francisco, Paranaguá, Santos, Vitória, and also more recently outside the region at Salvador and Belém. The South also produces Brasil's entire output of *erva-mate,* a green tea which is very popular is parts of South America.

In the North-east region, a number of vegetable waxes, oils and fibres are collected. The Carnaúba palm has traditionally supplied the rural *Nordestino* with a variety of materials including construction timber, thatching fibres and fodder; but the most commercial material is the hard, white wax yielded by the young leaves. The Babaçu palm yields a high quality vegetable oil, and the shell is now processed at Queiru in the state of Maranhão. In southern Bahia state, the coastal region produces fibres from

7.1. The Regional Distribution of Forestry, by Value, 1975.

Regions	Timber (%)	Charcoal (%)
North	6.3	2.3
North-east	16.5	18.5
South-east	13.6	75.5
South	53.2	2.7
Central-west	10.4	1.0

Major Producing States

Timber	Paraná: 22%
	Santa Catarina: 20%
	Rio Grande do Sul: 11%
Charcoal	Minas Gerais: 65%

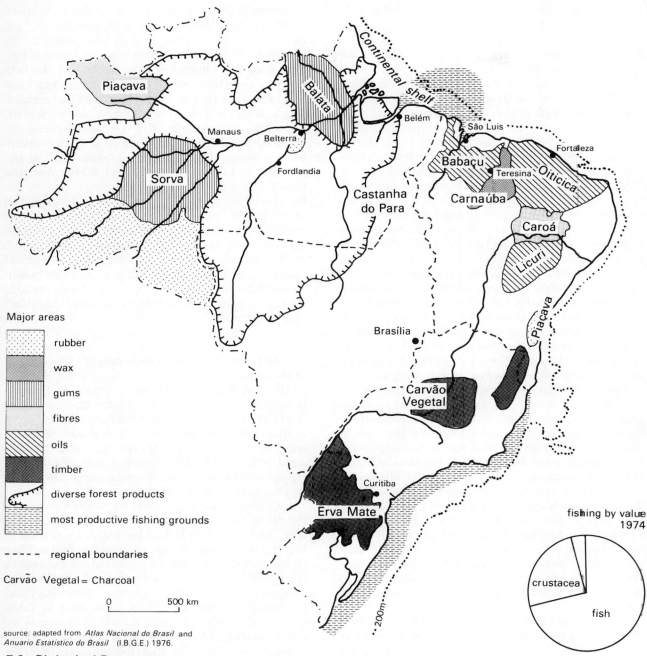

Major areas

- rubber
- wax
- gums
- fibres
- oils
- timber
- diverse forest products
- most productive fishing grounds

- - - - - regional boundaries

Carvão Vegetal = Charcoal

0   500 km

source: adapted from *Atlas Nacional do Brasil* and
Anuario Estatistico do Brasil (I.B.G.E.) 1976.

7.2. Biological Resources.

fishing by value
1974

crustacea

fish

the Piaçáva and Caroá plants, and 80 per cent of
Brasil's latex rubber produced on new plantations.

Until recently, Brasil's exploitation of vegetable
resources was at a primitive collecting level, but now
serious attempts are being made to establish plantations, and to create a system of planned development. This is true of the recently established
Carnaúba plantations of the North-east, rubber in
Amazonia and Bahia, and charcoal in the South-

east. The deforestation of Brasil's eastern forests
proceeded at such a rapid rate that eucalyptus plantations are being established, to provide a continuous
supply of wood for the charcoal used in iron smelting. Wood, bagasse (from sugar-cane) and charcoal
still account for about 25 per cent of Brasil's energy
output.

The distinction between the 'exploitation' and
'development' of forest resources is illustrated by the

contrasts between Amazonia's rubber boom and the Jari River Project.

The Rubber Boom of Amazonia—A case study of 'exploitation' in the selva.

As a result of Goodyear's discovery of the vulcanization process, and the increased world demand for rubber tyres and rubber for electrical insulation, there was a frantic rush in the nineteenth century to exploit the *Hevea brasiliensis* trees of Amazonia. Brasil's monopoly of this new resource led to a typically speculative response. From the mid-nineteenth century to the 1920s, the wealthy élite purchased large tracts of forest in the hope that they would contain sufficient numbers of wild rubber trees to make their fortune. From 1872 to 1920, Amazonia's population rose from 300 000 to 1 433 000. Thousands of *Nordestinos* were tempted to flee their drought-stricken home-lands; they were employed by the land-owners, equipped with tools and tinned-food, and sent into the forest to tap the rubber trees. The latex was brought back to riverside camps where it was solidified by smoking, and then collected by river craft owned by the land-owners. Rubber exploitation never developed beyond a primitive hunting and collecting level. A network of collecting posts developed at the major river confluences, and Manaus and Belém became the twin urban foci of the region's new found wealth. They were transformed by the *nouveau riche* into symbols of their social status. Lavish mansions and public buildings were built, including the famous opera house at Manaus. It was constructed of imported Italian marble, decorated with gold and diamonds, and was opened by the famous Italian tenor, Carouso. Every possible luxury was bought from the finest stores in Paris and London. Manaus became the first city in the continent to install trams. Attempts were made to develop a railway network, but many schemes were abandoned as the fatalities resulting from malaria became unacceptably high in financial as well as human terms.

No attempt was made to develop a rationalised plantation system, so that by 1920 the 'boom' was over. In 1876, Sir Henry Wickham had smuggled seeds to Kew Gardens in London, and these formed the basis of the successful plantations of Malaya. In 1910, Amazonia still produced over 90 per cent of the world's rubber, but by 1920 was producing less than 10 per cent. The collapse of the rubber economy left the new northerners stranded and impoverished, and Amazonia reverted to an economic back-water.

In 1927, the first major attempt to develop commercial plantations began when the Ford Motor Company purchased 1 million ha of land in the Tapajós valley. About 3 400 ha were planted at 'Fordlandia', but the site was ill-considered. Within a short period deforestation had resulted in soil exhaustion and erosion, and disease added to the problems. In 1934, a new area was developed at Belterra only fifty kilometres from Santarem. The land was more suitable, but this project also failed. Ford had estimated that in order to meet their requirements about 30 000 ha would have to be planted, requiring a labour force of 11 000. Despite generous financial and other incentives only 2 700 workers were attracted to the so-called 'green hell' of the rain-forest. Following the Second World War, the plantations were bought for a nominal sum by the Brasilian government, and were later developed as experimental areas. Preston E. James (1959) explains the collapse of the plantations in the following terms: 'It was not the equatorial climate which made the Ford Company abandon its experiment . . . , (it) was the scarcity of workers which meant that there was no hope that the plantations could ever provide more than a fraction of the rubber that was needed.'

The Jari River Project—A case study of 'development' in the selva.

In 1967 the American billionaire, Daniel K. Ludwig, bought an estate of over 1.2 million ha—equivalent to about a third of the area of the Netherlands—from a Brasilian land-owner who had produced Brasil nuts. Until recently the project was severely criticised because of Ludwig's secrecy, and allegations of slavery were made in the Brasilian press. These allegations have since been disproved.

Ludwig's major aim was to produce cellulose, but since the indigenous tree species were unsuitable, and the forest lacked homogeneity, a team of highly paid specialists were entrusted to find suitable species. *Pinus caribaea* was selected for the poorer sandy soils, and *Gmelina arborea* for the better soils. Despite the availability of advanced technology and the world's leading specialists, some early mistakes were made. These included the use of machines for forest clearing, which uprooted the trees and consequently disturbed the thin top-soil. By 1979, 74 million trees had been planted on 73 000 ha. The advantage of the *Gmelina* is that it grows at the phenomenal rate of 5 metres per year, can be frequently cropped yielding 38.5 m³ per hectare per annum, and then after 10 years is felled. In order to process the timber, Ludwig constructed a floating pulping factory in his own Japanese ship-yard. It was towed from Japan to Jari, and located in a prepared dock which was then drained. The mill has a capacity of 850 tonnes per day. A 220 km railway is being constructed from the new 'forest' to the mill, and an

80 km long stretch of the Jari is being dredged to take the 42 000 dwt ships which will export the pulp.

If the Jari project were judged on these facts alone it could be considered highly successful. It illustrates the potential of Amazonia when large-scale investment of capital, technology and labour is available. However, this is but one aspect. A chance discovery of South America's only proven kaolin (china clay) reserves of 40 million tonnes has led to exports of 220 000 tonnes per annum. The clay is mainly used in paper manufacture. Ludwig's ability to convince the Brasilian authorities as to his intentions was based on his concern about the problems of the 'Third World', and in particular possible future world food shortages. He set up a rice experimental station and tested 360 different strains. Having selected the most suitable—IR22—he then planted the *várzea* part of his estate. These flooded areas have been prepared using Dutch technology and technicians, and 14 000 ha are being planted. Yields of 10 tonnes per hectare—over six times the Brasilian national average—have been achieved by two harvests a year and by a very high degree of mechanisation and scientific control. Specially designed floating tractors have been developed, and planting and pest control is carried out entirely by light aircraft. On the same estate, Ludwig has developed a 4 500 ha cattle ranch which contains 11 500 crossbreed Charolais/Nelore cattle, and also buffalo. The aim is to develop a herd of 50 000 head and to export beef from the refrigeration plant at Monte Dourado. This is a new city and the planned centre for ten satellite settlements referred to as *silvavilas*.

The project has been highly successful in attracting peasant farmers from the North-east. The population is now in excess of 25 000. Families live in well appointed, specially designed houses which are rented at the equivalent of 25 pence per month, with free water and electricity. In order to maintain a stable and contented labour force, the project has excellent free facilities for child and adult education, community welfare and medical care. Ludwig encourages the cultivation of food crops by the workers themselves.

The Jari project has given a new meaning to the term 'potential' in Amazonia, and whilst it could not be repeated or copied elsewhere on such a large scale, it has placed the problems of rain-forest development in perspective. There has been ecological damage, particularly to wild-life, but one of the most hopeful developments is that the fragile soils are gradually being improved under the new forest. By 1983, total investments will have reached the equivalent of about £2 billion, new cellulose, plywood and veneer factories will have been completed, and it is forecast that 100 000 people will be employed.

Fishing

Fish is an important dietary supplement for Amerindians and other subsistence farmers along the Amazon and its tributaries, and along the North-east coast. The traditional *jangada* raft with a small triangular sail is still used in the North-east for catching crabs, shrimps, turtles and molluscs, and larger fish beyond the coral barrier reefs. Only about 5 per cent of the total recorded catch is provided by inland waters, though this could well rise to a significant level if the vast reservoirs associated with the hydro-electric power-stations were stocked. It has been estimated that the reservoirs of the Urubupunga hydro-electricity complex on the Paraná river alone could yield 400 000 tonnes per annum. This compares with a present total catch of about 750 000 tonnes from all sources. The Itaipu project could make an even greater contribution.

Brasil has claimed a 360 km fishing limit along its 5 600 km coastline. The areas with the greatest potential lie on the continental shelf off the mouth of the Amazon, and the inshore region of the South-east and South (see **7.1**). Motorised fleets are based only at the larger ports. The ports of the states of São Paulo, Rio Grande do Sul, Santa Catarina, Rio Grande do Norte and Pará account for 54 per cent of the total catch by value. Deep water trawlers are primarily used for catching tuna and for whaling.

Brasil is unfortunate that her continental shelf is relatively small in area as compared with the length of coastline. However, overfishing is not yet a problem. More serious is river and coastal pollution which in some areas has now reached critical proportions. The Rio Tietê, flowing through São Paulo city, is virtually anaerobic. There has also been much controversy concerning Brasil's recent nuclear power programme, and its possible effects on coastal areas.

Mineral Resources

Brasil has a vast proven mineral stock, and there is little doubt that new discoveries will continue to be made for some time to come. However, despite the fact that Brasil is a major world producer of a number of metallic minerals and gem-stones, mining makes a very small contribution to the national economy at present. In the mid-1970s, mining contributed only just over 1 per cent of the GNP, 3.5 per cent of industrial production by value, and employed only 63 000 people. Mining's major role is to provide the raw materials for industrial growth, and through exports to provide the foreign exchange to support it. Mining contributes over 13 per cent of exports by value, of which half is iron ore. Brasil possesses only

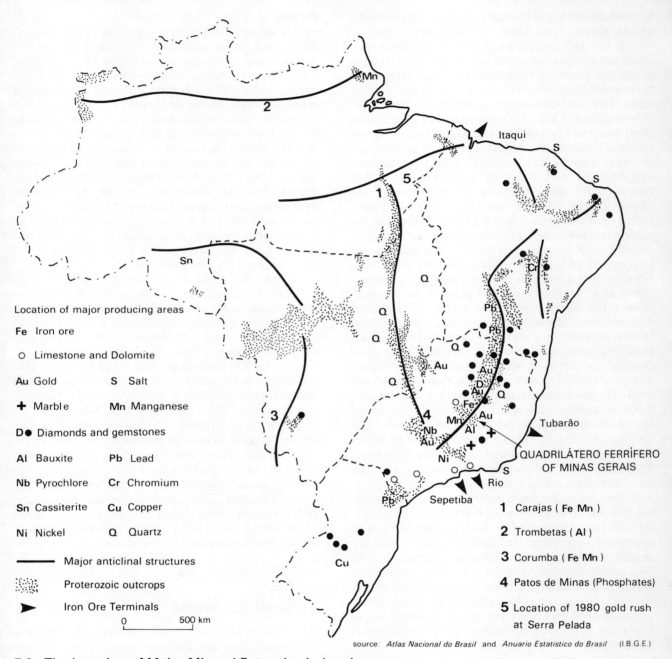

Location of major producing areas

Fe Iron ore

O Limestone and Dolomite

Au Gold   **S** Salt

+ Marble   **Mn** Manganese

D● Diamonds and gemstones

Al Bauxite   **Pb** Lead

Nb Pyrochlore   **Cr** Chromium

Sn Cassiterite   **Cu** Copper

Ni Nickel   **Q** Quartz

────── Major anticlinal structures

::::: Proterozoic outcrops

▶ Iron Ore Terminals

0   500 km

QUADRILÁTERO FERRÍFERO
OF MINAS GERAIS

1 Carajas (**Fe Mn**)

2 Trombetas (**Al**)

3 Corumba (**Fe Mn**)

4 Patos de Minas (Phosphates)

5 Location of 1980 gold rush
at Serra Pelada

source: *Atlas Nacional do Brasil* and *Anuario Estatistico do Brasil* (I.B.G.E.)

7.3. The Location of Major Mineral Extractive Industries.

sixteen of the sixty principal elements in abundance, the most serious shortage being copper. This is largely responsible for an overall trade deficit in minerals.

The mineral zones correlate closely with a series of geanticlines along which Proterozoic rocks outcrop. Two of these structures converge at the *Quadrilátero Ferrífero* of Minas Gerais (see **7.3** and **7.5** on pages 94–96). The state has dominated mining since the gold-rush of the eighteenth century. It pro-duces a third of minerals by value, employs a third of the mining labour-force and produces over 90 per cent of iron, zinc and nickel ores, and bauxite.

The mere possession of a vast minerals stock does not in itself guarantee its exploitation. Brasil does have some major advantages not possessed by some other major mining countries, such as a climate which permits all-year mining, and relative political stability. But the vast scale of the country poses problems of accessibility. It is significant that the exploitation of the minerals of Minas Gerais is primarily the result of its accessibility, with rail links to ocean terminals at Rio, Tubarão (Vitória) and Sepetiba. There are many other ore bodies in more remote locations with equally advantageous physical properties in terms of metal content, quantity and workable depth, and lack of impurities. The exploitability of ore bodies is particularly related to economic incentives. Because the manufacturing industries of the advanced countries have a wide choice of producing countries, exploitation is related to production and transport costs. Brasil's minerals policy is to produce sufficient to provide for domestic needs, to export in sufficient quantities to reduce the net trade deficit, and to provide surplus export revenue. In order to achieve this level of exploitation, Brasilian companies have had to seek partnership with foreign corporations.

Exploration techniques are becoming ever more sophisticated—Amazonia is being radar mapped under the RADAM scheme, and a geo-synchronous resources satellite is being planned. However, it is extremely unlikely that any major new discoveries of metallic ores in remote areas would result in their exploitation in the 1980s, with the possible exception of copper ores. New fossil fuel discoveries would be a different matter. Brasil has to import 40 per cent of her energy needs, because of very low proven stocks of coal, petroleum and natural gas.

Iron Ore: A case study in minerals exploitation and development

Brasil's iron ore reserves are estimated at over 60 000 000 000 tonnes—sufficient to meet the entire world demand for over two centuries. The ores are high grade haematite with a metallic content averaging 68 per cent, occur on the surface or at shallow depths, and are therefore open-cast quarried. The reserves are concentrated in two main areas—the *Quadrilátero Ferrífero* (Iron Quadrilateral) of Minas Gerais, and the Serra dos Carajás in Pará, which was only discovered in 1967 and has yet to be exploited.

From the mid-eighteenth century until the Second World War, iron ore mining was related to the iron industry of Minas Gerais which was small in scale because of the small domestic demand for iron. Major production dates from the formation of C.V.R.D. (*Companhia Vale do Rio Doce*), in which the government has majority control. Previously, mining had been hindered by political difficulties between Brasilian officials and British financiers, and also the decision by Bethlehem Steel (U.S.A.) to develop its Venezuelan resources rather than increase investments in Brasil. The formation of C.V.R.D. and the construction of the state steel-

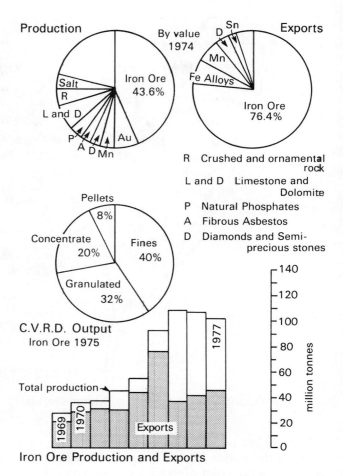

R   Crushed and ornamental rock
L and D   Limestone and Dolomite
P   Natural Phosphates
A   Fibrous Asbestos
D   Diamonds and Semi-precious stones

source: *C.V.R.D.* and *A.E.D.B.* various years.

7.4. Mineral Production, with special reference to Iron Ore.

works at Volta Redonda in 1947 initiated a period of major government involvement in industrial development.

The *Quadrilátero Ferrífero* is a large mining region over 600 km^2 in area, within which outcrop the ore-bearing rocks of the 'Minas' and 'Rio das Velhas' series of middle Pre-Cambrian age. In addition to iron, the rocks also yield manganese, bauxite and gold, non-metallic minerals such as dolomite and quartz, and to the north near Serro and Diamantina, diamonds. Within the quadrilateral, marked by the four towns of Belo Horizonte (the state capital), Itabira, Ouro Prêto and Congonhas, are about 90 iron ore mines and about 50 manganese mines; but the major mining centres are in close proximity to the afore-mentioned urban centres.

The single largest iron deposit is that at Cauê Mountain (see **7.5**) near Itabira, which lies within an isolated inlier of the Minas series. Its ore has an

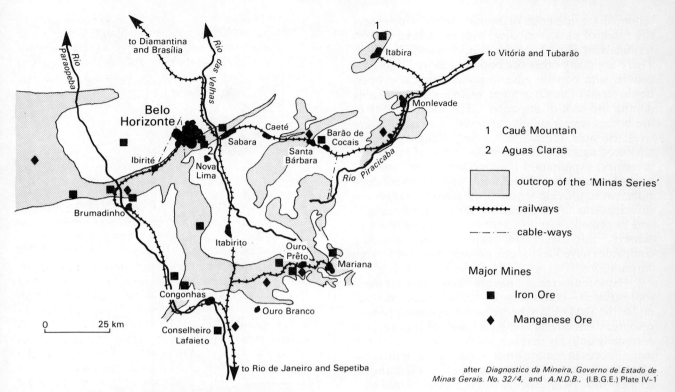

7.5. The *Quadrilátero Ferrífero* of Minas Gerais.

extremely low phosphorus and sulphur content, and like all the major bodies is open-cast mined. Its output is in the order of 40 million tonnes per annum and is mostly exported.

The ores of the eastern mines are exported via the railway which follows the Rio Doce and its tributary the Piracicaba. The railway was up-graded in 1947, resulting in a sixfold increase in exports by 1951. However, the increasing size of ore ships necessitated the construction of a new ocean terminal. This had to await the return of political stability after the 1964 'revolution', and a massive loan from the Inter-American Development Bank. The 550 km railway now ends at the ocean terminal at Tubarão, which was inaugurated in 1966. It has an annual capacity of 80 million tonnes, handles over 75 per cent of Brasil's iron ore exports, and like its feeder mines and the railway is run by C.V.R.D. In order to increase the value of ore exports, the terminal has its own benefication plants. Three new pelletization plants have been recently completed. At the terminal, hundred-thousand-tonne ore ships can be loaded at a rate of 6 000 tonnes per hour.

The western mines have traditionally used the Rio terminal, to which they are linked by rail via Brumadinho and Itabirito. The Rio terminal was however too small, so in 1973 a new terminal was completed at Sepetiba to the west of Rio. The development of the terminal was necessary to export the ores from the new mine at Aguas Claras (see **7.5**) which lies between Nova Lima and Belo Horizonte. In 1974, its first year of production, it produced over 11 million tonnes and this is likely to be doubled in the early 1980s. The Aguas Claras ore body is a tabular lens about 3 km long, containing an estimated reserve of 400 million tonnes. Mining is by means of thirteen-metre-high benches cut by large excavators. These load hundred-tonne trucks which transport the ore to a primary crusher. The ore is graded by filters, screens and 'cyclones', before being transported to Sepetiba by 125-truck ore trains which use the new track built by the federal railway company R.F.F. The Aguas Claras and Sepetiba project has involved a total investment equivalent to £200 million, 62 per cent of which has been supplied by foreign investors in the form of 10 and 15 year contracts. Exports are already at a level equivalent to £50 million per annum.

It is clear that Brasil has been extremely successful in attracting foreign investment for those mining projects which are demonstrably viable. However, the exploitation of the Serra dos Carajás ores is likely to be a long-term project. The discovery of the world's single largest iron ore body, with an estimated 18 billion tonnes of high quality haematite, and also vast quantities of manganese, led to feasibility studies by C.V.R.D. and U.S. Steel which themselves cost the equivalent of £30 million. The ores are situated in Pará state about 750 km from the coast. In order to develop the ores, an 870 km railway would be needed to link wih a new ocean terminal at Itaqui, a hydro-electric plant would have to be constructed to power the electrified railway, and mining equipment, and amenities such as housing and medical services, would have to be installed in what is an isolated interior region. All this would require capital investment equivalent to £2 500 million; and in order that the project would prove viable, 50 million tonnes would have to be exported per annum. In the mid-1970s it seemed likely that despite this massive investment, and the fact that world demand for ore was already being met by Australian and Liberian exports, exploitation would start in the late 1970s. But in 1977 U.S. Steel gave up its 49 per cent share in *Amazonica Mineracão*, the company formed to develop the ore.

Plate 20. Open-cast bench quarrying of iron ore at Aguas Claras near Belo Horizonte. The iron ores of the *Quadrilátero Ferrífero* of Minas Gerais have made a major contribution to the industrialisation of the South-east, and to exports. ***Hoa-Qui.***

Efforts have been made to interest other potential foreign investors such as British Steel, French and West German companies, and a Japanese consortium. It is possible that Carajás will be developed in the 1980s, but the planned scale of the project has already had to be reduced, and the project modified. In 1978, the Brazilian Trade Centre in London announced that forecast costs had been reduced by 37 per cent. Diesel locomotives and lighter gauge rails were to be used, and planned annual exports were consequently reduced to 8 million tonnes. The future of Carajás is still uncertain, but iron ore could become an even more important export commodity in the 1980s. Projected output for 1987 is 220 million tonnes, double the present output.

Other Mining Activities

Gold was the backbone of the economy in the eighteenth century, and still contributes over 5 per cent of mining output. The largest mine, at Morro Velho near Nova Lima, has been in continuous production since 1834, but small scale prospecting referred to as *garimpagem* still contributes a significant share of total output. Diamond mining is concentrated in the Diamantina district. The diamonds are not found in 'in-situ lodes', but in sedimentary placer deposits. The crystalline rocks of the shield yield a variety of gems and precious light metals, such as lithium, beryllium, beryl, emeralds and topaz. The diabase lavas of the southern plateau are very different and yield agates, amethysts, opal and citrine. Diamonds and emeralds are the most important gemstones by value.

The development of the steel, construction and light manufacturing industries has created a vastly increased demand for a variety of minerals. The steel industry demands minerals for producing special alloy steels. Manganese is one of the most important additives, as it is used for cleansing and increasing the tensile strength of steel. Minas Gerais is a major producer, but the main output is from the Serra do Navio district of Amapá. Following a chance discovery in 1944, these ores were developed by the Bethlehem Steel Corporation (U.S.A.). The ore is transported 200 km by rail to a terminal at Santana near Macapá. The region still produces over 80 per cent of national output, but the reserves are dwindling rapidly. This may give rise to intensified interest in Carajás, and lead to increased exports from the Urucum deposits in the Central-west. These are transported along the Paraná-Paraguay river system.

Aluminium is the most abundant metal in the earth's crust, but is only found in commercially viable concentrations in tropical regions. Bauxite—a hydrated oxide of aluminium—results from the intense weathering of crystalline rocks. Brasil has estimated reserves of over 10 billion tonnes. The mines of Minas Gerais accounted for Brasil's entire output in the 1970s, but recently discovered deposits at Trombetas—possibly the world's largest—are now being developed by a multi-national corporation controlled by Brasilian interests. Output is expected to reach 10 million tonnes per annum in the early 1980s. The development of Trombetas is not only providing a new 'growth pole' in Amazonia, but could make Brasil a net exporter of bauxite. Even more important than this is the potential for the development of a major aluminium smelting industry; this is an extremely attractive prospect for a country with a considerable hydro-electricity potential, as cheap electricity is necessary for aluminium smelting.

Brasil also has reserves of a number of other metallic minerals. If estimates of the cassiterite (tin ore) reserves of Rondônia territory are accurate, then Brasil has a stock 150 per cent larger than the entire reserves of the rest of the world. Other minerals include chromium and silver, and the world's largest reserves of pyrochlore (niobium ore). Niobium is used as a corrosion inhibiter in special steels. The major disappointment is that reserves of copper are very low. But recent discoveries of platinum are estimated at half the world's reserves.

Brasil's determination to be self-sufficient in metals is illustrated by the development of a new zinc processing technology since 1962. Previously, the oxidised zinc carbonates and silicates of Minas Gerais could not be used, but Brasil now produces significant quantities and is likely to be self-sufficient in the 1980s.

Salt is probably Brasil's most widely used and least industrialised mineral, having been produced by the evaporation of sea-water in the coastal pans of the North-east for a considerable period. Production is now sufficiently large to have justified the construction of a barge terminal at Areia Branca, with bulk-loading facilities. The 6 million tonne halite (rock-salt) reserves of Sergipe could also be developed.

The construction industry is developing rapidly and requires increasing quantities of limestone and dolomite in particular. These now rank second only to iron ore by value of production. Minerals are also required by agriculture, especially nitrogenous, phosphatic and potassic fertilizers. At present Brasil still has to import most of these, but the world's dwindling reserves are becoming increasingly more expensive. The phosphate deposits at Patos de Minas (Minas Gerais) are now being processed at Uberaba. The plant was constructed only a few years after the discovery of the deposits.

Mineral discoveries are being made at a bewildering rate, and the mining sector has been given a high priority. In 1969, C.P.R.M. (*Companhia de Pesquisas de Recursos Minerais*)—a joint venture between the federal government and private Brasilian companies—was set up to undertake and coordinate exploration, research and development, and to act as a financing and advisory agency. It has already been involved in 630 projects, including the RADAM project and in the establishment of the Institute of Mineral Technology at Rio's federal university.

Energy Resources

All forms of advanced economic activity are dependent on the availability of energy. Energy is produced either by burning wood or 'fossil fuels', or by harnessing the elements to generate power. Brasil's comparatively recent industrial development has depended heavily on petroleum, but domestic production is sufficient to meet only about 20 per cent of total requirements. Thus, Brasil has a major energy problem which has become severe since the quadrupling of world crude oil prices in 1974. The shortage of fossil fuels is, however, only one aspect of a greater problem, as table **7.6** illustrates.

Brasil has by far the greatest gross energy consumption in the continent, but because of its low reserves of fossil fuels and comparatively high population, per capita consumption is very low—in fact it ranks only eighth in the continent. Also, Brasil has to import a greater proportion of its energy than any other industrial country in South America, despite its large hydro-electricity capacity. Raw data

7.6. Energy Production and Consumption in Brasil, Argentina and Venezuela, 1976

	(1) Energy Production	(2) Energy Consumption	(3) Per capita Consumption	(4) Electricity Production	(5) Hydro-electricity as a % of (4)
Brasil	26.5	79.8	731	88 383	92
Argentina	41.8	46.4	1 804	30 328	16
Venezuela	199.0	35.1	2 838	23 276	45

Note: (1) and (2) in million tonnes coal equivalent; (3) in kg; (4) in million KWh.
Source: *United Nations Statistical Yearbook, 1977.*

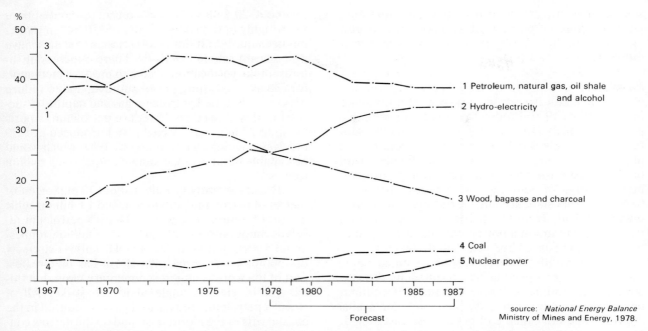

7.7. Percentage Contribution of Primary Energy Sources to Gross Energy Consumption, 1967–77, and Forecasts 1978–87.

is however misleading. Per capita energy consumption in the industrialised South-east is the highest in the continent.

There is a strong correlation between energy consumption and economic development. From Brasil's industrial 'take-off' in the early-1960s until the mid-1970s, energy consumption increased by over 85 per cent, and by 1980 it had more than doubled. The energy crisis of the 1970s has emphasised not only Brasil's dependence on imported petroleum, but also the danger of relying on fuels which are finite and are being rapidly depleted. Brasil has been forced to seek alternative sources, and to develop new energy technologies ahead of developments in the industrialised countries. If these measures are successful, then Brasil will be in a comparatively strong position in the late 1980s and 1990s.

It is clear from **7.7** that the traditional energy sources of wood, charcoal and bagasse (derived from sugar-cane) have a limited and declining role. It is clear, too, that despite a steady growth in hydro-electric power, petroleum and natural gas have been the primary sources of energy during the 'economic miracle'. A detailed break-down of the estimated gross energy supply for 1980 is given by **7.8**. It was the first year that both alcohol and nuclear power contributed to energy suplies. The graph also shows the contribution of imported petroleum and coal. Throughout the 1960s and early 1970s, the degree of dependence on imported energy increased. Before

the petroleum crisis of 1974, the average annual increase was in the order of 16 per cent. Since then it has slowed to 8.5 per cent, but even the most optimistic forecasts for 1985 give a 20 per cent dependence on imports. Whilst there may well be a significant reduction in the use of petroleum as an energy

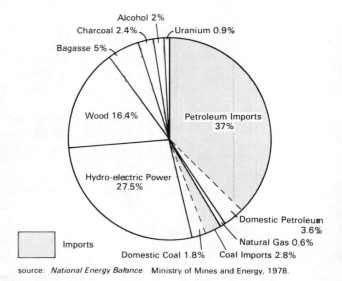

source: *National Energy Balance* Ministry of Mines and Energy, 1978.

7.8. Brasil's Gross Energy Supply and Imports in 1980 (estimated).

source, it is still required as a transport fuel and, perhaps more important, it is needed as a raw material for the rapidly expanding petrochemicals industry.

Fossil Fuels

Coal production is very low, in spite of a threefold increase since 1970. Production stands at less than 6 per cent that of Britain. Reserves are mainly sub-bituminous coals which contain sulphur and have a high ash content; they have to be blended with imported coal for industrial use. Mining costs are high because of faulting and igneous intrusions. Santa Catarina state accounts for 85 per cent of production, mainly from the Tubarão region. About a third is used in thermal power-stations, the largest of these being at Santa Cruz near Rio de Janeiro.

Until recently, future prospects seemed poor, but intensive prospecting has resulted in the discovery of an estimated 7 billion tonnes at Candiota, near Bagé in Rio Grande do Sul state. The seams are thick and are capable of being open-cast mined. New discoveries have also been made at Gravatai near Pôrto Alegre. Whilst proven reserves amount

to about 20 billion tonnes, recent estimates have been highly optimistic—a figure of 150 billion tonnes has been quoted. If this is correct then coal must have a significant role in the 1980s. There is increasing interest in the gasification of coal to produce methanol, for use as a substitute petrol additive, and to reduce imports of liquified petroleum gas and naptha. If successful, this in itself could reduce petroleum imports by up to 25 per cent. A coal plan introduced in 1979 involves opening 25 new mines by 1985, which would be capable of an average annual output of 35 million tonnes.

Brasil currently produces about 10 million cubic metres of petroleum per annum, and 1.6 billion cubic metres of natural gas. In 1973 Brasil's petroleum reserves amounted to only about 100 million tonnes, about 5 per cent that of Venezuela. This is extremely disappointing. In Amazonia Brasil has the greatest part of the world's largest sedimentary basin, but this has yet to yield a single major oil strike. All of Brasil's petroleum and natural gas is produced in the coastal rifts of the North-east, and on the narrow continental shelf, where it occurs in sandstones of Cretaceous age.

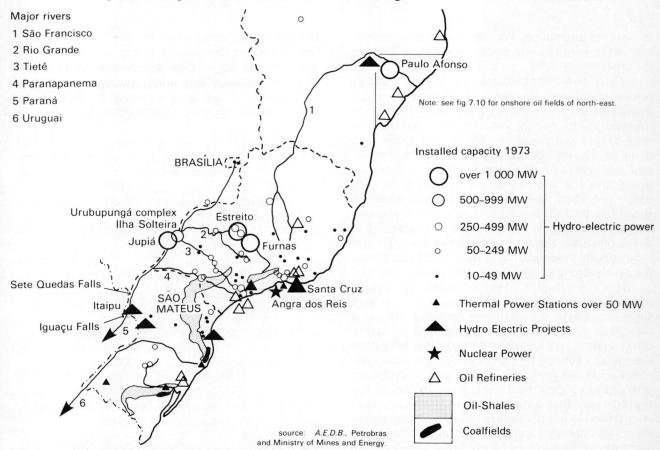

7.9. The Distribution of Power-stations, Fossil Fuels and Oil Refineries.

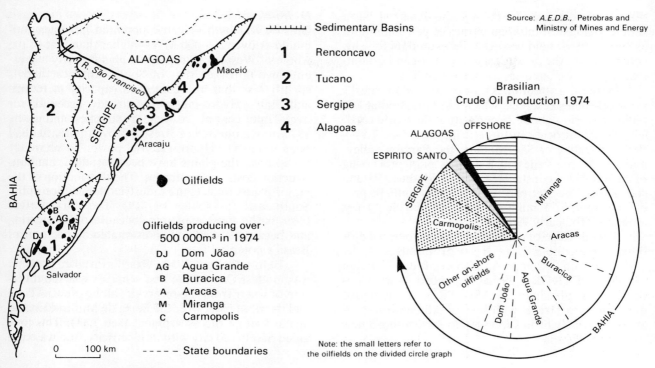

7.10. The Onshore Oilfields of the North-east.

The first oil strike was at Salvador in 1939, in the Reconcavo basin. From the beginning, the government took complete control of the industry. This is in sharp contrast to Venezuela, where foreign companies were encouraged to explore and develop the major oil fields. The overriding interest in Venezuela, stimulated by the large profits, was the main factor in the slow development of the industry in Brasil. In an attempt to stimulate exploration, the state petroleum company—PETROBRAS—was created in 1954. It has a monopoly of exploration, production, refining and imports. In 1955, oil was discovered at Nova Olinda near Manaus, but the well failed to maintain production, and the North-east continued to be the major producing area. In the mid-1970s, onshore wells in Bahia (60 per cent of output), Sergipe and Alagoas dominated production, whilst offshore wells accounted for about 20 per cent of output (see **7.9** and **7.10**). The quadrupling of world crude oil prices in 1974 by the O.P.E.C. countries, and other recent increases, has had a major effect on the balance of payments, as petroleum was and still is Brasil's major import. A massive exploration programme was launched, and in 1975 the government allowed the participation of the multi-national oil corporations, whilst preserving PETROBRAS's overall control. Several significant discoveries were made in the offshore region, using rigs and technology developed in the North Sea by British Petroleum and other companies. The offshore discoveries of the late 1960s and early 1970s were all predictable extensions of existing coastal oil fields in the North-east, but since 1973 several new fields have been discovered—eight small and medium fields were discovered in 1975 alone. The recent offshore discoveries with significant reserves include:

(a) A gas anticline trap off the mouth of the Amazon.

(b) A faulted anticline oil field (Ubarana) off the coast of Rio Grande do Norte,

(c) The Campos basin (Garoupa) oilfield, associated with salt domes and faulted anticlines. This is the largest offshore oilfield and is expected to produce 188 000 barrels per day by 1985.

Exploration is continuing at several locations within Brasil's 800 000 km² continental shelf, but as yet no major oilfields have been discovered. The exploitation of many medium-sized fields is proving difficult, for instance the oilfields of the Campos offshore basin occur in part of the continental shelf where the sea is over 150 metres deep.

It is difficult to estimate Brasil's oil potential. Sedimentary basins cover over a quarter of Brasil's land area, but the majority are of Palaeozoic rather than Mesozoic age. In theory, the Amazon basin should yield substantial quantities of petroleum, but as yet no major field has been discovered there. This contrasts with the *oriente* regions of Peru and Colombia, where estimated reserves are significant.

Increasing attention is now being paid to Brasil's large oil-shales reserves, which are estimated at 800 billion barrels—about 25 per cent of the world total. The oil-shales occur in three main areas (see **7.9**)—the Irati valley at São Mateus, the Paraíba valley, and the Marua valley in Bahia. A pilot processing plant has been constructed at São Mateus (Paraná state) using the 'petrosix' process. This could be producing about 2.5 million tonnes of petroleum per annum by the early 1980s.

The shortage of petroleum is likely to be a major brake on economic development throughout the 1980s. In an attempt to secure future foreign supplies, PETROBRAS has expanded its activities through its subsidiary BRASPETRO. It has signed exploration contracts with several African countries and has already been successful in discovering a new oilfield in Algeria.

Hydro-electricity

Brasil's vast hydro-electric potential has been estimated at over 209 000 MW—higher than that of the whole of Western Europe. Installed capacity represents two-thirds of that of South America, and is slightly less than the combined capacity of France and Italy. Hydro-electricity already accounts for over 27 per cent of gross energy supplies, and yet by 1975 only a quarter of Brasil's proven potential had been realised. Hydro-electric power is relatively cheap once the plants have been installed, but construction costs are enormous. The distribution of the major plants reflects the industrial dominance of the South-east, (as shown by **7.9**). The Paraná river basin is the most exploited, because of its location and because it contains an estimated 58 per cent of Brasil's potential (see **7.12**).

Before the mid-1950s, Brasil's installed capacity was modest.One of the first schemes was the diversion of water from the reservoirs along the Rio Tietê and its tributaries, over the Serra do Mar to Cubatão at the foot of the escarpment (see **7.11**). This provided São Paulo city with its electricity, and was vital

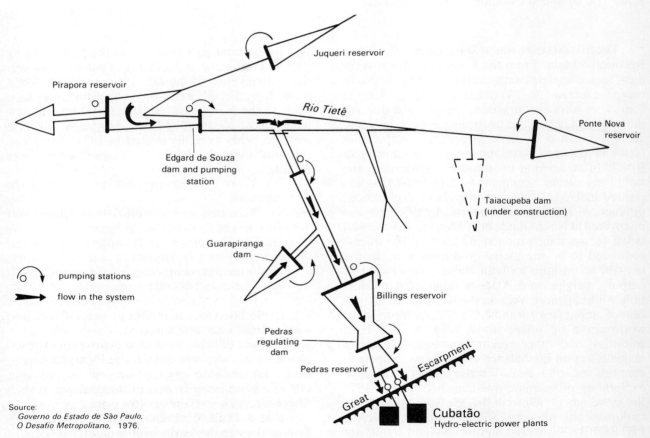

Source:
 Governo do Estado de São Paulo,
 O Desafio Metropolitano, 1976.

7.11. The Cubatão Hydro-electricity Scheme (São Paulo)–Diagrammatic.

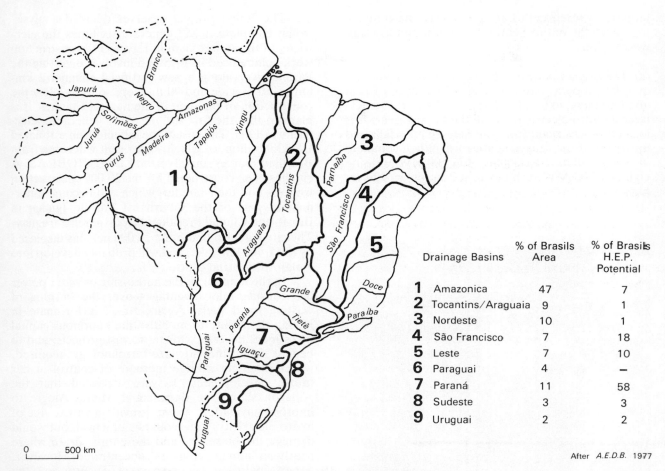

Drainage Basins	% of Brasils Area	% of Brasils H.E.P. Potential
1 Amazonica	47	7
2 Tocantins/Araguaia	9	1
3 Nordeste	10	1
4 São Francisco	7	18
5 Leste	7	10
6 Paraguai	4	—
7 Paraná	11	58
8 Sudeste	3	3
9 Uruguai	2	2

After *A.E.D.B.* 1977

7.12. River Drainage Basins and their Proven Hydro-electric Potential.

to its industrial development. The major dam construction programme dates from the late 1960s. From 1970 to 1975, installed capacity more than doubled. There are now over 70 hydro-electric plants.

The increased demand for power in the 1980s is to be supplied from four major hydro-electric complexes:

(a) The Paulo Afonso Complex on the São Francisco River. The first power-station commenced production in 1954, but there are now three separate plants with a combined capacity of 1 260 MW. Paulo Afonso serves the major cities and developing industrial centres of the North-east. Despite the irregular regime of the river, the São Francisco basin has an estimated potential of 15 000 MW. The Três Marias dam and power-station in the upper part of the basin was completed in 1962, and it serves the mining and manufacturing region of Belo Horizonte and the iron ore fields of the *quadrilátero ferrífero*. A further plant is to be developed at Itaparica.

(b) The Rio Grande Complex. This consists of seven separate dams on the Rio Grande, which is a tributary of the Paraná. The installed capacity is nearly 3 400 MW and is concentrated mainly at Furnas (1 064 MW) and Estreito (1 050 MW). There are also a number of other power-stations on the Tietê and Paranapanema rivers further south.

(c) The Urubupunga Complex. This complex alone will realise a total capacity of 26 000 MW, in excess of the nation's entire present capacity, and will develop into the world's second largest complex. The schemes are located along the Paraná river. Jupia, situated just below the Urubupunga falls, was completed in 1970 and has an installed capacity of 1 400 MW; Ilha Solteira, situated 60 km upstream, was completed in 1973 and has a capacity of 3 200 MW. The scheme is being developed by a consortium including the federal agency, ELECTROBRAS, and the state electricity agencies of Minas Gerais (CEMIG) and São Paulo (CESP). The latter is the

largest corporation in Latin America. The complex will serve the entire South, South-east and Central-west regions.

(d) The Itaipu Complex. This is a bi-national venture established by a joint treaty in 1973 between Brasil and Paraguay, to build and operate the world's single largest hydro-electric plant on the Paraná river. It is located downstream from the Sete Quedas falls and upstream of the Iguaçu confluence. When complete in 1986 it will have a capacity of 12 600 MW, utilising eighteen 700 MW turbines in a 2 km-long, 120 m-high dam.

Plate 21. The dam and turbines of the Itaipu hydro-electric project under construction on the dry bed of the diverted Paraná river. When complete it will be the world's largest, generating 12 600 MW. *Camera Press Ltd.*

The Itaipu project deserves detailed analysis. When complete it will generate six times the electricity of the Aswan dam in Egypt. The construction work commenced in 1975 and involves diverting the Paraná river along a new, artificial channel 2 km-long, 150 m-wide and 90 m-deep, so as to allow the construction of the dam in the natural channel. It is planned that the first turbine starts generating electricity in 1983. The cost of the scheme is an estimated US $3.9 billion, of which 90 per cent will come from Brasilian sources, mainly from ELECTROBRAS. A city has been constructed for the 20 000 construction workers and their families which will become a permanent part of the suburbs of Foz de Iguaçu in Brasil, and Ciudad President Stroessner in Paraguay. The city will also house the 20 000 persons displaced by the 1 460 km^2 lake, and will probably develop into a major industrial centre.

In the long-term, the harnessing of water power has considerable advantages over the burning of wasting fossil fuels. Again, Brasil is fortunate in having the ability to mobilise the enormous capital investment necessary for these vast projects, and to benefit from the advanced technology required, whilst retaining a large measure of control in her future development. It was suggested that the Amazon should be dammed at Monte Alegre to improve navigation, and to provide a vast source of hydro-electricity. This would be practical, but would damage the biosphere and the entire *várzea* where nearly all human activity is concentrated. However, a new hydro-electric project at Tucuriu, on the Tocantins river in Pará, is to be developed with an installed capacity of 3 800 MW; this is close to Serra dos Carajás.

Alternative Energy: New Fuels and Power Sources

It is clear from previous sections that Brasil's rapid economic growth is demanding increasing inputs of energy. In fact, gross energy supply must increase at a more rapid rate than economic growth, because the economy is becoming more energy-intensive. For example, the economy is now growing at a rate of about 6 per cent per annum, and yet electricity consumption is growing at a rate of about 12 per cent per annum. The same is true of fuels, but the heavy reliance on imported fossil fuels has forced the federal government to develop new energy strategies.

In the face of considerable domestic and international criticism by those who would wish to limit the spread of nuclear power, Brasil has signed an agreement with the German Federal Republic to build nine nuclear power-stations by 1990. These will have a total capacity of 10 600 MW, equivalent to about half the present hydro-electricity capacity. The

Plate 22. Brasil's first nuclear power station at Angra dos Reis. By 1990 Brasil will have nine nuclear power stations with a forecast total capacity of 10 200 MW. *Camera Press Ltd.*

first has already been commissioned; it is located at Angra dos Reis, on the coast near Rio de Janeiro. The government regard the nuclear programme as being essential in the long term because hydro-electricity is approaching its 'natural economic limits'. It has been forecast that by the year 2000, Brasil's gross electricity requirements will be greater than the entire hydro-electric potential. Also, it is unlikely that the full hydro-electricity potential will ever be realised because some potential sites would not be economically viable.

The relatively low domestic production of fuels is however a more pressing problem. This demands short-term remedial measures, and a major long-term programme. Fortunately, Brasil already has other sources of fuel which can be developed.

In 1975, the National Alcohol Programme—PROALCOOL—was launched, using the spare capacity of existing sugar mills. Alcohol has many advantages as a fuel. It can be mixed with petrol up to a ratio of one-in-four without the need for any modification to internal combustion engines; it can be used in much higher proportions with slight modification; and it can be used by itself in purpose built vehicles. Alcohol has a higher octane rating than

petrol, so that there is less need for lead-based additives. It is these which produce toxic exhaust gases, and thus the use of alcohol would reduce atmospheric pollution. Already petrol in Brasil contains 20 per cent dehydrated ethyl-alcohol, over 300 000 vehicles run entirely on alcohol, and as a result atmospheric pollution in São Paulo has fallen by over 18 per cent.

The use of alcohol is an extremely attractive proposition because Brasil is already the world's major producer of sugar and manioc, and a major producer of other suitable raw materials. At present, and in the immediate future, sugar will be the major raw material. The IAA (Sugar and Alcohol Institute) is developing a sugar planting programme which will produce over ten billion litres of alcohol per annum by 1985—equivalent to seven per cent of forecast petroleum demand, and forty per cent of petrol consumption. There are plans for 300 distilleries which will be privately owned, but will receive considerable government support. Many will use bagasse as a fuel. Whilst the alcohol programme could have a spin-off by increasing investment in agriculture, there are problems. About three per cent of Brasil's territory would have to be planted with sugar-cane to achieve self-sufficiency in fuels, though manioc grown in rotation with soya in the *cerrado* would decrease the reliance on sugar. In 1980, the estimated alcohol output was slightly less than four billion litres, five times the output in 1975, but still relatively insignificant in terms of present petroleum consumption. Also, large quantities of potash fertilizer and herbicides would be needed to maintain yields.

A further problem is that Brasil consumes more diesel oil than petrol. Ethanol (ethyl-alcohol) does not have a sufficiently high cetane index or calorific value to be used in diesel engines. It could be used up to a proportion of about 7 per cent in diesel fuel, but would increase fuel consumption considerably. However, there are other alternatives based on the use of vegetable oils. Rudolf Diesel ran his engines on vegetable oils as early as 1900, and recent research in Brasil has shown that vegetable oils from peanuts and the *dendê* palm can be used up to a ratio of one-in-three with diesel oil without the need for modification. Higher proportions result in increased

carbon deposits in diesel engines, with a resultant loss in efficiency. Other vegetable oils could also be used, such as those from the sunflower, soya bean, cottonseed, and castor oil, but peanuts are the most likely crop to be developed. The peanut is a nitrogen fixer, can be grown in rotation with crops such as sugar-cane, and yields three harvests a year.

Thus Brasil has the potential for producing a wide range of petroleum substitutes. The rate at which these are developed will depend not only on policy decisions, but on their cost effectiveness. At present imported petroleum is still cheaper than the substitutes, but this could change dramatically in the 1980s. Renewable biological raw materials, processed as fuels, will undoubtedly have a major role as the world's finite petroleum reserves become depleted in the not too distant future.

Brasil is developing alternative energy sources at a comparatively rapid rate, but whilst the potential for solar power is great, that of wind, tidal, wave and geothermal power are less attractive.

8 Industrialisation and Industrial Case Studies

As has been previously discussed in Chapter 2, Brasil had experienced industrial growth up until the First World War, but was not truly industrialised, as there had been little diversification of industry. Industrial growth usually begins as a result of an increased domestic demand for necessities. Thus the first manufacturing industries to develop are usually food processing, textiles and clothing, and later construction and metals industries. Infant industries are highly labour-intensive because of the primitive processing technologies and relatively unskilled labour force.

The development of a diverse and productive manufacturing sector requires the application of power, expanding domestic and foreign markets, a high level of technological development, and a 'money' economy. Before 1930, the 'coffee economy' provided the major impetus for industrial growth in Brasil. Not only did coffee export revenues provide the finance, but also indirectly the government's financial policies, which maintained those revenues through periods of crisis, had an adverse effect on the exchange rate. As imports of manufactured goods became more expensive, the expanding domestic industries became more competitive. After 1930, the government became progressively more involved in industrial growth. The diversification of industry was achieved by 'import substitution' policies, and by direct government action in stimulating and supporting the growth of key industries. Good examples of such initiatives include the inauguration of the state steelworks at Volta Redonda in 1947; the creation of the National Economic Development Bank (BNDE) in 1952; the establishment of the state petroleum company PETROBRAS in 1954; and the selection of the motor vehicles industry for priority development in 1956. Three of the world's major motor vehicle corporations were attracted to the south-east suburbs of São Paulo city by the low industrial wages, the well developed infrastructure, financial incentives, and high profit margins.

From 1947 to 1961, industrial growth accelerated to an average annual rate of about 10 per cent, and the volume of industrial production tripled. Brasil's planned reduced dependence on imports and its priority investment in manufacturing mobilised the vast mineral and energy resources of the country, and led to industrial 'take-off' in the 1950s and 1960s. By 1958, Brasil had become the continent's leading industrial country.

A central element in this process was the spatial concentration of industrial activity. In many advanced countries, urban and industrial growth are mutually supportive because of the economies gained from large-scale production in large cities. However, in Brasil the over-concentration of industrial development in the cities of the dominant South-east region has resulted in considerable regional imbalances. Even within the South-east there is a considerable imbalance between the major cities. Rio became the first major industrial city because of its status as the federal capital, and its role as the nation's major entrepôt. But it was by-passed when São Paulo emerged as the commercial centre of the new coffee lands. São Paulo became the nation's leading industrial centre in 1920, even before the industrialisation process had developed beyond its early stages.

Since the late 1950s, and especially since the military coup d'état of 1964, Brasilian industry has become more 'internationalised'. Foreign corporations in partnership with Brasilian firms have increased their investment in manufacturing; and the increasingly diversified and expanding manufacturing sector has increased its share of exports to such a level that it is now the single largest exporter.

The Structure of the Industrial Sector

The following tables (8.1 and 8.2) illustrate the contribution of manufacturing to the economy, and the structure of the industrial sector. Table 8.1 shows the

8.1. Industrial Growth by Classes, 1949, 1970 and 1975.

Industrial Class	Percentage share of GDP		
	1949	1970	1975
Mining	0.48	0.84	1.40
Manufacturing	20.28	23.84	30.20
Civil Construction	4.34	5.98	5.70
Public Service industries	1.13	2.08	2.20
Contribution of Industry to GDP	26.23	32.74	39.50
Index of Industrial growth, 1949=100.	100	512	2 672

Source: A.E.D.B., various years

8.2. The Manufacturing Industries, 1974

Classes in rank order of production by value.	A Value of Production (Cr$ million)	B %	C Value added by manufacturing (Cr$ million)	D Column C as % of A	E Number of Establishments	F Number Employed (000s)	G Column C Column F (Cr$)
1. Food processing & Beverages.	89 846	16.8	24 910	28	19 322	464	53 667
2. Chemicals & Pharmaceuticals.	84 087	15.3	26 845	32	2 658	186	144 331
3. Metallurgy.	75 578	14.1	29 296	39	6 186	405	72 274
4. Textiles, products, and footwear.	58 906	11.0	22 440	38	8 857	593	37 813
5. Transport Equipment.	45 608	8.5	14 287	31	1 685	204	69 887
6. Machinery.	40 525	7.6	19 719	49	4 902	337	58 513
7. Electrical and Communications Equipment.	26 909	5.0	12 013	45	1 864	196	61 408
8. Non-metallic mineral products.	18 608	3.5	11 213	60	5 652	226	49 576
9. Paper & Cardboard.	17 561	3.3	7 567	43	1 211	92	82 650
10. Timber.	13 104	2.5	6 628	51	6 078	162	40 802
11. Plastic products.	10 465	2.0	5 409	52	1 473	76	71 192
12. Printing & publishing.	10 347	1.9	6 594	64	3 194	112	58 976
Others.	36 499	8.5	18 120	—	9 095	343	—
Total	535 151	100	210 621	39	73 569	3 397	62 006

Source: After *A.E.D.B.*, 1977.

increasing dominance of manufacturing in an industrial sector which expanded over fivefold from 1970 to 1975. The low contribution of mining is misleading, as the resource base is vital for manufacturing and construction industries, and as a source of export revenue.

The increasing importance of manufacturing when related to the 'sector theory' (see Chapter 5) indicates that Brasil has not yet reached the level of a complex advanced industrial country.

Table **8.2** shows that the 'traditional' industries are still prominent, but that manufacturing is now diverse. It is difficult to achieve a simple index which can be used for either analysing industrial location or assessing the relative importance of various industries. Whilst employment, the number of establishments and the value of production can all be used, one of the best indicators is the value added in the manufacturing process (column *C*). When related to employment, this gives a useful measure of productivity and the stage of technological development. The table illustrates the great contrasts between traditional labour-intensive industries and the new highly capital-intensive industries which developed rapidly in the 1970s.

The Traditional Industries

The food processing and textiles industries together account for 27.8 per cent of the gross value of manufacturing, and account for 31 per cent of employment. Both are characterised by relatively inefficient production in a large number of older established factories of varying size. They produce a great variety of products. Despite a relative decline in both industries over the last fifteen years, they have benefited from 'spin-off' from growth industries, and from rapidly expanding domestic and foreign markets.

There has been a considerable rationalisation of food processing, and much investment in modern plant and improved technology. Government loans to the agricultural sector have increased productivity, reduced the real cost of foostuffs, and have attenuated seasonal price fluctuations. The location of the industry reflects the South-east's highly developed commercial agriculture, infrastructure and domestic markets. In 1970, the region accounted for 64 per cent of production by value, São Paulo itself contributing 43 per cent. The increasing technological sophistication of the industry is shown by its increasing share of exports, the relative decline in frozen and dried products, and the increased importance of canning. Two large canneries—at São Paulo, and at Pernambuco in the North-east—account for 70 per cent of the output of canned products. The São Paulo plant specialises in fruit products and it controls many plantations in several states. The most important recent developments have been in citrus fruit juices which are an important export, and also in soya and instant coffee. The coffee processing plant at Londrina, in the Paraná coffee lands, is the world's largest.

The textiles industry suffered a severe decline because of the inefficient production of poor quality cotton in the North-east, and the obsolete mills of the region. The industry was very slow to innovate. In 1960, nylon was the only synthetic fibre produced,

and polypropylene fibres were only produced after 1968. However, since 1964 government policies have succeeded in re-equipping the industry, with a resulting rise in productivity. This has been in part forced on the industry by a reduction of protective tariffs. The development of the petrochemicals industry has also increased the production of artificial fibres such as viscose and acetate, but the raw materials for many of the synthetic fibres such as nylon and polyester are still imported.

Some producers still specialise in processing locally available raw materials such as jute in Amazonia, and wool and leather in the South, but intense competition has closed many small factories in recent years. Others have survived by amalgamation. The net effect is that the industry is now even more concentrated in São Paulo. It accounts for 62 per cent of production by value, and of value added, and 54 per cent of employment. There has been a dramatic resurgence in the textiles industry in recent years; from 1974 to 1978 exports rose by 60 per cent.

Rapid industrial and urban development has resulted in a great expansion in the construction industry. Cement and structural steel have also been in large demand for dam construction at the new hydro-electric plants. The highly localised demand in the South-east is the major locational factor: the region produces over three-quarters of non-metallic mineral products. The Industrial Development Board (CDI) has introduced regulations aimed at rationalising the cement industry and concentrating

a) Output of the Food-processing Industry 1970, (by value).

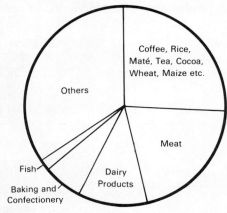

b) Output of the Textiles Industry 1970, (by weight)

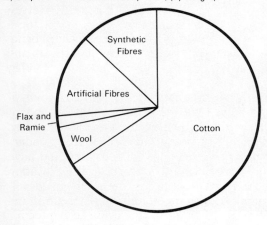

After – *Censo Industrial* 1970, I.B.G.E. 1974

8.3. The Food Processing and Textile Industries.

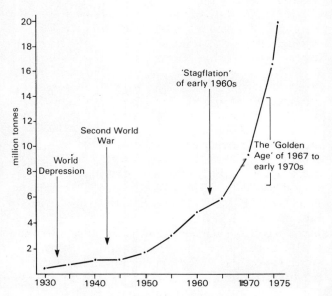

8.4. The Production of Cement, 1930–77: Illustrating the effect of Changes in the Rate of Economic Growth.

production in plants of over 2 000 tonnes kiln capacity. Cement production has increased at a phenomenal rate since 1945, making Brasil the world's tenth largest producer. The construction industry is the only user of constructional steel rod, which is produced by private firms. It has also resulted in a 'spin-off' in glass and ceramics industries, and in timber production which is increasing at over 10 per cent per annum.

Iron and Steel

During the twenty years following the construction of Brasil's first integrated steelworks in 1925, many new plants were constructed in the Velhas, Doce and Piracicaba valleys within the *'quadrilátero ferrífero'* of Minas Gerais. As a result, by 1945 the state dominated production, accounting for 83 per cent of pig iron, 57 per cent of ingot steel and 51 per cent of rolled products. However, these works were of small capacity and lacked capital. The development of a large integrated plant was advocated on industrial, political and military grounds. This was initiated by the formation of the National Steel Company— C.S.N. (*Companhia Siderurgica Nacional*)—in 1941, and was realised by the completion of its Volta Redonda works in 1947. The site had considerable advantages in terms of access to the iron and manganese ores of Minas Gerais, proximity to the port of Rio for imported coking coal, and further rail links with Greater São Paulo. During the 1950s, many older, inefficient works were incorporated into large-scale enterprises, and new plants were constructed to meet the rapidly expanding needs of the recently established motor vehicles industry at São Paulo. The *'Programma de Metas'*, instigated by President Kubitschek, established fifty-seven new 'mini' blast furnaces, located mostly in the vicinity of Belo Horizonte and using the then large reserves of charcoal. But more significant was the construction of three new plants, which together with Volta Redonda now dominate production. The Mannesmann company

Plate 23.   The National Steel Company's integrated steelworks at Volta Redonda in the Paraíba valley. This was Brasil's first large works, completed in 1947. It has an intermediate location, and uses imported coke.   *Hoa-Qui.*

controls the large works at the Cidade Industrial (Belo Horizonte), whilst the Cubatão (São Paulo) and Ipatinga (Minas Gerais) integrated plants were constructed by the newly formed state steel companies of COSIPA and USIMINAS respectively. By 1962, the Volta Redonda works was producing over half of Brasil's steel output. However, the completion of the Tubarão C.V.R.D. terminal, and the upgrading of the Doce valley railway, permitted return cargoes of coking coal from the U.S.A. and the German Federal Republic, which boosted production at Ipatinga. Despite its inland location it now accounts for nearly a quarter of total steel production.

8.5. Processes of Pig-iron and Ingot Steel Production.

Processes of Pig-iron Production	Processes of Ingot Steel Production
Charcoal blast-furnace 51%	Siemens-Martin/Open Hearth 33.3%
Charcoal-electric reduction furnace 3%	Linz Donawitz Basic Oxygen furnace 39.6%
Coke blast-furnace 46%	Bessemer convertor 0.2%
	Electric Arc 26.9%

Brasil's iron ore reserves are more than adequate to meet the needs of foreign and domestic steel producers for the foreseeable future, but other major inputs are in short supply. This is shown by the contribution of charcoal to pig-iron production (as shown by **8.5**), and by the need to import scrap. The mini furnaces have an uncertain future, despite the construction of Highway BR 040 which has improved access to the increasingly remote and dwindling forest reserves. The steel industry still uses over 3 million tonnes of charcoal per annum. It has been estimated that further deforestation at present rates could exhaust reserves within a decade. Only large-scale enterprises are capable of ensuring supplies by reforestation schemes; for instance Belgo Mineira, which operates the João Monlevade works, now has extensive eucalyptus plantations. This species is proving popular as it is capable of producing a regular output by 'cropping (i.e. without felling), thus preserving the mature tree.

Despite the promise of future coking coal supplies from the recently discovered deposits of Rio Grande do Sul, imports are likely to continue during the 1980s. Present supplies from Santa Catarina have to be blended with imported coal prior to use, because of their high ash content. In 1975, 40 per cent of coal requirements had to be imported, mainly from the U.S.A., Canada, South Africa and Poland. In 1979, steel output reached nearly 14 million tonnes, which necessitated even higher coal imports. Whilst the integrated plants of Volta Redonda, Cubatão and Ipatinga (which together account for 50 per cent of steel production) use minimal quantities of scrap, the remaining plants consume over four million tonnes annually. In 1975, 17 500 tonnes of scrap were imported and the situation is unlikely to improve. If it is assumed that steel products have an average life-span of some fifty years, then domestic scrap from discarded manufactured goods cannot provide more than 2 per cent of annual steel production for some time to come.

Brasil's industrial development during the 1970s has relied heavily on increasingly greater imports of steel (as shown by **8.6**) and this is likely to continue into the 1980s. Both state and private companies are now controlled by two major organisations. CONSIDER (The National Iron and Steel Council) is a planning and policy-making body which consists of the ministers of Industry and Commerce, Finance, Planning and Mines, and Energy. SIDERBRAS (Brasil Steel Ltd.) which was established in 1973, not only provides capital to its subsidiaries which account for 56 per cent of total output, but also co-ordinates policies. The state owned or state controlled plants specialise in flat products, whilst the more dispersed and generally smaller capacity private plants produce special shaped products.

8.6. Steel Production, Consumption and Imports.

Source: M.B.A. and CONSIDER.

Year	Production	Consumption	Imports	Steel imports as a Percentage of total imports
	(Ingot equivalent in million tonnes)			
1968	4.5	4.6	0.5	4.4
1970	5.4	5.6	0.8	6.0
1972	6.5	7.5	1.5	6.0
1974	7.5	12.7	5.5	12.2
1976	9.2	9.9	1.1	—
1980 (est).	17.9	18.1	—	—

8.7. The Major Steelworks.

Rank	Location	Company	Steel-Making Process	Fuel/Energy	Ingot Capacity tonnes	Main products
1.	Volta Redonda	CSN	SM	Coke	1 681 000	NCF, CF, HCS, MHS, R.
2.	Ipatinga	USIMINAS	LD	Coke	1 496 000	NCF
3.	Cubatão	COSIPA	LD	Coke	1 142 000	NCF
4.	Cidade Industrial (Belo Horizonte)	Mannesmann	EA/LD	Charcoal/ Electricity	629 100	B, W, SP.
5.	João Monlevade	Belgo Mineira	SM/LD	Charcoal	615 000	NFP

Key: NCF—Non-coated plates, sheets and coils; CF—Coated tin, terne and galvanised plate; HCS—High carbon sheets; MHS—Medium and heavy shapes; R—Rails and track; B—Bars; W—Wire rods; SP—Seamless pipes; NFP—Non-flat products.

Source: *Anuario Estatistico da Industria Siderurgica Brasíleira, 1975.*

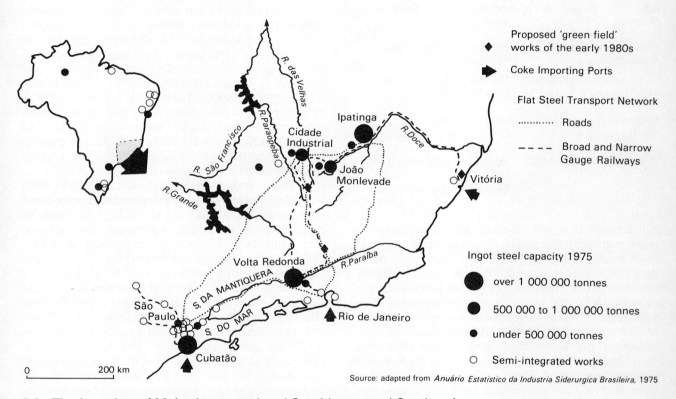

Source: adapted from *Anuário Estatistico da Industria Siderurgica Brasileira, 1975*

8.8. The Location of Major Integrated and Semi-Integrated Steelworks.

The iron and steel industry now employs 117 800 workers, of which 85 644 are concerned with production. This represents 4 per cent of the total employed in manufacturing. The industry is largely concentrated in Minas Gerais, São Paulo and Rio de Janeiro states, and consists of 18 fully integrated works, 22 semi-integrated works and 6 non-integrated works, the latter producing only non-flat products. Only 5 works have an installed capacity of over 500 000 tonnes.

Motor Vehicles

The production of motor vehicles requires high levels of technology, skills, massive capital investment, and large-scale production in large plants. It utilises a great variety of inputs such as steel, electrical equipment, capital machinery, rubber, textiles, numerous petrochemicals products, and power. Thus it is a key industry which has the potential for stimulating a variety of important ancillary industries.

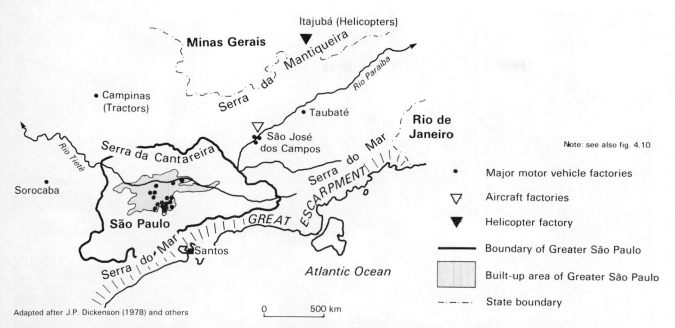

8.9. The Location of Motor Vehicles and Aircraft Industries in and around Greater São Paulo.

The first Brasilian plant was built by Ford in São Paulo city in 1919. By 1924 it was producing over 24 000 Model 'T's per annum from imported components. Thirty years later the industry was still in its infancy, as only spares were manufactured in Brasil. Up until the mid-1950s the future of the industry looked bleak, and Brasil had the status of a classic export market. However, today Brasil's motor vehicles industry produces over 1 million units per annum, and ranks first in Latin America and fifth in the world. It contributes 5 per cent of the GDP (10 per cent if ancillaries are included), about 5 per cent of exports, and employs about 8 per cent of the industrial labour force. Not only does Brasil export complete vehicles and components to more than 30 countries, but it even supplies the large American corporations based at Detroit with certain components.

This phenomenal transformation is entirely due to the success of President Kubitschek's decision to adopt a strategy similar to the Hirschman strategy of industrial growth. A. O. Hirschman (1958) views the development process as a 'chain of disequilibria', with the growth of leading industries being communicated to others. He also emphasises the role of 'non-market forces' in the process; this is particularly true in Brasil in terms of the extent of government intervention. The participation of the large multi-national corporations also was vital in achieving the high degree of necessary capital investment.

Kubitschek gradually nationalised the major domestic firms, and in 1956 a government agency was established to co-ordinate the industry and to stimulate its growth. Favourable tariffs and financial facilities encouraged the import of vital capital goods such as machinery, and import restrictions drastically reduced imports of vehicles. At first, eleven different foreign companies established works, but competition from the major corporations soon resulted in the closure of small inefficient firms. In 1957, the first 'Kombi' with over 50 per cent domestically manufactured components was launched, and production in that year reached over 30 500. Through the late 1950s and the 1960s, the growth of the industry was such that the profitability of ancillary industries increased, and thus 'spin-off' effects benefited a number of other industries. Despite a temporary fall in sales in the 1960s, production soared. Sales recovered as real wages began to increase and credit facilities improved. By 1966, domestic parts accounted for 99 per cent of new vehicles by weight, and from 1969 to 1974 in the 'Golden Age' average annual production increased by nearly 20 per cent. The energy crisis has since reduced this rate to about 7 per cent.

The motor car industry is now dominated by three large corporations, all located in the south-east industrial zone of Greater São Paulo. Volkswagen is the largest, contributing 55 per cent of production. General Motors contributes 19 per cent and Ford 17 per cent. Volkswagen has been particularly successful in exports: some 7 per cent of total production is exported, mainly in the form of CDKs ('completely-

Plate 24. One of the assembly lines in Volkswagen do Brasil's factory at São Bernardo do Campo in Greater São Paulo. Brasil now produces well over a million vehicles per annum, and the industry has had a key role in industrial development. *Camera Press Ltd.*

knocked-down' vehicles) for assembly in the importing countries.

Brasil now has 5.2 million vehicles, of which over 90 per cent were manufactured in Brasil. This constitutes an average of one motor car per 20 inhabitants, as compared with one car per 78 inhabitants in 1957. Most cars are based on established European or American models, but an increasing number of Brasilian designed or modified vehicles make up the 46 models marketed. Passenger cars now account for only 58 per cent of total vehicle production, whilst utility vehicles and small trucks have a 32 per cent share, and lorries 8 per cent. Mercedes Benz concentrate on buses, over which they have a virtual monopoly, and also specialise in heavy lorries.

In 1970, São Bernardo do Campo (see **4.10**) accounted for 43 per cent of Brasil's output of transport materials by value, and for 26 per cent of the employment in the industry. More recently, however, the success of the major firms has attracted other foreign manufacturers. In 1976, a new Fiat plant at Betim in Greater Belo Horizonte was completed, and it already exports to Bolivia, Chile and Paraguay. In 1978, Case International commenced production of heavy tractors at Sorocaba. Recently Japanese companies have shown increased interest, and Toyota already have a foothold in São Paulo. There are strong government moves to attract a large

Japanese factory to the North-east. If successful this could have a major and accumulating effect on the region's industrial development and diversification.

Shipbuilding

Brasil's first shipyard, built at Rio in 1850, lasted only eleven years because of foreign competition. For nearly a hundred years after that Brasil had no shipbuilding industry to speak of, and yet inland waterways and coastal shipping provided the only means of access to many commercial centres.

The establishment of the Merchant Marine Fund and SUNAMAM, in 1958, marks the beginning of the industry which now ranks first in Latin America. The fund is financed by a 20 per cent tax on imports, and is used to finance shipbuilding and the shipping lines. By 1960, four new shipyards had been constructed and the two major companies were established—the Japanese owned Ishibras (Ishikawajima do Brasil) and the Dutch owned Verolme. By 1966, 20 yards had been established. An emergency programme, initiated in 1967, succeeded in phasing out many obsolete vessels and improving construction technology, but only ten vessels were delivered in that year.

The economic recovery after 1967 and the implementation of the first Naval Construction Programme (1971–75) encouraged investment, and the industry was rationalised by a system of assigning contracts to specific yards on the basis of their comparative advantage. However, the industry is still totally financed by private capital. By 1974 the merchant fleet had increased to 565 vessels, of which 75 per cent were less than a decade old. In that year 42 new vessels were delivered. In July 1974 the *Docepolo* (130 000 dwt), the largest ship constructed in the southern hemisphere, sailed from Tubarão with her maiden cargo of iron ore. The second Naval Construction Plan (1975–79) envisaged a major expansion of the industry, involving 765 new ships totalling 5.3 million dwt. PETROBRAS is the major buyer and has ordered four 277 000 dwt supertankers for Fronape, the nationalised tanker fleet. Ishibras owns Brasil's largest shipyards which are situated in Guanabara Bay. With government aid it has recently completed a new slipway which will enable the construction of ships of 400 000 dwt. Three new sister ships to the *Docepolo* are being constructed for exporting iron ore and conveying return cargoes of crude oil. Brasil now has seven major shipyards—four of which are located in Guanabara Bay (Rio de Janeiro) and another at Angra dos Reis. The merchant fleet has 665 ships of which 119 are ocean going, and 117 are involved in coastal trade.

The Naval Construction Plan is Brasil's largest-ever construction programme. This emphasises the increasing importance of exports. Brasilian shipyards are producing over 90 per cent of the total tonnage required to expand the merchant fleet from 6 million tonnes in 1974 to 11 million tonnes in 1982. Only specialised ships, such as petrochemicals tankers, which require a very high degree of technological sophistication, will be constructed in foreign shipyards. Exports of ships will also be significant. In 1975, other countries were committed to receive more than 500 000 dwt, and a further 250 000 dwt were under negotiation. The industry is also producing a significant spin-off as 70 to 80 per cent of materials will be provided domestically. Only high-stressed steels, propeller shafts and some electronic equipment have to be imported.

Plate 25. A 'Jubilee' oil prospecting platform under construction near the Verolme shipyards near Rio de Janeiro. The shipbuilding industry has grown rapidly to meet the demands of greatly increased trade. *Camera Press Ltd.*

Aircraft

This industry is still in its infancy. Brasil manufactures small and medium sized aircraft only, and still has to import all the required aero-engines. Until the formation of EMBRAER (*Empresa Brasileira de Aeronautica*) in 1969, there were only four small companies which produced small aircraft and trainers for the Brasilian Airforce. The mixed economy company was formed to undertake larger projects than the other companies could cope with, and specifically to produce a replacement for the imported Douglas DC3 Dakota for civil and military use. The prototype EMB-110 'Bandeirante' got off the ground in 1968, and within four years the airforce had ordered 80. The twin-turbo-prop 'flying jeep' has been extremely successful because of its versatility and economic operating costs. It has now replaced larger foreign aircraft on less profitable 'air-shuttle' and 'air-taxi' services, and is also being exported in large numbers. In 1976, seventy-six were ordered by the Federal Express Co. (U. S.A.) and exports to other countries are increasing rapidly. EMBRAER also produces a number of other aircraft: the 'Xavante' jet trainer produced under license from the Italian firm Aeronautica Macchi; the 'Ipanema' crop-dusting light aircraft; the 'Araguaia,' 'Xingu' and 'Tapajos' passenger aircraft. In addition it signed an agreement in 1974 with the Piper Aircraft Corporation (U.S.A.) to produce five of their light planes.

8.10. Aircraft Production, 1976

Model	Numbers Produced
Bandeirante (all 6 models)	46
Ipanema (2 models)	101
The 'Piper models'	351
Xavante	16
Uirapuru	4
Xingu	1
Total	519

Source: *Anuario Estatistico do Brasil, 1976*

Production is located at São Jose dos Campos at a 400 000 m² installation which employs over 3 600 workers (see **8.9**). Most of these workers were recruited in the local area and trained at the factory.

Brasil's first helicopter factory has been constructed at Itajubá in the south of Minas Gerais. Two hundred will be produced each year from components supplied by the French company Aerospatiale, which has signed an agreement with the state government and Aerofoto Cruzeiro do Sul.

Petroleum Refining and Petrochemicals

Industrial development has necessitated the provision of petroleum products on a scale far in excess of Brasil's ability to provide the basic raw materials. The industry is therefore strongly market-orientated and relies heavily on imported crude oil (see **7.8** on page 99). In 1974, the Sudeste region contained seven of Brasil's eleven refineries and 90 per cent of refining capacity. It now ranks first in Latin America, tenth in the world, and employs nearly 10 per cent of industrial workers.

The development of the industry was initiated by the creation of PETROBRAS in 1954, and by the construction of the Presidente Bernardes refinery at Cubatão, which utilises a thermal cracking process to produce the largest possible volume of residual gases. This provided the raw materials for the first petrochemicals plant, constructed near the refinery in 1958 to produce ammonia and nitrogenous fertilizers. It has developed as a 'growth pole' attracting a number of ancillary plants since 1958, producing ethylene, styrene, polyethylene and propylene deri-

Plate 26. The recently completed Paulinia refinery near Campinas. Campinas like many other towns near Greater São Paulo is benefitting from recent industrial decentralisation. *Hoa-Qui.*

vatives. By the early 1960s demand had outstripped domestic supply so that a new refinery, Brasil's largest, was constructed at Duque de Caxias near Rio de Janeiro. In 1962 a synthetic rubber works was added to the factory, to use its by-products.

From 1959 to 1965 the development of the industry was hindered by the lack of suitable natural gas supplies, and by the inability of the industry to attract domestic private investment and foreign investment. This was mainly the result of the monopolistic control of the industry by PETROBRAS. In 1965 the new military government reversed previous policies, and encouraged private companies to develop the increasingly complex and diverse processes required to provide the products needed by other industries. In 1967 a new subsidiary—PETROQUISA (*Petrobras Quimica S.A.*)—was set up to aid this process. Within a year of Decree No. 56 971 in 1965, 49 new projects had been approved. Over US$1 000 000 000 was invested in the industry from 1965 to 1975.

Today the industry is concentrated at two major poles in São Paulo and Bahia, and at two sub-poles at Rio de Janeiro and Alagoas.

(a) The São Paulo Pole: This is based on the Presidente Bernardes, Paulinia and União refineries which contribute 45 per cent of total petroleum products; and on 24 ancillary plants which produce a great variety of products including, in addition to those products mentioned above, methanol, benzine, carbon black, plastics and synthetic fibres. The rapidly expanding União complex now has the largest annual turnover, and it exports to a number of other Latin American countries.

(b) The Bahia Pole: The North-east has traditionally supplied the South-east with a variety of raw materials, including natural gas and petroleum from Salvador and Sergipe, marine and rock-salt from Rio Grande do Norte and Alagoas, sugar alcohol from Pernambuco, and a variety of vegetable oils and waxes. In 1972 the construction of the Camaçari complex began as part of SUDENE's regional development programme. It has already attracted an investment of US$ 1.2 billion, as well as 27 separate projects, and has doubled Brasil's output of ethylene. The complex complements the Aratu industrial district, which is also at Salvador and is also supported by SUDENE.

(c) The Rio de Janeiro sub-pole: This is centred on the Duque de Caxias and Manguinhos refineries, and it produces sufficient synthetic rubber and methanol to satisfy domestic demand and to allow exports.

(d) The Alagoas sub-pole: The industry is based on salt and on access to hydro-electricity. One of the world's largest caustic soda and chlorine plants is being developed here by Du Pont, with the co-operation of SUDENE.

The development of the petrochemicals and pharmaceuticals industries has been of even greater significance since the increase in world crude petroleum prices in 1973/4. Without such an industry, Brasil would have to import even greater amounts of products at disproportionately higher prices. Crude oil price increases have so far been largely absorbed within the petrochemicals sector. The development of the Bahia complex is expected to reduce petrochemicals imports, which currently stand at about 13 per cent of total imports by value, but further developments are required in the early 1980s. In line with decentralisation and 'growth pole' regional development strategies, a new complex is to be developed near Pôrto Alegre (Rio Grande do Sul) to utilise the naptha already available from the Canoas refinery which is already located there. The complex will consist of over 30 separate plants, will produce ethylene, polyethylene, synthetic rubber and PVC, and will result in an estimated 40 000 new jobs.

9 Agricultural Regions and Regional Development

Brasil's contemporary agricultural systems, land-use patterns, crop distributions, and agricultural productivity show considerable regional variation. It is this great regional imbalance which is the dominant characteristic. Its causes are complex and result from the interplay of a number of factors such as:

(a) The historical sequence of occupation and agricultural development.

(b) the problems of environmental constraints, including those associated with scale and accessibility.

(c) The response to changes in domestic and world markets.

(d) The stagnation of traditional areas and the dynamic growth of new areas.

(e) The large-scale immigration of Europeans into São Paulo and the South.

(f) The dominance of the South-east, which resulted from the success of coffee, subsequent industrialisation, and technological progress.

(g) Urbanisation and rural depopulation.

(h) Spontaneous and planned colonisation of new areas.

(i) The gradual emergence of a large domestic market for food crops and industrial raw materials.

(j) The effect of policies of 'national integration' and regional development, and the developments in the infrastructure associated with the inauguration of a new capital city.

The regional subdivision of Brasil is traditionally based on physiographic or administrative criteria; usually the *Grandes Regioẽs* and state boundaries figure to a considerable extent. Despite contrasts within the administrative regions, and the emergence of 'cores' and 'peripheries', the use of these regions is appropriate because Brasil's regional development agencies are organised along similar lines. Also, the different planning regions have different problems, and different programmes.

Figure **9.1** represents a regional subdivision based on agricultural land-use and regional economic organisation, within the framework of the *Grandes Regiões*. It provides an useful framework for an analysis of contemporary patterns, agricultural development, and the regional development programmes.

The North-east: Crisis and Transformation

The administrative region of the North-east is indeed 'a nation within a nation' and is the 'largest underdeveloped area of the largest developing country in the entire western hemisphere' (R.K. Webb, 1974). It is larger in area and population than any other South American country. In 1970 it contributed only fourteen per cent of the national income yet contained over thirty per cent of Brasil's population. It now has a rural population of nineteen million, representing fifty-three per cent of the region's total population.

The North-east is Brasil's crisis region. From being the economic hub of the colony in the seventeenth century it has been by-passed by the rapid progress of the South-east, and has been subject to drought, chronic poverty, economic stagnation and massive population pressure.

The large rural population and predominantly agricultural economy are a legacy of the colonial era—the heritage of plantation *latifundio* farming and a 'patriarchal' society dominated by the landowner.

The North-east consists of four distinctive agricultural regions, as shown on **9.1** and by the crop distributions on **9.2**:

(a) The humid coastal lowlands of the *Zona da Mata*.

(b) The transitional eastern upland zone of the *Agreste*.

(c) The semi-arid plateau of the *Sertão do Nordeste*.

(d) The *Meio-norte* (middle-north) forested region of Maranhão state.

The Zona da Mata

Since 1945 the *terras umidas* (humid lands) of the littoral lowlands have been displaced as the nation's major sugar producer by São Paulo. The region now produces only a third of national production whilst Maranhão, Piauí and Ceará contribute a further four per cent. However, the relics of a sugar monoculture and a vast subsistence sector have persisted to the present.

The cocoa region of southern Bahia, centred on Ilhéus, produces 96 per cent of national output, and

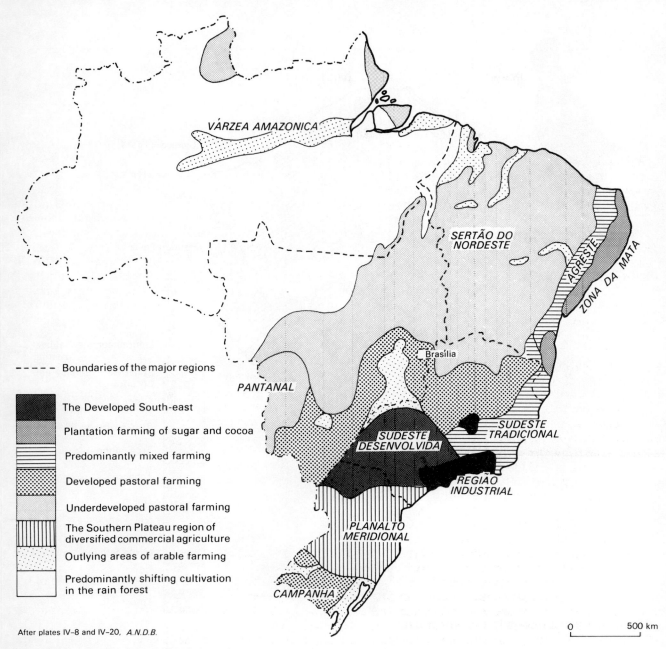

9.1. Major Agricultural Regions.

After plates IV–8 and IV–20, *A.N.D.B.*

Legend:

- - - - Boundaries of the major regions

The Developed South-east

Plantation farming of sugar and cocoa

Predominantly mixed farming

Developed pastoral farming

Underdeveloped pastoral farming

The Southern Plateau region of diversified commercial agriculture

Outlying areas of arable farming

Predominantly shifting cultivation in the rain forest

Map labels: VÁRZEA AMAZONICA, SERTÃO DO NORDESTE, AGRESTE, ZONA DA MATA, PANTANAL, Brasília, SUDESTE DESENVOLVIDA, SUDESTE TRADICIONAL, REGIÃO INDUSTRIAL, PLANALTO MERIDIONAL, CAMPANHA

0   500 km

is second in the world to Ghana. Cocoa is cultivated in the coastal valleys below 200 m, which possess a hot and humid climate, and deep soils. It was first cultivated in the mid-eighteenth century, but major production dates from 1907 when new trees were imported from Sri Lanka (then Ceylon). Like sugar, cocoa faced a long period of declining yields and quality, compounded by poor cultivation techniques, a dependence on migrant labour, and insufficient investment. However, since 1957 this decline has been reversed as a result of the formation of CEPLAC (Executive Commission for the Economic Recuperation of the Cocoa Region). CEPLAC was established by the federal government to provide credit to cocoa farmers, to enable them to purchase pesticides, insecticides and fertilizers, and to promote the planting of new varieties which have since quadrupled yields. Since 1967 about 150 000 ha have been planted, amounting to a third of the land under cocoa. Rubber is now also being successfully cultivated in the upland area west of the cocoa zone. It produces 95 per cent of Brasil's latex.

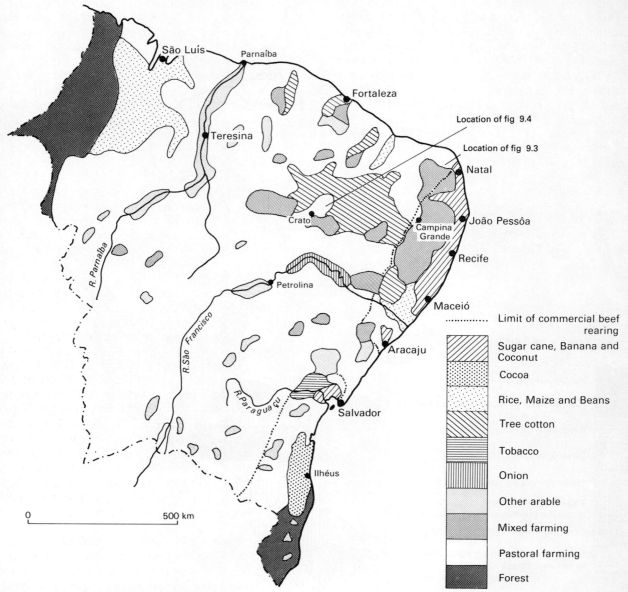

9.2. Crop Distributions in the North-east.

The *Zona da Mata* now produces a variety of crops. Tobacco is highly localised in the Paraguaçu valley west of Salvador. Its success results from a dramatic increase in the domestic market, and the relatively low investment needed. The deep red clay *massapé* soils, which developed under the formerly ubiquitous rain-forest cover, have been increasingly used for other crops since the 1940s. These include coconut, potato, cotton and agave (sisal). This diversification of agriculture was accompanied by an increase in the cultivated area, increased regional specialisation, and the increased use of labour. The use of more land to increase production is a method

typically associated with a low level of agricultural technology, and with the *latifundio* system of land tenure. However, this has been reversed. From 1960 to 1975, small farms of less than 10 ha increased by over 70 per cent in number, and by 50 per cent in area, and the *latifundio* are now employing fewer labourers. For the first time since the sugar boom of the sixteenth and seventeenth centuries, agriculture in the North-east is growing at a faster rate than the national average. The transformation was helped by the 1970 drought, which forced federal involvement, and initiated a new phase of investment.

The pattern of land-use of the sugar zone north

of Natal in the state of Rio Grande do Norte, is illustrated by **9.3**. The coastal dunes and swamplands are unsuitable for cultivation. The sugar areas correspond with the deepest soils of the valleys, whilst manioc and fruit cultivation predominate on the valley sides and coastal slopes. Subsistence *roça* farming is relegated to areas of poor soils, and the humid uplands are used primarily for extensive livestock rearing. Beef cattle and pigs are the most important livestock, but significant numbers of goats and sheep are also reared, especially on subsistence farms.

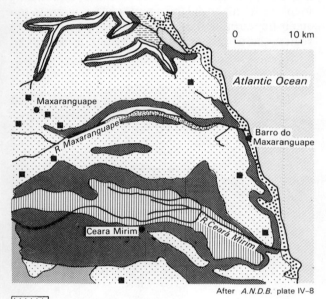

After *A.N.D.B.* plate IV–8

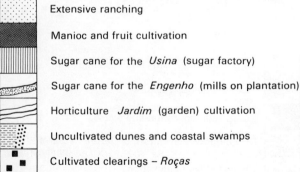

Extensive ranching

Manioc and fruit cultivation

Sugar cane for the *Usina* (sugar factory)

Sugar cane for the *Engenho* (mills on plantation)

Horticulture *Jardim* (garden) cultivation

Uncultivated dunes and coastal swamps

Cultivated clearings – *Roças*

9.3.   The Land-use of the Northern *Zona da Mata/ Agreste* Region

The Agreste

The *Agreste* is an upland transitional zone between the *Zona da Mata* and the *Sertão do Nordeste*. It has been described by R.K. Webb, as, 'a cultural invention of the twentieth century'. It developed as a zone of convergence because it was settled both by

drought-stricken *sertanejos* from the west, and by *favelados* from the coastal cities. The region was largely ignored by the wealthy land-owners, so that a *minifundio* system developed. Eighty-six per cent of the farms are under 20 ha in size. Whilst the majority of farmers are subsistence farmers, the farming systems are untypical. The *roça* system is here replaced by subsistence 'polyculture', combining livestock such as cattle, sheep, goats and pigs, with a mixed-plot garden type of cultivation known as *jardim*, which produces a great variety of crops. These include tree cotton, coffee, sugar, agave, black pepper, oranges, mango and avocado. The *jardim* system is regarded as being one of the most ecologically beneficial methods for food production. It can often be carried on in relatively small clearings, and because inter-cropping is practised it does not make excessive demands on the major soil nutrients.

Before the 1920s, the traditional crops of the *Agreste* were manioc and coffee. Coffee was virtually wiped out by the 'plagues' of the 1920s and the output of the entire North-east is now less than 3 per cent of national production. Arboreal (tree) cotton is well suited to the region, as it requires a long dry season. Since it is a long fibre variety, it is not in competition with the herbaceous cotton grown at the edge of the coastal zone and in São Paulo state. Ceará is the major producer, accounting for 48 per cent of national production. The 'boom' crop of the region is agave. Its production increased dramatically in the 1940s and 1950s because of the trade restrictions of the Second World War, and because of the development of new processing techniques which enabled its use as pulp for paper manufacture, in addition to its traditional use as sisal fibre and as fodder.

Within the *Agreste* there is a marked contrast in land-use between the mountain flanks, where *roça* farming is still dominant, and the low damp areas with alluvial soils, known as the *brejos*. The *brejos* are often associated with specialised agriculture including the cultivation of manioc, tomatoes and sugar-cane. The rural villages lie within the spheres of influence of a number of market centres where the produce is collected and marketed. The major market is at Campina Grande which is the regional centre of the *Agreste*.

Dairy cattle are usually found in small numbers on most farms, mainly providing for the needs of the family, with a small surplus for sale at the market. Beef cattle, however, are reared on *fazendas*. These estates are much smaller than those of the *cerrado* and *caatinga*. The cattle are driven to the mountains in the dry season and return with the first rains in March. This seasonal movement of cattle is referred to as 'transhumance'. The *Agreste* cattle have been considerably improved in recent decades by cross-breeding with '*zebu*', Dutch and Swiss breeds.

The Sertão do Nordeste

This dry, and in places, semi-arid, backlands plateau region has a virtually inert economy. R.K. Webb considers that it is a region which, 'absorbs people, money, animals and government efforts to change it with hardly any visible difference'. It is regarded by Brasilians as a primaeval and mystical land. It has bred the infamous bandits or *cangaceiros*, and religious fanatics, some of which still foster the cult of *Sertãoejismo*, the worship of the backlands.

Aridity has resulted in a discontinuous vegetation cover of thorn scrub, the *caatinga*, with sandy saline soils and bare, deeply-rotted rock pavements.

The region's traditional role is as a supplier of beef, hides and draught animals to the coastal areas. The dominant economy is semi-nomadic subsistence cattle rearing, though the region contains less than ten per cent of the nation's cattle. In numerical terms, goats and sheep are equally important. The coarse grasses are of low nutritional value, supporting only one cow per five hectares, but cattle rearing gives the highest return for the minimum investment of capital and labour. The *vaqueiros* (North-east cowboys) tend herds of up to 2 000 head on the open range, but even a short drought can reduce herds by over 50 per cent. In the past, the major product was dried meat (*charque*) because the drove routes to the coastal cities (see **9.13** on page 134) were generally over 250 km long. The average weight loss of over 1 kg per cow per day prohibited large-scale cattle movements. However, two major drove routes persist: those from Recife to Fortaleza and from Recife to Crateús. The *vaquieros* who worked on a cattle estate used to be paid by the *sorte* system, by which they received one calf in every four from the cattle they tended. Today wages are the rule, but they are very low. Many *vaqueiros* also cultivate small plots during the period when the cattle are on the estate.

Cultivation within the semi-arid areas is confined to low damp lands, known as *vazante*. These are usually dessicated lake beds, the beds of ephemeral streams, or floodplains in the areas of more reliable rainfall. The major crops are manioc, maize, beans, melons, sugar, fruits and short-cycle cotton. Like the *Agreste*, the region also experienced a boom in agave cultivation, but it suffered a decline following the fall in world prices in 1966. In some areas, small dams known as *açudes* have been built to provide water for irrigation; until recently these small-scale projects were the only method of irri-

gation, but major advances have been achieved through regional development programmes.

The following map (**9.4**) shows the land-use in the region around Crato, Juàzeiro do Norte and Missão Velha in the south-east of Ceará state. Within the area shown, altitude falls from above 800 m in the Chapada do Araripe to below 300 m in the north-east. There is a marked break of slope at the *pé de serra* (piedmont). On the *chapada* (high plain) some 60 000 head of cattle are reared. They provide the single largest source of farming income. The rocks of the *chapada* are permeable so that there is little surface drainage. Cultivation is concentrated at a few sites which have access to water, and mainly involves manioc and pineapples. The scarp is too steep for farming, but at its base in the *pé de serra* region there is a spring-line, feeding a number of

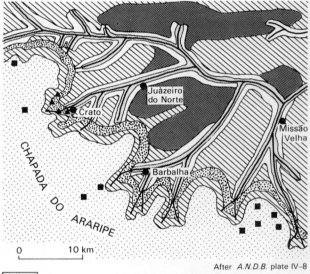

After *A.N.D.B.* plate IV–8

⣀⣀	Intensive sugar cane and rice cultivation
〰〰	Continuous polyculture
▓▓	Crop rotation–cotton and staples
⣿⣿	Continuous polyculture of the *Pé de Serra* (piedmont)
▲▲	Irrigated fruit cultivation
////	Uncultivated land
⣿⣿	Extensive ranching
■■	Crop rotation–manioc and pineapples

9.4. The Land-use of the *Sertão* and *Vazante*: The '*Ilha Agricola*' (agricultural island) of Juàzeiro do Norte, Ceará State.

streams which combine to form the Rio Jaguaribe. The lowlands are densely populated, averaging over 70 inhabitants per square kilometre, and are intensively farmed. Tree cotton and bananas are the two most valuble crops. They are cultivated on the interfluves, whereas sugar-cane and rice are cultivated on the valley floors. The *pé de serra* and valley sides are zones of polyculture, the former specialising in pineapples. The great variety of agricultural produce is not typical in the region. Cultivation in this particular area is intense because of the availability of water, and the needs of a relatively large urban population. Juàzeiro do Norte has a population of 96 000, and Crato 71 000. Their textiles and food processing industries exceed the value of agriculture. Both towns have grown rapidly in the 1970s because of new road construction which has given the area access to the larger urban markets to the south-east.

Within the *sertão do Nordeste* there is evidence of major changes in the *caatinga* vegetation. It is possible that like the *cerrado* it has been considerably modified by burning and grazing. Some cacti and succulents have been used as fodder for centuries. The area of bare rock surface is increasing, and the vegetation is becoming less diverse and even more discontinuous.

The agriculture of the north-east is closely associated with the exploitation of tree species in some areas (see Chapter 7); but only recently have attempts been made to establish plantations.

The Meio-Norte

This region corresponds to Maranhão state. It lies on the eastern fringe of the Amazon rain-forest and its economy is dominated by beef rearing, the cultivation of rice, maize, manioc cotton and beans, and the exploitation of forest products. As shown by **5.10** on page 68, the *Meio-Norte* is served by both the SUDAM and SUDENE regional development agencies. Because of its high rainfall and forest cover it is considered to be an area particularly suited to colonisation. A major colonisation project was begun at Alto Turi in the early 1970s, with the aim of attracting colonists from the *sertão* and establishing commercial agriculture and forestry. The project reinforces earlier attempts in the region, and has been heavily financed by SUDENE.

Regional Development and the 'Drought Problem'

The *zona da mata* is chronically overpopulated, with widespread poverty, and relatively low levels of both commercial agriculture and industrial development. Up until the 1950s, however, the drought problem was considered the major cause of the region's prob-

lems and consequently virtually monpolised the attention and investment of the state, regional and federal governments.

As was discussed in Chapter 1, the drought is a natural phenomenon. Total annual rainfall over much of the interior is sufficient for farming, but it occurs in a relatively short period giving a dry season lasting over 8 months. It also varies considerably from year to year. Only in a relatively small area is annual rainfall less than 500 mm per annum (see **9.5**). However, because of the colonisation of the *sertão do Nordeste*, it has long been considered a 'human' problem. The combined rural and urban population of the region is still over eleven million.

The first organised attempts to assist the poverty stricken *sertanejos* were forced by the great drought of 1877 to 1879, which followed a thirty-year period of adequate rainfall. The drought claimed an estimated 500 000 lives in Ceará state alone, about half of its population. The response was a dam and road construction programme—the so-called 'hydraulic solution'. This was ineffective as the dams were small

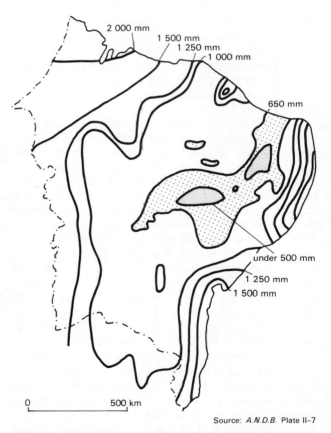

Source: *A.N.D.B.* Plate II-7

9.5. Annual Rainfall in the North-east and part of Northern Minas Gerais.

and dispersed, and merely expanded existing subsistence farming practices. In 1909 the Inspectorate of Works Against the Droughts was established. But from then until 1935, a period within which three other major droughts occured, expenditure on the programme fluctuated wildly. Much of it was concentrated on drought relief, and little was spent on lasting projects.

In 1936 the 'Drought Polygon' was designated. It was enlarged in 1951 to include part of northern Minas Gerais, after the fifth major drought of the century. The area of the polygon now totals 940 000 km², representing about half the area of the Northeast. It was established for the purpose of legally deliniating the region entitled to benefit from drought relief and associated programmes. In 1945 the 'Inspectorate' was re-designated as the National Department of Works Against the Drought (DNOCS). The 1946 constitution allocated 3 per cent of annual federal tax revenues for the works, providing that the states made an equal provision; also, a third of federal investment was held for emergency relief. By 1959, over 600 reservoirs had been constructed, and over 5 000 wells drilled to tap artesian water. Also, many new unmetalled roads were constructed and a 2 000 km highway connecting Fortaleza with Brasília was completed. However, developments in irrigation were relatively minor— the new works expanded the irrigated area by only 6 000 ha as compared with 12 000 ha of *vazante* farming, and the estimated 250 000 ha capable of being irrigated.

The 'hydraulic solution' failed in its major aims because it did not recognise the reality of the drought, and DNOCS faced numerous problems such as withdrawal of funds, and pressure from influential land-owners. By the mid-1950s, investment was being channelled into the industrial development of the South-east, and to the construction of Brasília. The 1951 and 1958 droughts exposed the fallacy of the hydraulic solution, compounded the chronic poverty of the *flagellados* ('beaten ones'), and led to peasant revolts against the land-owners. The peasant leagues were led by the communist lawyer Francisco Julião, who had close links with the Castro regime in Cuba. Political pressure became so great that unions of rural workers were legalised, the Bank of the North-east, was established, and in 1959 the Superintendency for the Development of the North-east (SUDENE) was established. R. Roett (1972) states that SUDENE faced considerable opposition from right-wing politicians who considered it to be 'a tool of international communism'.

SUDENE's first and most ambitious project was to re-route the *flagellados* to colonisation areas in Maranhão. It was hoped to settle 25 000 families

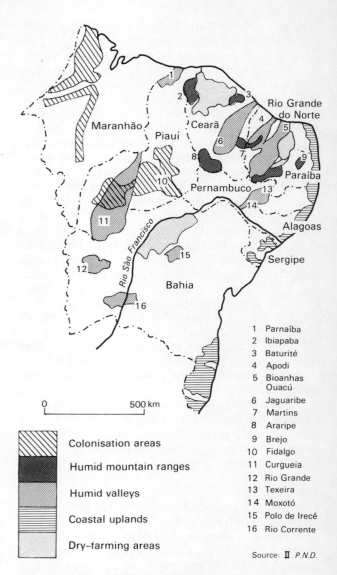

1 Parnaíba
2 Ibiapaba
3 Baturité
4 Apodi
5 Bioanhas Ouacú
6 Jaguaribe
7 Martins
8 Araripe
9 Brejo
10 Fidalgo
11 Curgueia
12 Rio Grande
13 Texeira
14 Moxotó
15 Polo de Irecê
16 Rio Corrente

Source: II *P.N.D.*

Colonisation areas
Humid mountain ranges
Humid valleys
Coastal uplands
Dry-farming areas

9.6. POLONORDESTE—The Development Programme for Integrated Areas in the North-east.

and to develop a co-operative system. The first 6 000 colonists were established in 1962 at Pindare, but the scheme was of limited success. Roett considered that, 'The six months of rain that Maranhão has every year made the task of setting up an agricultural program more difficult; isolation from markets (and little basic pre-study) compounded the feeling of frustration among the settlers . . . and not long after its initiation, the boldly conceived project became little more than a social assistance program for the bewildered settlers'.

SUDENE also extended two major existing projects, both based on the water resources of the São Francisco river. CVSF (The São Francisco Valley

Commission) and CHESF (The São Francisco Hydro-electric company) had been established in the 1940s. CVSF was a multi-purpose commission based on the highly successful Tennessee Valley Authority in the U.S.A., which had been a major instrument of President Roosevelt's 'New Deal' for the American south. One of the T.V.A.'s engineers made a survey of the agricultural and hydro-electric potential of the valley, but many of CVSF's projects were small in size and did little to promote an integrated and co-ordinated plan for the valley. CHESF, though faced with many problems, has developed the hydro-electric potential of the river at Paulo Afonso, and more recently at Moxotó, so that these hydro-electric plants now serve all the major urban/industrial centres of the region (see **9.7**). CHESF, a mixed economy corporation heavily funded by the World Bank, has been a major success, and this success in turn has contributed greatly to a change in emphasis from the 'hydraulic solution' to a more balanced regional development programme. The CHESF programme also involved industrial developments, and these are discussed in Chapter 10.

SUDENE made relatively little impact in the early 1960s, but gained considerably from a politically motivated US$131 million investment programme funded by the American Aid Mission at Recife. Since the coup d'etat of 1964 it has also benefitted from the funds of other programmes, from direct transfers by the federal government, and from the support of the Federal Banks. From 1960 to 1974, the region's per capita GDP grew by an average annual rate of 4.6 per cent, as compared with a national average of 4.2 per cent.

The Second National Development Plan (1975–79) earmarked an investment equivalent to one per cent of total national investment for development in the North-east; but like previous investments, industrial development absorbed the major share. However, since 1970 agriculture has been growing faster than the national average, so that the North-east is experiencing a gradual agricultural, as well as industrial, transformation. By 1972, twenty-six irrigation projects were in operation or under construction, and a further 50 were planned or under study. As maps **9.6** and **9.7** show, most of these are related

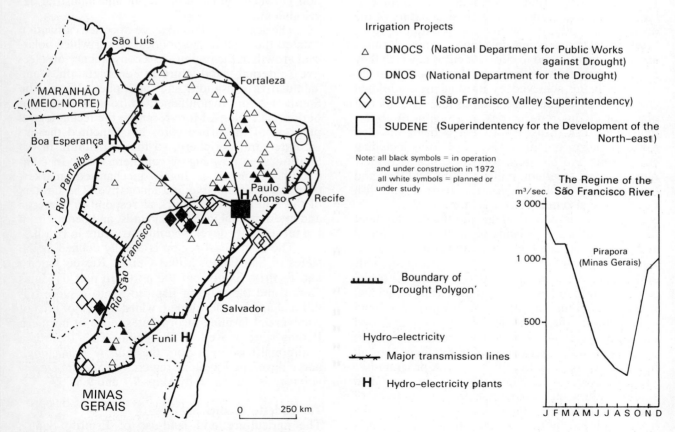

9.7. Irrigation and Hydro-electricity in the North-east.

to 'humid valleys', particularly those of the rivers Piranhas-Açú, Parnaíba, Ceará Mirim, Jaguaribe, Moxotó-Gorotuba and the São Francisco and its drainage basin. In the early 1970s SUVALE was established to co-ordinate development and investment in the São Francisco Valley. As part of the POLONORDESTE programme, 130 000 ha of new irrigated land was to be created and 21 000 families were settled. Irrigated farming has a major future here as the valley is capable of producing a variety of crops. It is already responding to new market demands and is beginning to share in the production of soya, Brasil's current 'boom' crop.

Whilst the irrigation programme has achieved considerable success in increasing the production and productivity of a large number of communities throughout the *sertão*, and associated projects have provided much needed medical and educational services, the POLONORDESTE programme recognised that irrigation is only a partial answer. The solution to many of the problems of upland regions and areas with little potential for irrigation lies in the short-term in Project *Sertanejo*, which gives special aid to the driest areas. In the longer term, the solution must be the development of efficient and well researched 'dry-farming' methods. Dry-farming is based on an acceptance of the physical nature of the drought. In addition, twenty-four separate agricultural projects are being developed, where farmers are being encouraged to cultivate crops in which they have a comparative advantage. Increased diversification is being achieved by introducing traditional crops into new areas, and establishing a number of new crops. This reduces risk in a region of abnormally high risk. Most investment is being directed towards maize, onions, a variety of fruits including citrus fruits and bananas, tomatoes, beans, cashew nuts, manioc, sorghum, millet, cotton, and rice, and *faveleira* for fodder. Livestock rearing and fish farming are also being strongly stimulated.

The growth pole strategy and the development of 'integrated areas' is being scientifically developed and planned, so that the agricultural potential, selection of crops and/or livestock, agricultural methods and infrastructure are planned as a whole. Also, the reorganisation of land tenure is increasing individual incentive. Within the North-east, the process of land redistribution, the promotion of agriculturally-based industries, and the provision of credit for farmers who would not otherwise qualify for loans, are all being undertaken by the PROTERRA programme.

However, A.L. Hall (1978), after detailed studies of three major irrigation projects, is critical of many practices. He states that many people have been displaced by the projects. If a farmer cannot prove his ownership of his land he may not receive any compensation. In some cases new colonists have displaced a formerly higher rural population. Hall found that the conclusions drawn from feasibility studies of the areas to be irrigated were over-optimistic, so that production targets have not been met. Thus, many colonists are heavily in debt. He criticises the 'showpiece' Morada Nova project for not producing highly marketable products such as tomatoes; instead traditional crops account for about 90 per cent of its total production. A further criticism is that some irrigation projects are only improving the areas where the rural population was never in any great danger from drought.

The South-east Heartland: The Dynamic Commercial Core

The South-east region contains forty-two per cent of Brasil's population but accounts for only eleven per cent of its area. It is Brasil's urban and industrial core, as well as being its most productive agricultural area. Eighty-four per cent of its population is classed as urban. It is no coincidence that there is a correlation between agricultural, urban and industrial development.

The success and dominance of coffee cultivation created the wealth and political power which polarized growth in the region. As a consequence of selective internal and foreign immigration, and 'cumulative causation' and 'multiplier effects', the South-east core region benefited from the decline of peripheral regions. More recently, the technological progress of the urban cores has benefited the immediate rural periphery, so that agriculture in the South-east is now highly commercialised. In comparative terms it is highly mechanised, market-orientated, productive and innovative. The farmers of the South-east are quick to respond to domestic and international market demands, and benefit from the most highly developed infrastructure in Brasil.

The South-east region is usually defined as the states of São Paulo, Minas Gerais, Rio de Janeiro and Espírito Santo, but the northern part of Minas Gerais and the state of Espírito Santo is more traditional and less developed, whilst the major area of commercial farming incorporates much of northern Paraná state as well as São Paulo. Thus there is a traditional eastern region, the *Sudeste Tradiçional*, and a developed western region, the *Sudeste Desenvolvida*, as illustrated by Maps **9.1** and **9.8**.

The Sudeste Tradiçional
The agriculture and land-use of Espírito Santo, south-eastern Minas Gerais and eastern Rio de

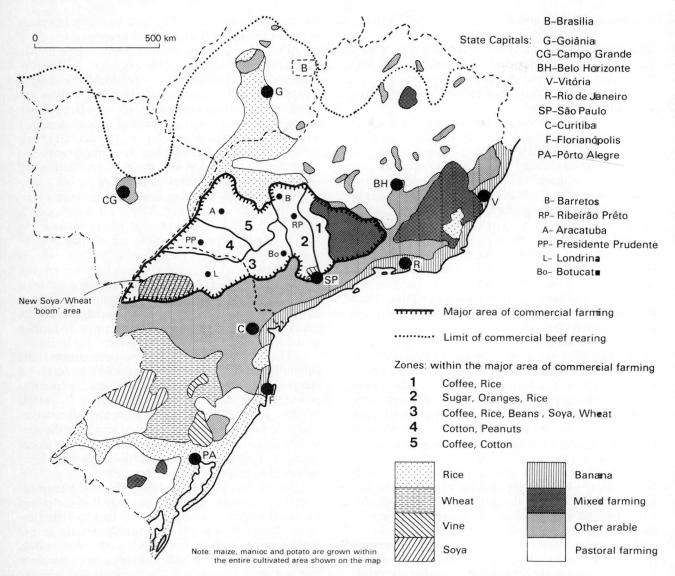

State Capitals:
B–Brasília
G–Goiânia
CG–Campo Grande
BH–Belo Horizonte
V–Vitória
R–Rio de Janeiro
SP–São Paulo
C–Curitiba
F–Florianópolis
PA–Pôrto Alegre

B– Barretos
RP– Ribeirão Prêto
A– Aracatuba
PP– Presidente Prudente
L– Londrina
Bo– Botucatu

New Soya/Wheat 'boom' area

|̅|̅|̅|̅|̅|̅|̅ Major area of commercial farming

·········· Limit of commercial beef rearing

Zones: within the major area of commercial farming
1 Coffee, Rice
2 Sugar, Oranges, Rice
3 Coffee, Rice, Beans , Soya, Wheat
4 Cotton, Peanuts
5 Coffee, Cotton

Rice
Wheat
Vine
Soya

Banana
Mixed farming
Other arable
Pastoral farming

Note: maize, manioc and potato are grown within the entire cultivated area shown on the map

9.8. Crop Distributions in the South-east, South, Mato Grosso do Sul and Southern Goiás.

Janeiro states is the product of a number of speculative crop cycles involving different localities. The coastal deltas, plains and valleys shared in the sugar boom of the seventeenth and eighteenth centuries, and the Paraíba valley became the major coffee producing region in the early nineteenth century. But in both cases over-cultivation and soil exhaustion, combined with the success of São Paulo, caused a decline. The region then reverted to subsistence farming and pastoralism. The middle Paraíba valley and the delta region around Campos became important centres of rice cultivation in the early twentieth century, but production was greatly affected by the uncontrolled and irregular regime of the Rio Paraíba. During the 1930s oranges became the boom crop, but progress was curtailed by the Second World War.

The traditional South-east was unable to compete with the developing plateau lands of São Paulo, so that in the case of each boom crop it was eclipsed by them. Today, the region is primarily an area of mixed farming, with a significant subsistence farming sector; 'spread' effects from Rio and Vitória are, however, beginning to transform the agricultural zones within the immediate spheres of the major urban centres.

The states of Rio de Janeiro and Espírito Santo today produce significant quantities of only six major crops—bananas, tomatoes, oranges, sugar, coffee and pineapples.

The Sudeste Desenvolvida

This region has the most highly developed commercial agriculture in Brasil. It is dominated by São Paulo state, but also overlaps into northern Paraná, and into Minas Gerais, approximately as far as the Rio Grande.

The success of São Paulo is largely the result of the success of the cultivation of coffee on the *terra roxa* soils of the plateau (see Chapter 6). It was coffee which stimulated the construction of the railways, the commercial centre of São Paulo and the port of Santos; and which created the wealth that in turn stimulated immigration, industrialisation, technological development, a large domestic market, and the further development of commercial agriculture. The preoccupation with marketing rather than mere production results in a dynamic agricultural economy and rural land-use, responsive to the changing demands for different agricultural commodities. Thus the land-use of São Paulo is inherently unstable and constantly changing.

The movement of the coffee frontier towards the Paraná river in the west, as well as into northern Paraná state, has been the most important single factor which has affected land-use in São Paulo state. Declining yields in the traditional eastern producing areas was not countered by attempts to solve the problem, but by the establishment of new *fazendas* in virgin areas; one result was that as the coffee frontier expanded it left in its wake a 'hollow frontier' of exhausted and in places eroded land. Since the 1930s, over-production of coffee and the increasing demands of the domestic textiles industry have tempted many farmers to change to cotton production. Cotton was cultivated on the *fazenda do café* by tenant farmers (*colonos*) and share-croppers (*parçeiros*), but hired labour is now most common. Its use as a substitute for coffee was quite successful, as the climatic requirements of the short and medium staple herbaceous cotton grown in São Paulo were very similar to that of coffee. Since 1960 cotton has declined in the state, not because of production or marketing problems, but because a great variety of more profitable crops have been introduced. However, São Paulo still contributes 37 per cent of the total production of herbaceous cotton, closely followed by Paraná with 28 per cent.

The present broad distribution of coffee and cotton is shown by **9.8**. The pioneer zone—between the Rio Paraná in the west and the scarp of the Serra do Botucatu in the east—is still a major coffee producer, though now second to northern Paraná. Cotton is produced in western São Paulo, and is cultivated with rice in the north along the valley of the Rio Grande. It is also grown with more recently introduced frontier crops such as peanuts, especially between the rivers Tietê and Paranapanema.

The rehabilitation of the eastern region of São Paulo reflects a number of factors. Here, coffee production had stimulated the most highly developed transport network in the country. The well developed infrastructure, proximity to very large urban markets, and access to the port of Santos, together with massive rural depopulation, the relatively low price of land and the influx of new immigrants, has transformed the region into the most productive and commercial agricultural zone in Brasil.

Since the 1940s, these lands have become an important producer of sugar. The sugar zone extends northwards from Campinas and Bauru to Ribeirão Prêto, and is now responsible for 43 per cent of national production. Yields are exceeded only by those of Bahia which is not a major producer, and are significantly higher than those of the traditional areas of the *zona da mata*. The success of sugar led to Brasil regaining its position as the leading world producer in 1972, and sugar temporarily displaced coffee as the major agricultural export.

The eastern zone has now been successfully rehabilitated by immigrant farmers who by terracing steep land, applying fertilizers and improving pastures have made it the new boom area. It also has benefited from 'spread' effects from the urban areas. The new immigrants were the first to accept the new technology developed in the core region. In recent decades agricultural diversification has also been achieved in response to new markets.

In the Jundiai micro-region, the vine was introduced by farmers of Italian descent. It is cultivated on smallholdings averaging from two to four hectares. Production is geared towards dessert grapes for the urban market, in contrast to the vineyards of Rio Grande do Sul which produce grapes for wine production.

The recent dramatic growth in the cultivation of oranges is an excellent example of the rapid speculative response of the farmers of eastern São Paulo to changes in the world market. Oranges had been cultivated in the Paraíba valley for some time, but until the 1960s were not highly profitable because of the dominance of the more productive groves of Florida (U.S.A.). In São Paulo, oranges were cultivated as a supplementary crop on the coffee *fazendas*, and were frequently inter-cropped with the coffee bushes. However, in 1963 Florida experienced a disastrous frost, and this led to a rapid and dramatic increase in the world market price. The response of Brasilian farmers was immediate. From 1965 the region between Campinas and Ribeirão Prêto increased its share of national output from 39 per cent to a current 70 per cent. Output increased by an

Plate 27. An oblique aerial view of the farmscape near Campinas. This traditional coffee producing area now has a more diversified agriculture, producing sugar-cane, tomatoes, oranges and tangerines, grapes, cotton and maize. ***Hoa-Qui.***

average annual rate of about 20 per cent, which is double the rate of the increase of world demand. Brasil is now the world's major exporter of orange juice. However, at present only about 10 per cent of production is consumed in Brasil, and there is therefore a danger of overproduction. The domestic market is far too small to provide a 'safety valve' for large surpluses, and whilst projections of future world demand are high, if there was increased competition or a change in the world market, then producers would be in serious difficulty. At present there is virtually no investment in domestic storage

and distribution facilities, so that surpluses could not be easily diverted to the domestic market.

As previously stated, large urban markets have contributed greatly to the development of agriculture in the region. Greater São Paulo's eleven million inhabitants represent over half of the state's urban population. This has stimulated the development of a highly mechanised and high technology market gardening zone around the built-up area, which provides the metropolitan region with vegetables, poultry and eggs. About three-quarters of the intensively farmed smallholdings are owned by

Japanese immigrants. Many of these first settled in the western pioneer zone, but found that this was too remote from the markets and could offer only a precarious livelihood. Others had been employed as labourers on the *fazendas*. The Japanese are now highly organised, and have developed co-operatives along the western edge of the built-up area of São Paulo, such as at Cotia. The Japanese still form a distinct ethnic and social unit, and have developed into a new rural middle-class.

The *Sudeste Desenvolvida*, therefore, consists of five distinct zones as shown by **9.8**, although throughout the region subsistence farming co-exists with commercial farming. The subsistence cultivation of maize, rice and manioc as staples is widespread. In the coffee lands of northern Paraná, kidney bean is also in important crop, but in recent years the area centred on Maringa (see **9.8**) has experienced a dramatic boom in soya and wheat which are grown in rotation with each other. This boom has been so great that a 'soya railway' is being constructed to Paranaguá, to maximise exports. In Minas Gerais, the region of commercial farming south-east of the Rio Grande is characterised by mixed farming. Here, coffee and maize are the most significant crops.

Land-use in the Serra do Mar and the *baixada* below the great escarpment contrasts markedly with that of the plateau. A relatively small proportion of the land is cultivated, and banana, rice, maize and manioc are the major crops. Banana accounts for nearly sixty per cent of the cultivated area.

São Paulo is also a leading livestock producer. The fattening and breeding pastures of the western frontier zone (see **9.3** on page 121) contain 11 per cent of Brasil's beef cattle. The state also contains 22 per cent of Brasil's poultry and accounts for over 40 per cent of the country's egg production.

The expanding urban markets have also created an enormous demand for liquid milk. Indeed, Brasil currently produces over seven billion litres of milk per annum. The dairy herds originated from Friesian cattle brought to Brasil by Dutch immigrants since 1945. The main 'dairying basin' (see **9.9**) covers much of south-eastern São Paulo, southern Minas Gerais and the northern part of Rio de Janeiro. Its shape reflects the three urban foci of São Paulo, Rio de Janeiro and Belo Horizonte. Milk production is greater and the lactation period longer near the cities, where dairying is most mechanised and methods are technologically superior. Paraná and Rio Grande do Sul states are also major producers (see **9.10**).

A measure of São Paulo's dominance in commercial agriculture is its 40 per cent share of the nation's tractors. It has been able to maintain this proportion since 1950. From 1950 to 1970, the

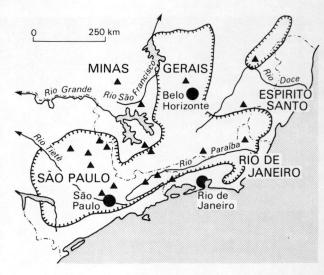

------- State boundaries

⊥⊥⊥⊥⊥ 'Dairying basin'

▲ Milk processing factories   After *A.N.D.B.*

9.9. The Dairy Farming Basin of South-east Brasil.

numbers of tractors in Brasil increased from 8 372 to 157 346. São Paulo has, therefore, been able to mechanise its agriculture at a time when its agricultural labour force was in rapid decline because of rural depopulation.

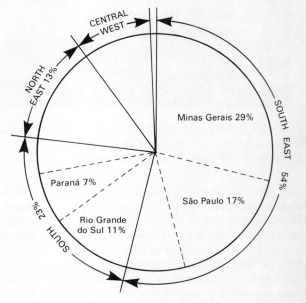

Note: Those states producing over 500 million litres/annum are specified

After *A.E.D.B.* 1977

9.10. Brasilian Milk Production by volume, 1974.

It is clear that both the milk producing area and the market gardening zones around the cities of the South-east reflect the importance of access to markets, and approximate to a von Thünen system of concentric zones. Outer zones also display this to some extent—the intensity of arable farming decreasing westwards to the beef rearing and fattening zone along the frontier of cultivation. However, as has been shown, there are also marked sectors reflecting the opening up of new frontiers as land became exhausted, forming the 'hollow frontier', which itself is now being transformed.

The South: European Colonisation in Temperate Brasil

The *Sul* region consists of the states of Paraná, Santa Catarina and Rio Grande do Sul. It contains eighteen per cent of Brasil's population on seven per cent of its area. Forty-nine per cent of its population is classed as urban, the main settlements being Pôrto Alegre (1.9 million) and Curitiba (1 million). Only two other settlements exceed 200 000 inhabitants—Londrina in the coffee belt of northern Paraná, and Pelotas some 220 km south-west of Pôrto Alegre on the western shore of the Lagõa dos Patos. Florianopolis, the capital of Santa Catarina state, ranks only eighth with a population of 140 000.

The South is unique in Brasil. Its distinctive temperate climate, forested plateau and southern grasslands contrast with the remainder of tropical Brasil, but its major characteristic is the great variety in farming which is the result of an immigrant population of almost entirely recent European origin.

At the beginning of the nineteenth century, the region was remote from the economic centre of the colony and was sparsely populated, despite the fact that no part of the region is further than 600 km from the Atlantic coast, and that its western frontier coincides with the Paraná and Uruguay rivers. However, like the rivers of the South-east, drainage over much of the area is westwards, the notable exception being the Jacuí. Compared with São Paulo, immigration in the nineteenth century was relatively small, but its effects were far reaching. Whilst northern Paraná was colonised directly by *Paulistas* crossing the Rio Paranapanema, the rest of the region was colonised independently. At first, Germans formed the major national group, and settled at colonies organised by the government at São Leopoldo, Rio Negro and São Pedro de Alcantara. The first German colonies (see **9.11**) skirted the southern edge of the plateau; further official emigration was stopped by the Prussian government in 1849, but privately sponsored emi-

gration continued and new colonies were established at Blumenau and at other eastern locations in Santa Catarina. At first the land grants to settlers were satisfactory—77 ha—but after 1851 they were reduced to about 48 ha and by 1890, 25 ha became the official size. Thus, the pattern of *minifundio* was established. The German colonists introduced mixed farming to Brasil, specialising in maize, rye, potatoes, cattle and pigs. They lived in typically linear '*strassendorf*' villages following the roads, and the farms employed crop rotation and manuring.

Italian immigration in the 1870s and 1880s resulted in the development of the vineyards around the settlements of Alfredo Chaves and Caxias on the plateau edge. The vineyards of Santa Catarina now produce over 60 per cent of Brasil's grapes, and are responsible for rapidly increasing wine exports.

By 1930, immigrant colonies had been established throughout northern Rio Grande do Sul, Santa Catarina and southern Paraná as far west as the Uruguay and Paraná rivers. The wave of immigration after 1850 had introduced a number of other national groups into the south, such as Austrians, Swiss, Spaniards, Dutch, and liberated slaves from other coastal areas of Brasil. The result was a diverse agriculture which included poultry, dairy farming, market gardening near the towns, rice cultivation along the coastal *baixada* and Jacuí floodplain, and tobacco cultivation. As previously stated, northern Paraná became an extension of the coffee lands of São Paulo, and is very different in character from the rest of the South which was settled earlier.

The last major wave of immigrants consisted mainly of Portuguese and Japanese, and introduced further expertise in temperate agriculture. More recently IBRA (The Brasilian Institute for Land Reform) has established four nuclei for colonisation—three in western Santa Catarina, and one in western Rio Grande do Sul. The entire western area has become a zone of spontaneous colonisation which is being aided by SUFRONTE (Superintendency for the Frontier Region of the South).

Whilst the influx of Europeans has radically affected farming in the South, and has been responsible for a diversification of Brasilian agriculture, agriculture has faced many problems. Many of the early immigrants adopted the *roça* system system of cultivation and forest clearing, and grew traditional crops such as manioc, rice and maize. Thus the development of commercial agriculture was delayed. A further problem was that demographic growth among immigrants was high, so that after two or three generations the system of inheritance had reduced the size of farms to a level which made them economically unviable. Many were therefore forced either to adopt a subsistence livelihood, or were

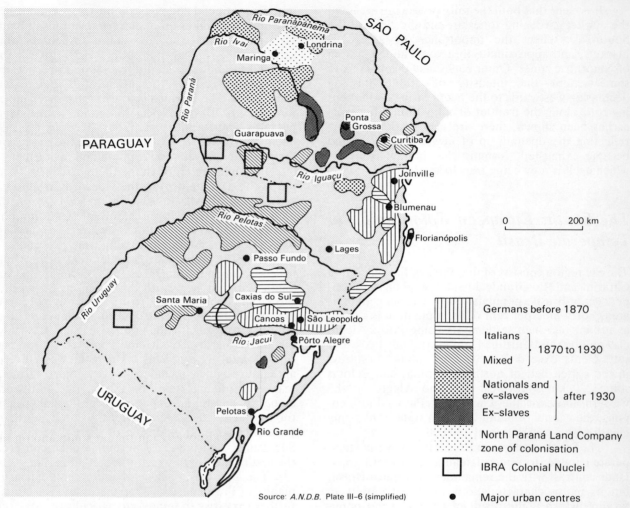

Source: *A.N.D.B.* Plate III–6 (simplified)

Legend:
Germans before 1870

Italians
Mixed } 1870 to 1930

Nationals and ex-slaves
Ex-slaves } after 1930

North Paraná Land Company zone of colonisation

☐ IBRA Colonial Nuclei

● Major urban centres

9.11. The Colonisation of the South.

driven to colonise new areas in the west. These new areas were more remote, generally forested and frequently too far from the major markets to be successful. However, deforestation was rapid so that there are now few areas of *Araucaria* forest intact.

Agriculture on the *planalto meridional* is, therefore, characterised by widespread *roça* cultivation, with highly localised commercial farming in favourable areas. These are mainly areas of recent colonisation, and areas serving towns and processing industries.

The land-use of the eastern part of the plateau can be illustrated by a brief sample study of the Curitiba basin (see **9.12**) in south-east Paraná state. The Curitiba micro-region has a population of 1 013 300, of which Curitiba, the state capital and regional centre, contributes over 766 000. No other settlement is larger than 40 000. It was colonised by central Europeans, Dutch, and freed slaves. Above the escarpment, marking the eastern edge of the Serra

Paranapiacaba, pastoralism is the dominant activity—about 120 000 head of cattle are reared which are the single most important source of farming income. The value of livestock, which includes pigs and chickens reared on lowland mixed farms, represents about 44 per cent of total farming income within the region. On the plateau, *erva mate* (Paraguay tea) is also collected, and there are isolated areas of agriculture. Below the escarpment edge, maize and pigs dominate the unimproved land, whilst near Curitiba intensive farming employing crop rotation is practised, the major crops being maize, potatoes, beans and oranges on permanently cultivated land. Curitiba's industries reflect the agricultural and forest resources of its region, the most important being food processing, furniture and forestry.

The general land-use of the southern plateau (see **9.8**) is dominated by *roça* cultivation, but this gives way to specialised farming regions in western

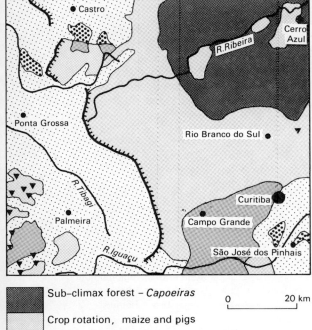

Sub–climax forest – *Capoeiras*

Crop rotation, maize and pigs

Crop rotation on improved land–cereals and potatoes

Extensive grazing and low density cultivation

Intensive cultivation of cereals

▼ Paraguay tea (*Erva Mate*)extraction

⊤⊤⊤⊤⊤ Escarpment of the Serra Paranapiacaba

0   20 km

After *A.N.D.B.* Plate IV–8

9.12. The Land-use of the *Planalto Meridional* and Curitiba Basin, Paraná State.

Santa Catarina and northern Rio Grande do Sul, the three most significant crops being soya, wheat and the vine, with rice cultivation dominating the Jacuí floodplain and littoral regions.

Soya is Brasil's current boom crop. In the 1950s soya production was insignificant, and even by 1965 total production was only 500 000 tonnes. But by 1975 production was nearly 10 million tonnes. In that year, Brasil overtook China to become the world's second largest producer, contributing 16 per cent of world production, and soya temporarily became Brasil's single most important source of export revenue. Whilst yields per hectare are only 60 per cent that of the U.S.A., which is the world's major producer, production costs per hectare are about half. By 1977 production had increased to over 12.5 million tonnes, Rio Grande do Sul contributing 45 per cent and Paraná 38 per cent. However, produc-

tion is now also expanding rapidly in São Paulo, Mato Grosso do Sul, and in the São Francisco valley. Soya bean has many advantages over existing crops. It is extremely rich in protein, with a higher protein content than beef by weight. It can be used for livestock feed or it can be reconstituted into a variety of different forms for human consumption. Its high protein content makes it invaluable in a country where a diet of starchy staples can lead to dietary deficiencies. The soya bean is also easily cultivated, requires a relatively small investment, and has a wide climatic tolerance.

The South is also Brasil's leading producer of wheat, which is the only staple crop which has to be imported. Until recently, imports from the pampas of Uruguay and Argentina have been on favourable terms, but domestic demand has grown rapidly as a result of the increasing popularity of 'western' foods. Unfortunately this has happened at a time when the world market price has also risen. Rio Grande do Sul was the major producer until recently, but its share is now only a third, whilst the major producer is now Paraná, contributing over sixty per cent. Whilst Paraná has increased its output, the decline of Rio Grande is not only relative, but absolute. Its 1977 output was less than forty per cent of the previous year. This emphasises the vulnerability of the temperate south to frost. The average number of days of frost per annum increases from less than 5 in northern Paraná, to over 25 in the far south and on the highest part of the plateau.

Government incentives to increase the domestic wheat production involve maintained market prices and low interest credit. There are also attempts to improve storage facilities. Wheat production is also greatly affected by pests, and by diseases such as stem-rust and mildew. Further problems are the acidity of the soils, and the high amounts of free aluminium necessitate heavy manuring. Major efforts are being made to introduce better varieties—for instance, short-straw Mexican wheats. They have already proved their worth in the Indian subcontinent. Wheat production has also been boosted by soya production, especially in Paraná state, because there wheat is grown in association with soya as a winter crop. Increased mechanisation is also raising production. This is facilitated by the size of the wheat farms, which average from 150 to 300 ha.

The *Campanha* temperate grasslands of the far south contrast greatly with the forested plateau. They proved far less attractive to European colonisation, so that they are relatively underdeveloped. The major early incentive for colonisation resulted from Brasil's need to reinforce her claims to the lands which were disputed by Argentina. Later, Uruguay was established as a 'buffer state'. Spanish influence

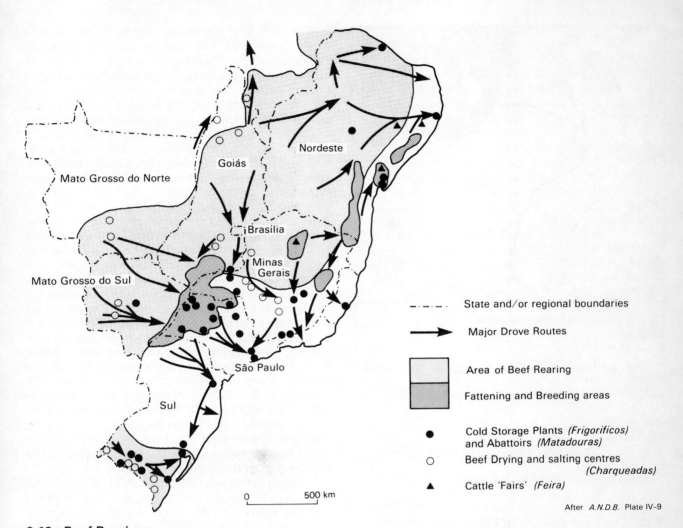

9.13. Beef Rearing.

survives to the present in the form of the *estancia* (estate) and the distinctive *gaucho* (cowboy). The Brasilian *pampas* support 13 million cattle, and 12.5 million sheep (fourteen and sixty-six per cent of the national herd and flock respectively). The region has major advantages over the *cerrado* for beef rearing. The temperate climate provides a more disease-free environment, and the grasslands are more nutritious. The climate is sufficiently warm and wet to allow all-year outdoor grazing. Commercial beef rearing dates from 1914 when the first *frigorifico* (refrigerating plant) was established. Since then a further seven have been built, and they now outnumber the traditional *charqueadas* (meat drying plants) (see **9.13**). Selective breeding of the beef herd, and especially the introduction of Hereford and Aberdeen Angus bulls, has improved the quality of beef considerably in recent years. This has justified meat packing plants at Pelotas, Pôrto Alegre, Rio Grande and Bagé.

The region also produces 34 000 tonnes of wool, representing virtually all of Brasil's production. Much of the annual clip is used in the domestic textiles industry. Pigs are also reared in the eastern regions.

The *Sul* is distinctive in terms of its agricultural diversity, and has a considerable potential. In general, the potential of temperate lands is more readily realised and requires less capital investment. It therefore has considerable advantages for future development.

The Central-west: The Productive Occupation of the Cerrado

The western interior *cerrado* region consists of the states of Mato Grosso and Goiás, and the Federal District of Brasília, although in order to facilitate planning, much of northern Minas Gerais is also included. Mato Grosso was divided into two new states in January 1979, as it was served by SUDAM in the north and SUDECO in the south. The Central-west accounts for 22 per cent of Brasil's territory, but only 6 per cent of its population; however, its population has more than doubled since 1960. Whilst 42 per cent of the population is classed as rural, many urban settlements are essentially rural in character. Brasília and the three state capitals—Goiânia, Cuiabá and Campo Grande—have a combined population of 1.6 million; only four other settlements have a population over 100 000 (see **9.4**).

The early colonisation of the interior followed a similar pattern to that of Minas Gerais. Cuiabá and Goiás became the centres of a short-lived gold-rush in the eighteenth century, and Corumbá developed as a port on the River Paraguay. However, the development of the region was retarded by its inaccessibility. Much of the states of Mato Grosso do Norte and Mato Grosso do Sul is an empty backlands region, whilst in marked contrast southern Goiás is now developing as a region of very rapid colonisation. This has gained momentum since the inauguration of the new federal capital in 1960, and its subsequent development as the focus for the new roads of the region.

Beef Rearing on the Cerrado

Pastoralism is the major element in the land-use of the *cerrado*, and also dominates the rural economy. Brasil has over 100 million beef cattle—the largest herd in South America, and the fourth largest in the world. The Central-west contains 24 per cent, and Minas Gerais a further 20 per cent. The *cerrado* has an enormous potential for commercial beef rearing, but the realisation of this potential will require considerable investment to offset a number of physical constraints, to develop adequate pastures and improved herds, and to evolve effective transport and marketing.

The high plateaus and ranges lie within the catchments of four major drainage basins and have a predominantly grassland vegetation, whilst the valleys are forested. The climate is continental in character, with a dry 'winter' and a wet 'summer'. In terms of the potential of the *cerrado* ecosystem, the high insolation, generally adequate rainfall (1 250 to 2 000 mm) and lack of extreme climatic hazards are more than offset by the high acidity of the highly weathered plateau latosols. They support a discontinuous grassland cover which is of low nutritional value. Even more significant in the past has been the inaccessibility of much of the *cerrado*, which has

Plate 28. Zebu cattle on the fattening and breeding pastures near Barretos in northern São Paulo state. *J. Allan Cash Ltd.*

prevented the production of high quality beef in Mato Grosso especially. Here, the cattle are mostly unimproved 'zebu' stock, which are low yielding and are affected by disease, and by parasites such as ticks. Though Corumbá is now linked by rail to São Paulo and is strategically situated along the road link between São Paulo and La Paz in Bolivia, its pastoral products are still largely traditional, i.e. hides, skins and dried beef. The relative development of beef rearing is illustrated by the distribution of the *charqueadas* (meat drying and salting centres) and *frigorificos* (refrigeration plants), the former being the traditional meat processing centres, and the latter the more technologically advanced (see **9.13**).

Traditionally, the production of higher quality beef has been the result of droving cattle from the Central-west to the improved pastures of western São Paulo, the *Triangulo Mineiro* of western Minas Gerais, and southern Goiás. This region is still the main fattening region and has also become an important breeding centre. Its proximity to the urban centres of the South-east has not only resulted in improved transport and marketing, but also the diffusion of pastoral technology. São Paulo itself now contains 11 per cent of Brasil's beef cattle. Both Minas Gerais and São Paulo have vastly better road and rail networks, and a large fleet of refrigerated trucks. In recent years this has also begun to spread to southern Goiás, and even to the seasonally flooded *Pantanal* region of western Mato Grosso do Sul, which is drained by the River Paraguay and its tributaries.

Beef rearing is now beginning to develop rapidly as there is a vast domestic market; this incidentally explains the low contribution of pastoralism to exports. A considerable amount of research is being carried out, and technological diffusion has passed the early stage when relatively few ranchers were prepared to risk change. The fundamental need is to correct the acidity of the latosols, so as to improve the pastures. Fifteen different sources of calcareous rocks have been identified within the region which could supply the lime needed to correct the soil acidity. Phosphatic fertilizers are now being processed from the recently discovered, large and easily exploited phosphate deposits at Patos de Minas. The University of Rio de Janeiro has completed experiments with Brachiaria grass which, apart from being superior to the natural grasses, is capable of fixing atmospheric nitrogen in the soil. These developments could have far reaching repercussions, the most significant being a reduced dependence on chemical fertilizers produced by the petrochemicals industry.

The introduction of new hybrid cattle is proceeding rapidly, the most successful being the Santa Gertrudis breed which combines the drought tolerance of Indian Brahman with the high yield of quality beef from the British Shorthorn.

Beef is now Brasil's major agricultural product by value. About 10 million head are slaughtered annually producing 1.6 million tonnes of beef. In recent years various measures have been adopted by CONDEPE (National Council for Live-stock Development), including credit facilities to help promote the genetic stock, storage facilities to regulate supplies to the market, and fiscal incentives to promote ranching in new areas. PRONASA (National Programme for the Protection of Animal Health) has a minimum annual budget equivalent to £15 million, which is largely invested in methods of eradicating foot-and-mouth disease and brucellosis.

The Development of the Central-west

The first major movement of the frontier of cultivation into the Central-west occurred in the 1940s. In 1937, the new planned state capital of Goiânia replaced Goiás which is situated in the malarial lowlands of the Araguaia valley. However, it was Anápolis that became the centre for spontaneous colonisation by smallholders, as it was the rail-head. The uplands of southern Goiás have since developed into a flourishing agricultural region producing rice in large quantities, and to a lesser extent maize, beans, manioc, sugar, tobacco, coffee, cotton, oranges and pineapples. The variety of agricultural products have given rise to regionally important food processing industries.

The major boost to the development of the region was the inauguration of Brasília as federal capital in 1960, and its subsequent development as the focus of the new national road network which was planned to speed the process of regional integration. The *raison d'être* of Brasília was to provide a magnet in the interior, capable of encouraging the 'March to the West' (*O Marcha Para O Oeste*) and stimulating a new interest in the development of the *cerrado* and *selva*. Since the early 1960s, a number of new roads have been constructed linking the capital with Belém to the north and Cuiabá in the west, in addition to its links with the industrial triangle of the South-east. Brasília is now the major urban centre of the region, and is being developed as a major growth pole as part of PRODOESTE (Programme for the Development of the Central-west) and POLOCENTRO (Programme for the Development of the Cerrado).

The POLOCENTRO programme has identified twelve agro-pastoral growth poles which are related to road and rail routes (see **9.14**). It is hoped to increase the cultivated area of the region by over 10 million ha in the long-term whilst also promoting pastoralism and forestry. Initially some 3.7 million

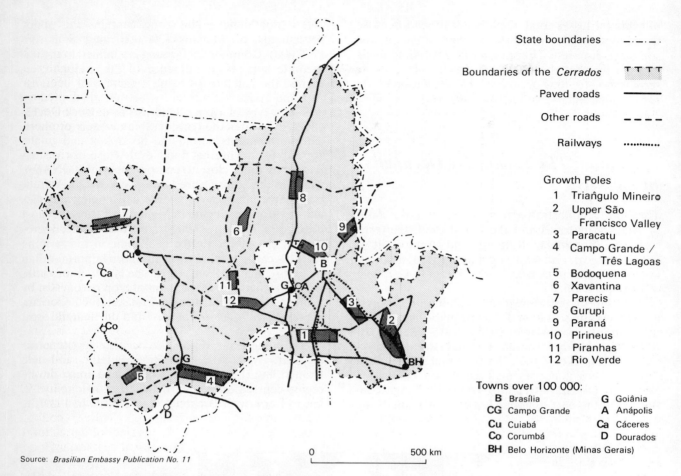

State boundaries — · — · —

Boundaries of the *Cerrados* ⊤⊤⊤⊤

Paved roads ⸻

Other roads – – – –

Railways ···········

Growth Poles

1 Triângulo Mineiro
2 Upper São
   Francisco Valley
3 Paracatu
4 Campo Grande /
   Três Lagoas
5 Bodoquena
6 Xavantina
7 Parecis
8 Gurupi
9 Paraná
10 Pirineus
11 Piranhas
12 Rio Verde

Towns over 100 000:

B Brasília   **G** Goiânia
CG Campo Grande   **A** Anápolis
Cu Cuiabá   **Ca** Cáceres
Co Corumbá   **D** Dourados
BH Belo Horizonte (Minas Gerais)

Source: *Brasilian Embassy Publication No. 11*

0   500 km

9.14. The POLOCENTRO Programme.

ha have been selected, of which 50 per cent is to be cultivated, with a special emphasis on priority crops such as rice, soya, maize, cotton, pineapples and peanuts. The programme was launched in 1974 and had a number of other priorities: these included the provision of credit and loans; the development of transport, the electricity grid, refrigeration and beef processing industries; the regularising of land titles; and the provision of technical assistance and research.

Two special development areas were established:

(a) The 'Geo-Economic' Area of Brasília. Since 1960, Brasilia has been successful in attracting spontaneous colonisation. Flourishing new colonies have developed along its road links—especially at Ceres—in response to the capital's food requirements, but the population growth of the federal district has been considerably faster than anticipated. By 1970 it had reached over 530 000, and by 1975 over 760 000—a

growth rate five times the national average. The Second National Development Plan allocated funds to develop five areas around the federal district, which would reduce migration to the capital itself, absorb many of the unemployed and underemployed, and produce a more balanced regional economy. The five areas are the Ceres-Anápolis axis, the dairying region to the south, the mining area centred on Niquelândia, the upper Paraná valley, and the area to the east centred on Paracatu which has the potential for pastoralism and irrigated agriculture. It is ironic that even Brasília now has to be 'decentralised'.

(b) The Pantanal. The *Pantanal* is literally a 'swampland' resulting from the seasonal flooding of lands with an impermeable subsoil. The region is remote and underdeveloped, but with the application of the major policies of the POLOCENTRO programme it would have an enormous potential for beef rearing. The region already contains over five million cattle,

but annual losses total some 300 000 head because they are allowed to graze the swamps untended, and some are diseased. The summer floods last up to six months, so that the cattle are driven to the *pé de serra* region for long periods. Flood regulation would result in greater use of the wet pastures.

Amazonia: The Productive Occupation of the Selva

The *Norte* administrative region consists of the states of Acre, Amazonas and Pará, and the three territories of Rondônia, Roraima and Amapá. It is Brasil's largest, and least populated region, accounting for 42 per cent of Brasil's area but only 4 per cent of its population.

Within the rain-forest the exploitation of forest products is important, and in some micro-regions it is the dominant economic activity (see Chapter 7). Farming is highly localised, the main areas of cultivation being along the *várzea* region. There is a discontinuous zone of small-scale *roça* cultivation and poor pasture, stretching from the Xingu confluence in the east to about 100 km upstream of the

Negro confluence. This zone contains the major settlements of Manaus (390 000) and Santarem (165 000). Commercial farming is confined to the immediate spheres of influence of the major settlements, the chief crops being manioc, rice, banana, jute and maize.

The typical *várzea* land-use is shown by **9.15**, which illustrates the considerable diversity of physical environments within the floodplain and in the zone above the normal flood level. The crops are cultivated in zones close to and parallel with the rivers, whilst in the areas cleared of forest cattle are raised, frequently for milk. The Careiro municipality lies within the micro-region of Manaus, which is the most developed region of the state. Within the micro-region, the major source of income in the farming sector is cattle rearing, which is more important than the entire income from crops. The major crop is jute, which accounts for 82 per cent of crop production by value. The cattle are reared on natural floodplain pastures—*campos de várzea*—and on cleared forest land.

Commercial farming also occurs near the towns of Pôrto Vehlo on the Rio Madeira, and Rio Branco, but the most highly developed area is in the region centred on Belém (820 000) and along its 150 km rail link with Bragança to the east. In 1929 the

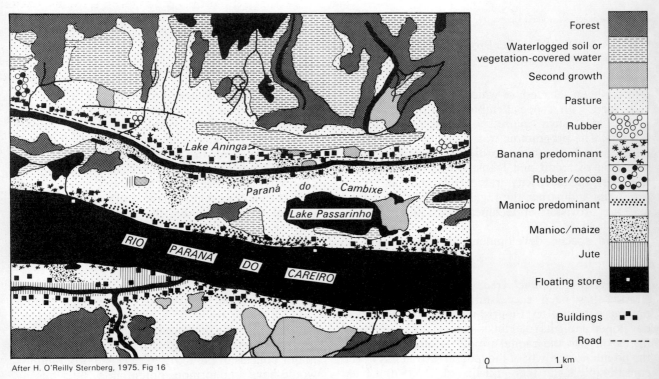

After H. O'Reilly Sternberg, 1975. Fig 16

9.15. Land-use on the *Várzea* near the Confluence of the Solimões and Negro, Amazonas State.

land of the Tome-Açu colony was given as a free grant by the Pará state government to Japanese immigrants. The colony now produces a large proportion of Brasil's black-pepper (*Piper nigrum*) raised from seedlings smuggled from Singapore in 1935. The Japanese also cultivate cocoa, sugar, tobacco, manioc, rice, banana, maize, and most important of all, jute. Jute cultivation was introduced entirely by the Japanese in the 1930s, and such has been its success that Brasil has been self-sufficient since 1953.

Map **9.16** illustrates the land-use of the area situated about 30 km west of Bragança (69 000). The micro-region has an average population density of 23 per square kilometre, and is within the immediate sphere of influence of Belém. Here, manioc, maize, rice and beans are the staples, and are cultivated by the *roça* system. Pepper and tobacco are the major cash-crops, and over 1.5 million cattle and pigs are reared.

Boa Vista is the centre of a pastoral farming region within the Rio Branco basin, but because of the remoteness of the region beef rearing has not yet developed beyond semi-nomadic herding. Cattle are also reared on the natural pastures of Marajó Island, at the mouth of the Amazon. Despite its relative accessibility and an estate system, it contributes little to the regional economy. The entire Amazon region contained less than 3 per cent of Brasil's cattle in the mid-1970s. Its only major share in livestock was its 118 000 buffalo, which represented 53 per cent of the national total. However, cattle are now increasing rapidly in number because of the implementation of some of the projects under the aegis of SUDAM.

Regional Development

The productive occupation of Amazonia, long regarded as Brasil's 'last frontier', has been a recurring theme ever since the expulsion of French and Dutch colonists in the early seventeenth century. The political integration of the region was established by the Treaty of Madrid in 1750, and Acre territory was ceded by Bolivia in 1903 in return for a railway link from Bolivia to Pôrto Velho which was never completed. The short-lived rubber boom (see Chapter 7) stimulated the growth of the settlements of Manaus and Belém, but also exposed the myth of the supposed fertility of the forest soils, and demonstrated the fragility of the *selva* ecosystem.

President Getulio Vargas who created SPVEA (Superintendancy for the Economic Evaluation of Amazonia) in 1953, stated at Manaus in 1940 that, 'To conquer the land, and tame the waters, subjugate the jungle, these have been our tasks. And in this centuries-old battle we have won victory upon victory'. It is unfortunate that the development of the *selva* is still regarded as a battle against a hostile environment. The dangers of such an attitude have been outlined in Chapter 1.

SPVEA laid the foundations for development by the construction of the Belém-Brasília highway in the 1950s, but many schemes were shelved because of inadequate government investment. Private investors have never involved themselves to any great extent in Amazonia, as the South-east offers quicker and higher returns. In 1966 'Operation Amazonia' was launched, and SUDAM (Superintendency for the Development of Amazonia) was created, along similar lines to SUDENE. It was funded by the Bank of Amazonia (BASA). Fifty per cent tax deductions were granted to registered companies willing to invest in approved agricultural, pastoral and mining projects. Manaus was declared a 'Duty-Free Port'—previously, smuggling had been

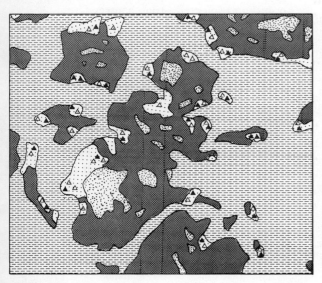

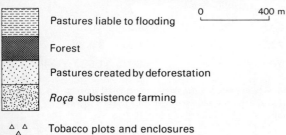

0   400 m

Pastures liable to flooding

Forest

Pastures created by deforestation

Roça subsistence farming

△ △
 △   Tobacco plots and enclosures

▲ ▲
 ▲   Tobacco farmer's houses   After *A.N.D.B.* Plate IV-8

9.16. Land-use between Belém and Bragança, Pará State.

described as the major industry of Amazonia (see Chapter 10). SUDAM's sphere of influence extends beyond the *Norte* region to include Mato Grosso do Norte state, and much of Maranhão state, and thus encompasses 60 per cent of national territory.

In 1968 a decision was taken to bisect the 'lung of the Earth' by the construction of the Trans-Amazonica Highway. The 6 370-kilometre-long road was to link with the Pan-American Highway and to join the heads of navigation of the Amazon's southern tributaries. By 1973 it had been completed as far as Pôrto Velho, and in the same year plans were announced for a northern 'perimeter highway' to skirt Brasil's northern and north-western frontier and to join the Trans-Amazonica at Cruzeiro do Sul.

The new roads were planned to serve as 'growth corridors' along which colonies were to be established. As previously stated, the concept of a geometrically planned hierarchy of 'Ruropolis', 'Agropolis' and 'Agrovila' was severely criticised on the grounds that it took no account whatsoever of the environment, and would therefore have disastrous ecological repercussions. From 1967 to 1974 SUDAM established a number of development priorities, set up the administrative and technological organisation for determining priority areas, and carried out feasibility studies to assess the potential for forestry, rubber and nut production, ranching, and the development of co-operatives. It also involved the CPRM (Company for Mineral Resources Discovery) in mineral resources evaluation using the RADAM (Radar mapping of Amazonia) project. Furthermore, it accelerated the Curua-Una and Coroaçy Unes hydro-electricity projects, improved the region's airports, and initiated a considerable investment in social services.

The Second National Development Plan (1975–79) stressed the challenge and potential of the region, and particularly its potential for making a major contribution to domestic and external markets. The Plan also established a new development strategy—the POLAMAZONIA programme (The Programme for Agricultural and Agro-Mineral Nuclei in Amazonia). The Plan involved an investment equivalent to about £1 billion over a five-year period. Its major aims were:

(a) To increase the cattle herd to five million.

(b) To support the region's traditional crops and to finance research into agriculture.

(c) To rationalise agriculture, and legalise the land titles of squatters.

(d) To extend credit and technical assistance to the *minifundio* farmer in an attempt to increase pasture and improve the breeding stock.

(e) To achieve a more equitable distribution of wealth and create 800 000 new jobs.

(f) To accelerate exports to a level 15 times greater than that in 1963.

(g) To concentrate development in 15 'growth poles' and selected urban centres.

The fifteen 'growth poles' are shown on **9.18**, which also summarises their major features.

There is no doubt that Amazonia could support a considerably larger population, and could make a significant contribution to the national economy. However, as has been shown previously, the major problem relates to the nature of future development. There are a number of conflicting priorities, and the conservation of the *selva* is but one of these. In the past the shortage of capital investment delayed development. Domestic and foreign investors could

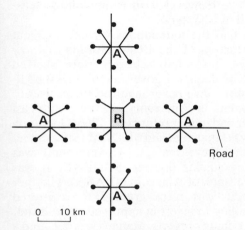

Urban-Rural Plan based on a Ruropolis:

Hierarchy	Area in ha	Area of influence	Population
1 Ruropolis	1 600	70 km	10 000 to 20 000
2 Agropolis	200	10 km	1 500 to 3 000
3 Agrovila	50–100	5 km	600 to 1 500

Each Ruropolis was to have primary, secondary and technical schools, each Agropolis, primary, and secondary and each Agrovila a primary school

Note: Other plans were drawn up for industries and cities

After *José Geraldo da Cunha Camargo* (Goodland and Irwin Fig 3.)

9.17. Part of the Geometric Colonisation Plan for the New Highways of Amazonia.

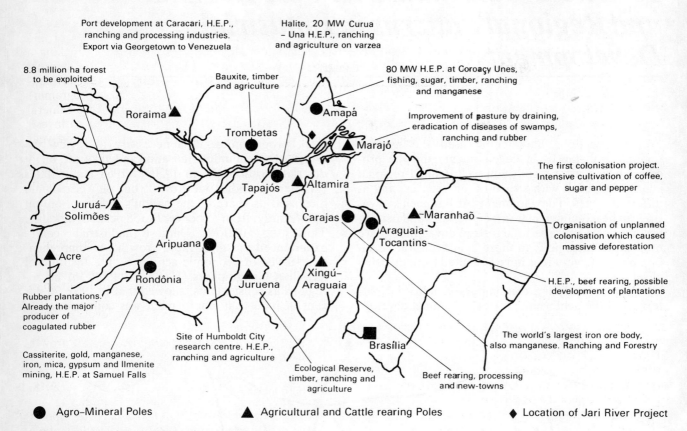

Port development at Caracari, H.E.P., ranching and processing industries. Export via Georgetown to Venezuela

8.8 million ha forest to be exploited

Bauxite, timber and agriculture

Halite, 20 MW Curua – Una H.E.P., ranching and agriculture on varzea

80 MW H.E.P. at Coroaçy Unes, fishing, sugar, timber, ranching and manganese

Improvement of pasture by draining, eradication of diseases of swamps, ranching and rubber

The first colonisation project. Intensive cultivation of coffee, sugar and pepper

Organisation of unplanned colonisation which caused massive deforestation

H.E.P., beef rearing, possible development of plantations

The world's largest iron ore body, also manganese. Ranching and Forestry

Rubber plantations. Already the major producer of coagulated rubber

Cassiterite, gold, manganese, iron, mica, gypsum and Ilmenite mining, H.E.P. at Samuel Falls

Site of Humboldt City research centre. H.E.P., ranching and agriculture

Ecological Reserve, timber, ranching and agriculture

Beef rearing, processing and new-towns

Roraima
Trombetas
Amapá
Marajó
Tapajós
Altamira
Juruá–Solimões
Carajas
Maranhaõ
Araguaia-Tocantins
Acre
Aripuana
Rondônia
Juruena
Xingú–Araguaia
Brasília

● Agro–Mineral Poles   ▲ Agricultural and Cattle rearing Poles   ◆ Location of Jari River Project

9.18. The POLAMAZONIA Programme.

make much higher and shorter-term profits elsewhere, but this is changing. Amazonia is now becoming a leading region for investment. In many ways the colonial entrepreneurial tradition is still alive in Amazonia; many government-sponsored projects, and those being financed by the multi-national corporations, are beginning to prove viable in cost-benefit terms.

Cattle rearing in particular is expanding rapidly. Amazonia now has five million head, reared on seven million hectares of artificial pastures. Production targets have been exceeded.

It is easy to be critical of many of these projects, but an assessment of the development and potential of Amazonia must take into account a number of other factors, such as those involved in national development. It is significant that the Third National Development Plan stresses the need for a 'non-predatory' occupation of Amazonia, and the advantages offered by the *cerrado*.

10 The Urban/Industrial Core Regions and Regional Patterns in Industrial Development

Previous sections have emphasised the marked regional imbalances in development, and the processes which have resulted in well defined regional economies: each with structural differences, and at different stages in development. As has been shown, this can be explained in terms of the 'core and periphery' model. Contrasts in industrial development are even more extreme than those in agricultural development, as fewer areas have benefited from industrialisation.

Before analysing contemporary industrial patterns and the achievements of the regional develop-

ment programmes, it is necessary to review the effects of recent industrialisation and 'take-off' on industrial location. From 1920 to 1968 many states experienced industrial growth, but only São Paulo increased its share of the nation's industrial output significantly, from 35 per cent to 58 per cent by value. Thus the nation's largest industrial centre experienced the most rapid growth. A comprehensive survey of economic activity by the Institute of Brasilian Geographers (1968), using all 361 microregions as census units, showed that in 1965, 75 per cent of industrial employment was concentrated in

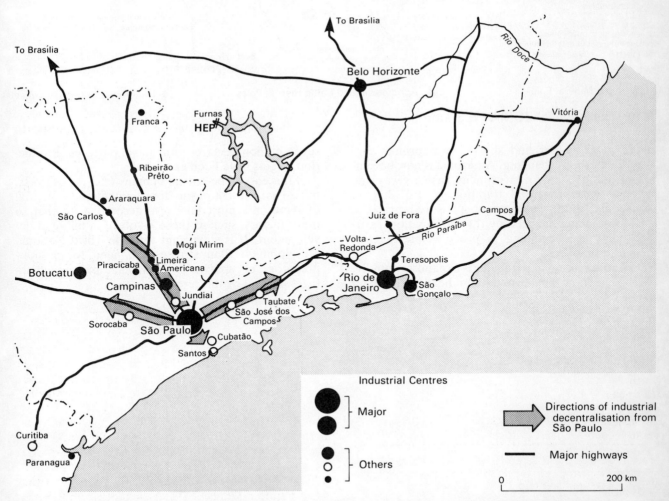

10.1   The Industrial Triangle of the South-east: Location of the Major Manufacturing Centres.

only 29 micro-regions, and only three contributed over 5 per cent—Greater São Paulo (32 per cent), Rio City (Guanabara, 9 per cent) and Pôrto Alegre (6 per cent). No other micro-region exceeded 3 per cent, and the next four in rank order were all associated with core regions in the South-east—Campinas and Botucatu near Greater São Paulo, São Gonçalo near Rio, and Belo Horizonte which is the industrial hub of Minas Gerais.

Brasil's industrial 'take-off' was therefore not a national phenomenon. It was strongly polarised in the dominant urban core regions of the 'industrial triangle' of the South-east. The location of manufacturing and tertiary industries is closely related to urban development, though this link was more tenuous in other regions. No micro-region in the North-east contributed more than 2 per cent, and none in the North and Central-west more than 0.5 per cent of industrial employment.

By the mid 1970s, industrial growth had been dramatic but was still strongly polarised. However, two processes are now beginning to modify contemporary regional patterns. In the South-east, diseconomies of spatial industrial concentration are leading to planned industrial decentralisation within the region. (This could also be regarded as a process leading to greater maturity in the dominant region.) Secondly, the revitalisation of existing industries and the diversification of the industrial sectors of the peripheral regions are gaining momentum, as a result of regional development programmes.

The precise measurement of industrial location is problematic as there are a variety of criteria which can be used. The single best index is that of the value added by manufacturing, as this is related to a number of factors including the level of technological development. The following table (**10.2**) shows the dominance of the South-east and São Paulo in particular.

10.2. Regional Contrasts in Manufacturing; The Value Added by Manufacturing, 1974

Region	Value Added by Manufacturing (Cr$ thousands)	Percentage of National Total
North	2 113 728	1.0
North-east	7 953 266*	3.8**
South-east	162 070 292	77.5
(São Paulo)	(118 491 771)	(56.6)
Central-west	not available	3.4**
Brasil (Total)	209,223,195	100.0

*1973   **Approximate

Source: *A.E.D.B., 1978*

The South-east: The Industrial Heartland

The South-east is larger in area than any European country and has a population of 51 million. Its population will surpass that of the most populous European country in the 1980s. Like most advanced countries it is not 'one massive complex of industrial activity' and 'is far from being uniformly industrialised' (J. P. Dickenson, 1978).

Manufacturing and tertiary industries are highly concentrated in the urban cores of the three metropolitan regions of Greater São Paulo, Greater Rio de Janeiro and Greater Belo Horizonte. Secondary centres have developed at Santos/Cubatão, in the '*Paulista*' zone which extends from Sorocaba in the south to Ribeirão Prêto in the north, and along the transport linkages between the metropolitan regions. (See **10.1**).

Greater São Paulo

Greater São Paulo has been described as the 'locomotive which pulls the rest of Brasil'. Its industrial dominance and its role as the nation's 'Supercap' ('Super Capital') has been the result of many factors. It virtually monopolised the coffee economy, and therefore became the commercial capital and centre of investment, as well as establishing a focal position in the developing infrastructure, including transport systems and hydro-electric power. It was closely associated with a large hinterland and with its port of Santos, and has experienced phenomenal urban growth. Thus is it also the nation's major market centre.

Its early industries were largely traditional and dominated by textiles and food processing factories, located east and west of the *Triangulo* on the south bank floodplain and terraces of the Rio Tietê (see **4.10**). The developing transport networks allowed it to serve the needs of a vast hinterland and it was able to capture not only local and regional markets, but later a major share of the national market and industrial exports. As the region developed into the continent's leading and most diverse industrial complex, São Paulo was able to capture a major share of new industries such as petrochemicals and engineering, to a lesser extent steel, and most significant of all, the motor vehicles industry.

The congestion of the inner city, and the locational advantages offered by the transport links with the port of Santos, caused the emergence of the south-east 'ABC' industrial complex as early as the 1920s. This zone was selected for the location of the major motor vehicles factories in the mid-1950s, when President Kubitschek decided to adopt the

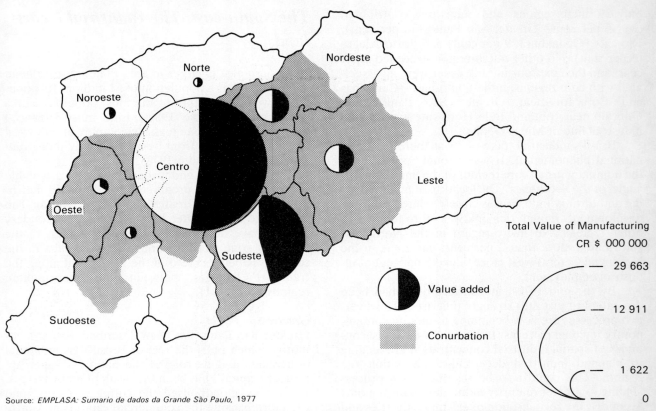

Source: *EMPLASA: Sumario de dados da Grande São Paulo,* 1977

10.3. Greater São Paulo Manufacturing Industry: The Total Value of Manufacturing and Value Added in the Manufacturing Process by, Sub-regions, 1970.

strategy of heavy investment from domestic and foreign sources in this key industry (see Chapter 8). Maps **10.3** and **10.5** show that the *Centro* or 'city' region still dominates industrial output and industrial employment; it contains a complete cross-section of Brasil's manufacturing industries, in over 20 000 establishments of varying sizes. In contrast, the

south-east sub-region, including the 'ABC' complex of Santo André, São Bernardo do Campo and São Caetano do Sul, contains less than 2 300 establishments; but these are large-scale units using modern production techniques.

Within Greater São Paulo, the industrial satellites show a high level of specialisation. São

10.4. The Industrial Dominance of São Paulo

	São Paulo City		Greater São Paulo		São Paulo State		Brasil
		(%)		(%)		(%)	
Number of Industrial Establishments	20 543	12.5	25 788	15.7	50 556	30.7	164 793
Number of Industrial Employees	643 672	23.8	906 907	33.6	1 295 810	48.0	2 699 969
Value of Production*	28 604	24.2	46 261	39.1	65 517	55.3	118 428
Value of Industrial Transformation*	14 908	27.2	23 162	42.2	31 059	56.6	54 837

Notes: *Cr $'000,000.
        All percentages are of the Brasilian total.

Source: *Censo Industrial Brasil, 1970,* I.B.G.E. 1974.

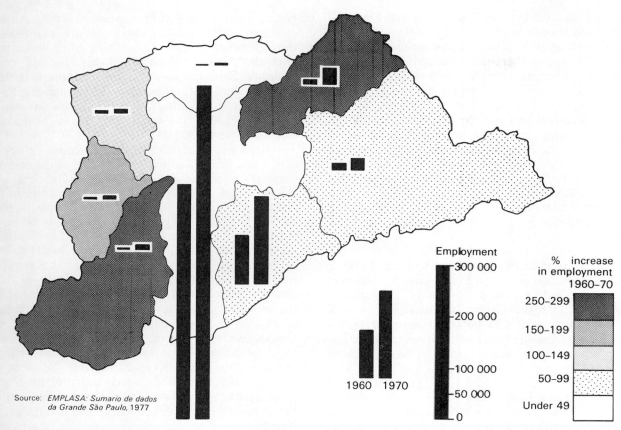

Employment

—300 000

—200 000

—100 000

1960 1970

—50 000

—0

% increase
in employment
1960–70

250–299

150–199

100–149

50–99

Under 49

Source: *EMPLASA: Sumario de dados
da Grande São Paulo*, 1977

10.5. Greater São Paulo Manufacturing Industry: Employment in Manufacturing in 1960 and 1970, and Percentage Increase, by Sub-regions.

Bernardo is the main motor vehicles centre, São Caetano and Santo André specialise in metalworking; Santo André also specialises in chemicals, and Guarulhos in the north-east in mechanical and electrical engineering and metals. The other major centre—Osasco, to the west of the *Centro*—has a mix of traditional and new industries.

Whilst the metropolitan region dominates manufacturing (see **10.4**), it does not have a monopoly of the state's industries. A number of industrial centres, located along the railways and roads radiating from the city, shared in the city's industrial growth, and became industrial centres in their own right. However, the excessive industrialisation of the metropolitan region has recently resulted in a policy of industrial decentralisation along four major axes which are orientated along these existing centres (see **10.1**). The four major axes are:

(a) The Coastal Zone centred on Santos and Cubatão. Santos (400 000) is Brasil's leading port, handling over a third of imports and exports. It developed as the main coffee exporting port, but since 1945 its trade has diversified as São Paulo's industries have

diversified. Santos's major industries are still closely related to its primary function, and are dominated by traditional port industries processing import and export commodities such as cereals, sugar, meat and fish. These and brewing account for over 55 per cent of industrial employment. The new industries of the zone are concentrated at Cubatão (66 000) where the first hydro-electric plants were developed. Like Santos, Cubatão benefited from its 'break of bulk' location below the great escarpment. In 1955, the Presidente Bernardes petroleum refinery was completed and this has in turn stimulated petrochemicals. Its industrial development was assured by the growth of São Paulo's motor vehicles industries, which required a new integrated steelworks in close proximity. This COSIPA works was completed in 1963; it is Brasil's third largest in terms of ingot steel capacity, and the only one with a strong market orientation. Unfortunately the lack of pollution controls has had chronic effects on the health of the inhabitants of Cubatão.

(b) The Campinas/Ribeirão Prêto Axis. Towns such as Campinas, Jundiai, Americana, Piracicaba,

Limeira, São Carlos, Ribeirão Prêto and Franca—with populations ranging from 100 000 to 500 000—form part of a north-south industrial belt some 500 km in length. These industrial centres developed along the railways serving the earliest *Paulista* coffee region. These early industries were typically those processing agricultural raw materials (textiles and food-processing) and those serving the needs of the *fazendas* such as small-scale engineering and metal-working. These industries have since expanded and have been diversified by the changes in agriculture (see Chapter 9), and by improved transport links with São Paulo. The larger towns are developing a number of new industries including those producing components for motor vehicles. Campinas also has a plant manufacturing tractors.

(c) The Sorocaba Axis. Linked to São Paulo by three major highways, Sorocaba is a flourishing commercial centre and like the entire South-east region is well served by hydro-electricity. It has been less successful in attracting new industries, so that textiles and food-processing dominate. However, there has been some recent success, notably the aluminium smelter at Mairinque.

(d) The Paraíba Valley. The Paraíba valley with its transport links is one of the most rapidly developing industrial zones of Brasil, as it connects the two major urban/industrial core regions which are about 500 km apart by road and rail. The valley has two distinct parts—an eastern section in Rio de Janeiro state, and a western section in São Paulo state. The western section has developed separately in association with Greater São Paulo, as this is the main axis of decentralisation. The zone's traditional industries have benefited from technological 'spin-off' from greater São Paulo, and the major towns have developed some specialised industries since the completion of the Dutra highway in 1951. São José dos Campos, about 100 km from São Paulo city, is the centre of Brasil's aircraft industry which is developing rapidly, though still in its early stages. The town also produces synthetic fibres, telecommunications equipment, pharmaceuticals and motor vehicle components. Taubaté (131 000) is also a flourishing centre.

As yet, decentralisation from São Paulo has not affected the eastern section of the valley in Rio de Janeiro state, the only industrial centres being Volta Redonda and Barra Mansa.

Greater Rio de Janeiro

Rio has been described as the '*Cidade Maravilhosa*' (the 'Marvellous City') and '*Belacap*' (the 'Beautiful Capital'). Its early growth resulted from its central position on the coast of Portuguese America, and its monopoly of the gold exports from Minas Gerais in the eighteenth century. Its position as the dominant port and commercial centre at this time led to it replacing Salvador as the colonial capital in 1763. The excellent natural harbour in Guanabara Bay ensured its growth after the mining boom was over, and from 1800 to 1900 its population increased tenfold to nearly 700 000.

Rio's site is remarkable, being wedged between ocean and beach and the massive crystalline domes (*morros*) such as the Corcovado ('Hunchback', 704 m) and Pão de Açucar ('Sugar Loaf'). It justifies the *Carioca*'s claim that his is one of the world's most beautiful cities. However, it is the very nature of its site, and the fact that Rio lies within a discontinuous coastal basin below the escarpment, known as the Baixada Fluminense, that has caused numerous planning problems. At the turn of this century, work started on excavating tunnels through the *morros* to link the commercial centre with the south-west coastal area. This stimulated the now famous select suburbs of Copacabana and Ipanema. Much of the excavated material was used to reclaim sections of the shores of Guanabara Bay, for the construction of a number of projects including the city's first airport (Santos Dumont), Flamengo Park, and the Avenida Beira Mar which is the main coastal highway.

Several attempts were made to reorganise the urban fabric, the most noteworthy being that of Passos in 1903, who initiated a massive renovation programme based on the principles used by Haussmann in Paris from 1853 to 1870. A number of monumental avenues were constructed, such as the Avenida Rio Branco which runs diagonally through the business district, and which is now the commercial heart of the city. However, many well researched projects were shelved because of frequent changes in municipal administration.

Rio's industries developed as a consequence of its function as federal capital, and its role as the then leading Brasilian city and chief port. But by 1960 it had lost all three roles. It is still a major industrial centre, but its industrial momentum has slowed. In 1920 it contained about 20 per cent of the nation's industrial labour force, but by 1970 this had fallen to less than 9 per cent. The port still handles about 20 per cent of the nation's imports, but only a mere 6 per cent of exports; Rio's declining share of the latter is partly explained by the development of the new ocean terminals at Vitória in the State of Espírito Santo, and in Sepetiba Bay to the west of the city. The port area and inner industrial areas still produce traditional commodities, notably two industries related to its former function as federal capital—

Plate 29. Rio de Janeiro, *Cidade Maravilhosa.* This view from the Corcovado shows the district of Botafogo and the famous Pão de Açucar, the sugar loaf. Behind the ridge on the right (south) is Copacabana, in the left background Niteroi and in the left foreground the favela shown on Plate 11. *J. Allan Cash Ltd.*

printing and publishing, and high-class clothing. Textiles industries and food processing are still significant.

The restricted site and congestion of the former federal district of Guanabara, and the development of the select south-western suburbs, has forced more recent industrial growth to take place in less central locations. Examples of these new centres are Nova Iguaçu (932 000) and São João de Meriti (366 000) in the northern zone along the shores of Guanabara Bay, and Niteroi (376 000) and São Gonçalo (534 000) on the eastern shores. A number of industrial satellites have also developed along the northern edge of the Baixada Fluminense (see **10.6**), and at the coastal centres such as Santa Cruz. This is the site of Brasil's largest thermal power-station and a semi-integrated steelworks. Angra dos Reis is the site of Brasil's first nuclear power-station, and has a major shipyard. However, there has been little movement towards the Volta Redonda steelworks in the Paraíba valley, which is still underdeveloped.

Duque de Caxias is the single most important industrial centre, as it has Brasil's largest oil refinery with ancillary petrochemicals plants, and a motor vehicles plant now owned by Alfa Romeo.

Rio is also a major centre for two other expanding industries. Guanabara Bay and Angra dos Reis account for five of Brasil's six large shipyards; this industry now ranks first in South America (see Chapter 8). Also, Rio is the major tourist centre of Brasil. Brasil has attracted an increasing number of tourists in the late 1960s and 1970s, the total number increasing from a mere 53 000 in 1959, to 300 000 in the early 1970s and an estimated 2.5 million in 1980. Tourism now brings in to Brasil the equivalent of about £250 million per annum in foreign exchange. Over eighty per cent of tourists spend at least one night in Rio, and the majority also spend most of their holiday within a short distance of the city. The ninety-six hours non-stop carnival in February, famous for its 'samba schools' from the *favelas*, is the major attraction; north of the city lie the old imperial summer resort of Petrópolis, the mountain resorts

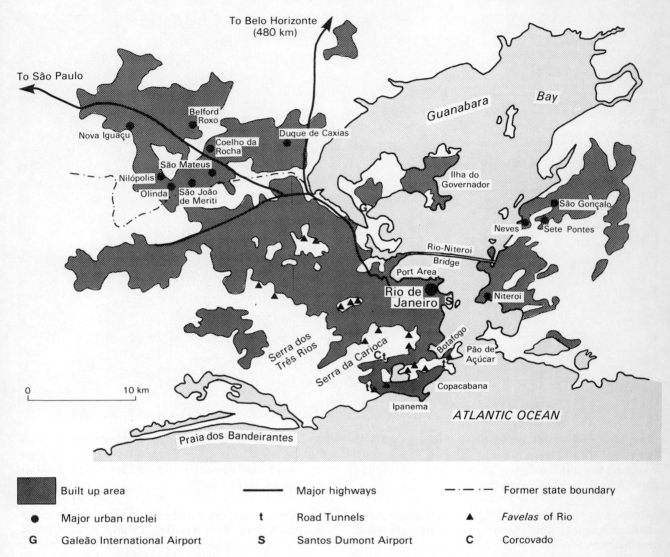

10.6. The City of Rio de Janeiro.

and spas near Pocos de Caldas, and the historic mining towns of Minas Gerais.

Throughout the 1960s and early 1970s it became increasingly apparent that the states of Guanabara (the former federal district) and Rio de Janeiro could not develop under separate administrations. On 15th March 1975 the states were amalgamated to form a new 'super-state' of Rio de Janeiro, which now accounts for about thirteen per cent of Brasil's industrial output, and seventeen per cent of the national income. Thus, the Greater Rio Metropolitan region is now an autonomous administrative unit, and is a much closer rival to Greater São Paulo. The integration of the separate urban/industrial centres on either side of Guanabara Bay was made possible by the construction of the fourteen-kilometre-long bridge which links Rio with Niteroi, the former state capital. The bridge is only one of a growing number of major public works boosted by the 'super-state'. Rio's other major project is the Galeão international airport, being constructed on the Ilha do Governador. This 'supersonic airport' is planned to handle up to ten million passengers per annum by the year 2000.

Belo Horizonte

The regional economy of Minas Gerais is dominated by the *Zona Metalúrgica*, centred on the metropolitan region of Belo Horizonte, which is thus the hub of the major mining state in Brasil. The vast reserves of relatively accessible resources (especially haematite iron ores and manganese), the development of

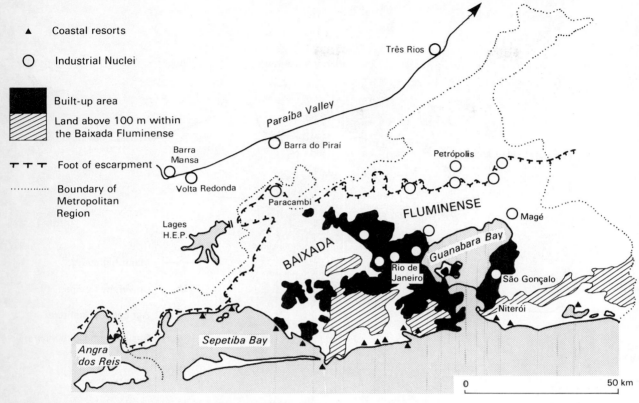

10.7. The Greater Rio de Janeiro Metropolitan Region.

hydro-electricity, the availability of charcoal, and the improved rail and road links have fostered the development of a dynamic manufacturing sector within the *quadrilátero ferrífero*. A comparison of **7.5** and **8.8** shows the close relationship between the mining and smelting centres, and also the transport links which not only allow the export of iron ore, but also supply São Paulo and Rio de Janeiro with ore and semi-finished steel products. The same links have allowed return movements—in particular of imported foreign coking coal, and sub-bituminous coal from the South—via the new ocean terminals.

As has been previously discussed, the mining boom of the eighteenth century laid the foundations for the broad settlement pattern, but the first urban centre—Ouro Prêto—was ill-sited. In the late nineteenth century, plans for a new urban centre and state capital were discussed, and in 1893 the site of this 'City of Minas' was selected. The new city, Belo Horizonte, was inaugurated in 1897. Its centre was planned in a geometric form along similar lines to Washington D.C., the capital of the U.S.A., with a grid street pattern overlaid by broad diagonal avenues focussing at several nodal *praças*. In sharp contrast to the 'colonial' cities, its plan is open and spacious reflecting the environment and culture of

the *Mineiros* (see **10.8**). It proved so attractive that the *sertão mineiro* was rapidly depopulated, forcing the import of foodstuffs from a wide area. However, it was not until the early 1960s that it reached its planned population of 500 000. By 1975 the city's population had reached over 1.5 million, and it was the centre of a large metropolitan region with over 2 million inhabitants (see **10.9**). Thus, Greater Belo Horizonte shared in the nation's industrial 'take-off' and attracted an increased population, despite the massive net migratory loss of the state as a whole.

Both urban and industrial planning have been of a high standard. The urban structure is highly organised into several distinct sectors amongst which are the *Cidade Jardim*, (Garden City), and the administrative and business districts centred on the Praça da Liberdade and Praça de Setembro respectively. In 1941, the *Cidade Industrial* (Industrial City) was created in the municipality of Contagem to the west of the city. It is now the single largest manufacturing centre in the state. In 1970 Contagem and Belo Horizonte together contained over 2 000 industrial establishments, which employed 35 per cent of the state's manufacturing labour force and accounted for 23 per cent of manufacturing output by value. It is significant that mining, though accounting for only 6 per

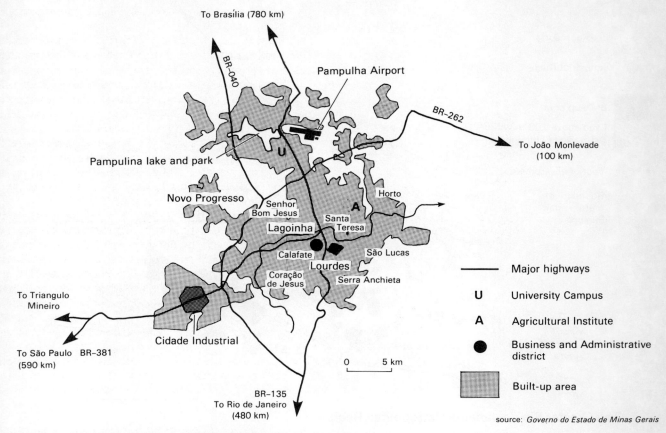

10.8. Belo Horizonte City and the *'Cidade Industrial'*.

cent of Minas Gerais' total industrial output, is the foundation for the steel and other metals industries which account for 37 per cent of the total output of the state's manufactured goods.

However, traditional industries still have a significant role in the metropolitan region, and other centres such as Juiz de Fora, Cataguases, Pocos de Caldas and Uberaba are still dominated by cotton textiles and food-processing. At present, Belo Horizonte is the only industrial centre with a diverse manufacturing sector, and there has been an increasing need for the establishment of new industries, both within the metropolitan region and at other dispersed centres, as much of the state is still predominantly rural and underdeveloped. State intervention has continued, notably in the development of its hydro-electric potential. CEMIG (Central Electricity Commission of Minas Gerais) was established in 1952, and has since raised installed capacity to over 1.5 million kW, of which three-quarters is used by industry. The availability of electricity has proved a major incentive for industrial growth and diversification. Also, the state has formed a company—CDI-MG (Company of Industrial Estates)—which has

established fourteen industrial estates, and is in the process of establishing a further fifteen. The company offers potential investors standardised pre-fabricated multi-purpose buildings, land, and a support structure including financial incentives, planning, research and technology consultants, together with a degree of financial security for infant industries (see **10.9**).

These measures have had considerable recent successes. They include the Fiat motor vehicles plant and the PETROBRAS refinery at Betim; Brasil's first helicopter factory at Itajuba, which assembles components supplied by Aerospatiale of France; and other new metallurgical, engineering, electrical and chemicals industries.

As yet, relatively few major industrial centres have emerged along Belo Horizonte's linkages with Rio and São Paulo, and much of northern Minas Gerais is still underdeveloped. However, meat and rice processing centres have developed at the towns of the *Triangulo Mineiro*, in the north-west of the state adjacent to southern Goiás; and SUDENE has been successful in attracting some firms into the zone north of Montes Claros.

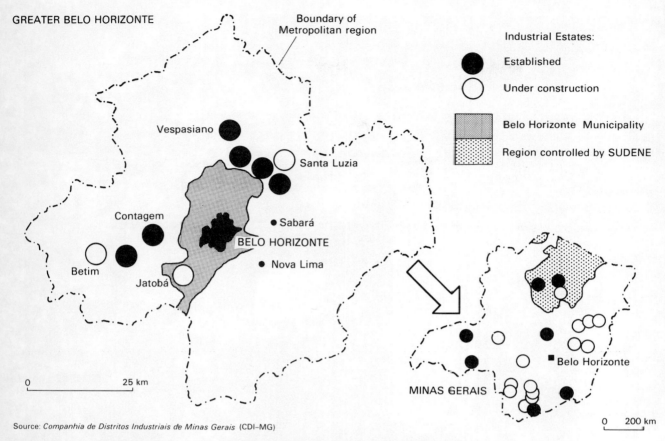

10.9. The Industrial Estates of Greater Belo Horizonte and Minas Gerais.

The three industrial cores of the South-east are spatially separate, and though they form the vertices of an 'industrial triangle', the centre is as underdeveloped as other areas. Only Greater São Paulo has a diverse economic base and well developed industrial satellites as yet. Few major satellites have developed along the linkages which form the edges of the triangle. Thus even within this, the nation's dominant industrial region, industrial development is strongly polarised. It is clear that the phenomenal growth of Greater São Paulo has to some extent slowed the industrialisation process in the other states. Thus it has now reached a level where diseconomies of spatial concentration and political pressure may well force future development into other centres; not only within the South-east, but also in the North-east and South. Thus industrial decentralisation may well have a major role in developing the underdeveloped regions in the future.

The South

The comparatively late colonisation of the region by Europeans has had a major effect on industrial devel-

opment, as it had on agriculture. Not only are the major urban/industrial centres related to the major areas of colonisation, but the manufacturing industries in all but the dominant centres are closely related to agriculture and forestry. The agro-industries account for over 40 per cent of employment and industrial output. Throughout the forested plateau forestry dominates. It employs over half the labour force in a number of small towns, whilst in Rio Grande do Sul food processing is equally dominant. The major manufacturing centres are concentrated in the east in two major regions.

Pôrto Alegre with a population of 1.8 million is the major industrial city. It is part of an industrial belt which includes a number of other centres such as Canoas, Novo Hamburgo, São Leopoldo and Caxias do Sul. In the 1960s it was Brasil's third ranking industrial city, but it has now been overtaken by Belo Horizonte. It is the focus of a number of German colonies whose industries are dominated by woollen textiles, clothing and leather footwear. Despite its name, it is not a major port as the Guaíba estuary on which it is situated can handle ships of only 5 m draught (see **10.10**). Pelotas and Rio Grande, at the mouth of the Lagõa dos Patos,

Plate 30. Pôrto Alegre. This is the major industrial city of the *Sul* region, and the centre of a large productive hinterland. It is not however a major port because of its estuarine site at the head of the 250 km long Lagoa dos Patos. *Hoa-Qui.*

compete for the region's trade and are both important food processing centres. Pôrto Alegre's dominance arises from its role as the hub of the above mentioned towns and a productive agricultural region. Its energy needs are supplied by the São Jeronimo coal mines and by hydro-electric power from the Jacuí river. More recently work has begun on a nuclear power-station to the south of the city. Pôrto Alegre like many of the larger towns has also developed metallurgical, engineering and transport industries to serve the needs of a large agricultural hinterland. As shown in Chapter 8, it also has a rapidly expanding petrochemicals industry based on the production of naptha from the Canoas refinery. Despite its peripheral location and distance from the South-east, its industrial future is assured.

The region's other manufacturing centres lie between Curitiba and Florianopolis, the state capitals of Paraná and Santa Catarina respectively. Whilst Curitiba is the industrial hub of its state, and

its forestry and food processing industries reflect the economy of southern Paraná, Florianopolis—situated on Santa Catarina Island—has no major function other than as state capital, and it accounts for less than 2 per cent of the state's industrial labour force. Curitiba, however, is linked to its port of Paranaguá which exports coffee from northern Paraná, and is also connected to the industrial South-east by road and rail.

Despite the recent diversification of the industries of the South, it is unlikely that the region will increase its share of Brasil's industry significantly in the future, though it has a major role to play in the production and processing of agricultural and forestry products for the domestic market and for export. The region is relatively prosperous as its population is comparatively small and productive. It is likely that the grossly overpopulated and underdeveloped North-east will consume much of the industrial investment outside the South-east.

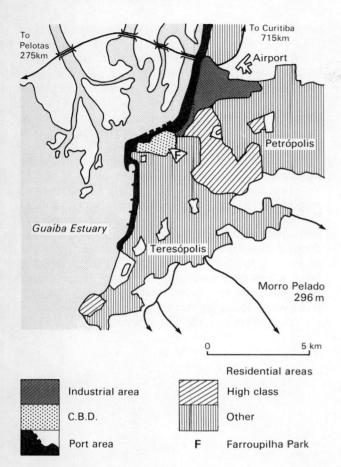

To Pelotas 275km

To Curitiba 715km

Airport

Petrópolis

Guaíba Estuary

Teresópolis

Morro Pelado 296 m

0   5 km

Industrial area

C.B.D.

Port area

Residential areas

High class

Other

F   Farroupilha Park

10.10 The Site and Urban Structure of Pôrto Alegre.

The North-east

From its once dominant position as Brasil's major industrial region, the North-east has gradually lost ground. The most disturbing aspects of its industries is that they have been too closely linked to an agricultural and forestry base which has not grown at the same pace as that of the South-east and South. From 1920 to 1970 the region's share of the nation's industrial labour force fell from 20 per cent to under 10 per cent. From 1960 to 1970 there was a partial recovery of the regional economy, with per capita GDP, manufacturing and services growing at a rate faster than the national average. This growth has continued, largely because of the many industrial, energy, and transport projects financed by SUDENE. However, growth has been greatest in high technology, capital-intensive industries such as petrochemicals, and whilst this has effectively diversified the industrial sector, it has made little contribution to

employment. The North-east is still characterised by many small-scale industrial establishments employing less than a dozen workers. Many of these are craft industries related to local materials, or suppliers of staple food products in 'pre-industrial' settlements.

SUDENE's first success in industrial development came from attempts to modernise the textiles industry, but greater efficiency resulting from re-equipping the industry also caused a loss of 35 per cent of the jobs in the industry from 1960 to 1970. The North-east had some major advantages for industrial development, including a large relatively low paid labour force, and a wide range of raw materials. Also, the Paulo Afonso hydro-electricity projects had given a readily available power base. SUDENE's main task was attracting capital investment. A law passed in 1961 contributed greatly to this. It enabled companies to bank half of their taxes with the *Banco do Nordeste*, and this allowed the bank to finance many new projects. This fund and other financial incentives enabled firms to raise up to 87.5 per cent of investment capital from public sources within the North-east. The expansion of existing plants and construction of new ones effectively diversified manufacturing, as 45 per cent of new investment was in metallurgy, electrical and mechanical engineering, and transport equipment. However, again the overall effect on employment was minimal. J. P. Dickenson (1978) states that, 'the North-east would need between 40 000 and 50 000 new industrial jobs annually to absorb new entrants to the labour market, let alone those already unemployed or under-employed', but that 'the region's labour force increased by only 55 000 over the whole decade (1960–70)'. In 1969 SUDENE recognised the impossibility of substantially increasing the labour force and concentrated its efforts on capital-intensive industries in the major industrial centres. The North-east's three metropolitan regions—Recife, Salvador and Fortaleza—together with the cities of João Pessoa and Natal contain a large proportion of the region's industrial labour force, and have virtually monopolised recent industrial growth. The only inland centres which have benefitted from industrial investment are the market towns of Campina Grande and Feira de Santana.

Like Minas Gerais, the state governments of the North-east attempted to concentrate new developments in industrial estates near the cities, such as Aratu near Salvador and Cabo and Paulista near Recife. Thus, industrial regional development in the North-east has accentuated intra-regional imbalances, and the dominance of the urban/industrial cores.

Recife is Brasil's fourth largest city, although its metropolitan region ranks third in population just above that of Belo Horizonte. The city's reef site, from which it derives its name, divides the built up area into three distinct sectors linked to each other by bridges. Its proximity to Europe, a natural lagoon harbour, and a sugar producing hinterland, enabled it to develop as a major port and commercial centre. At first manufacturing was restricted to the processing of cotton, sugar and vegetable oils. But more recently it has expanded and diversified its industries to include engineering, chemicals, electrical and telecommunications equipment, oil refining and a semi-integrated steel plant.

Salvador, Brasil's sixth ranking city, was Brasil's 'Primocap', the first capital. It is the state capital of Bahia, the largest state in the region, which is about the same size as France. It was at Salvador that Brasil's first oil strike was made in 1939. The region is still the nation's major oil producer, but it is ironic that it has a relatively minor role in petroleum refining. The necessity for massive petroleum imports has made refining strongly market orientated, so that the

South-east has seven of Brasil's refineries and about ninety per cent of refining capacity. However, the North-east, and in particular Salvador, has increased its share of the rapidly expanding petrochemicals industry since 1972 when work started on the Camaçari complex north of Salvador (see **10.11** and Chapter 8). The region produces a number of raw materials other than petroleum and natural gas, such as marine salt, halite, and sugar alcohol; but petrochemicals and steel still form the region's only heavy industries.

The decision by the Bahia state government to respond to SUDENE's incentives and to establish the *Centro Industrial de Aratu* within Salvador's metropolitan region, has had a major effect on industrial development. The CIA has been carefully planned into distinctive sectors. There is a naval base, a new port area, and zones for commerce and light, medium and heavy industries. Aratu is supplied with electricity from the Paulo Afonso hydro-electric complex on the São Francisco river; it is the

Plate 31. Salvador. This was Brasil's first capital. After many years of economic stagnation, it is now a rapidly expanding 'growth pole'. This view shows the market and harbour in the foreground, and in the background, the high or *alta* section above the scarp. ***Hoa-Qui.***

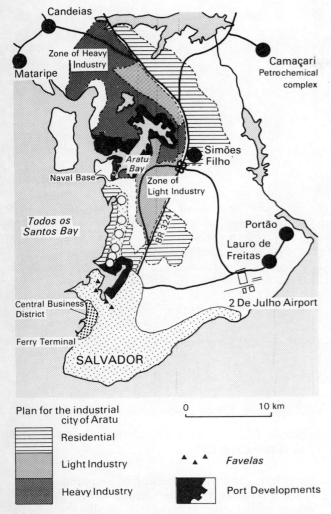

Plan for the industrial
city of Aratu

▤ Residential

▨ Light Industry

▦ Heavy Industry

0   10 km

▲ ▲
▲   *Favelas*

◼ Port Developments

10.11 The Site of Salvador, Aratu and Camaçari.

state's major rail focus; and it has new highway links with the major urban centres of the region, and with those of the South-east. The planning of the industrial centre allowed for the establishment of about 120 separate projects; by 1970 it had attracted over 50, including a cement works, an aluminium cable factory run by ALCAN (a Canadian corporation), the Sibra steel works, and a number of other factories producing bus chassis, spark-plugs, carbon black, laminated timber, plastics, special alloys, and pressed wood panels. Associated with the industrial developments are well planned standardised housing developments. The houses are provided with full services and are sold on easy terms to the workers.

The lower rates of industrial growth in the North-east since 1970 reflect the failure of regional development programmes to combat the dominance of the South-east, but this cannot detract from the

significant advances achieved. The North-east has experienced an absolute increase in industrial output and employment. From 1960 to 1970, the poorest 40 per cent of the population raised their share of the region's income from 8.9 per cent to 9.4 per cent, and regional unemployment fell from 18.6 per cent to 12.3 per cent as compared with a national average from 14.7 per cent to 9.7 per cent.

Amazonia and the Central-west

Industrial development in the Central-west and Amazonia is on an entirely different scale to the rest of the country. The high rates of industrial growth are deceiving as there is a low industrial base. Also, many industrial developments receiving support from SUDAM and SUDECO are related to mining activities rather than to manufacturing. Within the entire area of these regions—64 per cent of Brasil's area—there is only one metropolitan region, Belém. Its main function is as an entrepôt for the riverside settlements of the Amazon system, exporting forest products, jute, cocoa, and cotton, and importing fuels and manufactured goods. Its manufacturing industries are dominated by food processing and textiles, but the city now also has a steelworks.

Manaus is strategically situated at the centre of the Amazon basin, but until the mid-1950s was a shadow of its former self during the years of the rubber boom. It was selected as a priority area in 1957 when its free trade zone was established. This consists of a commercial nucleus of bonded warehouses and processing industries. It had little effect until 1967 when SUFRAMA was established (The Superintendency for the Manaus Free Trade Zone). Manaus was exempted from federal taxes and import duties, and this stimulated investment in the electronics industry and tourism. From 1967 to 1970 the built-up area increased sevenfold and the construction industry became of major importance. By 1972, SUFRAMA had approved eighty major industrial projects. In addition to an integrated steelworks and oil refinery there are now a great variety of industries including ship-building, jewellery, clocks and watches, toys, optical instruments, fishing equipment, cold storage and refrigeration equipment, chemicals, and new food, hides and textiles processing plants. Support for industry has been staggering, including measures such as direct long-term financing of projects by providing from 40 per cent to 75 per cent of the total investment; complete exemption from income, municipal, and other taxes; and the provision of prepared industrial sites with services at minimal cost.

Plate 32. The waterfront district of Manaus on the Rio Negro. Manaus is over 1500 km from the mouth of the Amazon, and at the centre of the *Norte* region.   ***J. Allan Cash Ltd.***

Thus Manaus, situated 1 500 km from the sea, is now experiencing a boom far in excess of that of the nineteenth century, and one which is likely to prove of considerable importance to the region. One of the major developments resulting from the combined attractions of the 'virgin' forest and the free trade area, has been the phenomenal development of Manaus as a tourist centre. Manaus has an international airport which now brings thousands to shop at the numerous duty-free shops which sell a variety of luxury articles from Brasil and abroad, and in particular from Japan and the Far-East. Tourism is now much more highly organised, and Manaus has become a staging post to and from Rio and other developing tourist centres.

The Central-west still suffers from remoteness and relatively expensive transport hauls to the South-east. Industrial development is based mainly on the exploitation of mineral bodies and the traditional food processing industries of the main urban centres of Goiânia, Anápolis, Cuiabá and Campo Grande. In 1970 the Federal District had just over 400 industrial establishments of all types and sizes, the most important being food processing, printing and publishing, and the processing of non-metallic minerals. It is unlikely that the Central-west will develop major manufacturing industries in the foreseeable future.

In isolation the projects outlined above are undoubtedly successful, but in comparison with the industrial might of the South-east they are relatively minor. The Second National Development Plan estimated that industrial growth in the North-east would have to average over 15 per cent per annum from 1975 to 1979 to give the region sufficient industrial employment to close the poverty gap; yet the locational advantage still lies in the South-east, and in particular within the 'industrial triangle' formed by São Paulo, Rio de Janeiro and Belo Horizonte. It is possible that the North-east will secure a large Japanese motor vehicles plant, but it is clear that industrial employment will only be increased to a significant level by investment in traditional and labour-intensive industries, as well as in the 'new' industries.

It could well be argued that industrial decentralisation into the underdeveloped regions in Brasil is an economic luxury, but that it is also a political and social necessity.

Conclusion: Brasil 'land of the future?'

Brasil has long been regarded as a country of enormous potential. The term 'potential' reflects that which is capable of being developed, and also that which is likely to be achieved in the future. A *cariocan* proverb states that 'Brasil is the land of the future, and always will be'. Whilst it is relatively easy to substantiate such a cynical view of Brasilian development, in that Brasil still has many characteristics common to the underdeveloped world, the statement has a more fundamental truth. All countries have alternative futures because the future is not predetermined. Some underdeveloped countries have few possibilities for future development, because of a narrow resource base. Brasil, however, has a wide range of economic, social and political options. Throughout the text the reader has been introduced to a wide range of problems, numerous examples of Brasil's rapid development in recent years, and also the effects of government policies on development.

It is clear that Brasilians have an enormous appetite for material advancement and that government policies have been directed towards maximising economic growth, and achieving 'first world' economic status by the year 2000. Throughout the last forty years the military have maintained a major interest in politics and therefore in policies. Since 1964 they have been the major factor in perpetuating the dominance of the 'executive', and centralised authority and decision-making. They consider that Brasil's future destiny is not only that of a major economic power, but also that of an increasingly influential political power.

Brasil has already increased its international political status considerably through membership of the United Nations organisations, the Organisation of American States, the Latin American Free Trade Association (LAFTA), and more recently the *Sistema Economico Latinamericano*. It has also been strengthened by trade links with many countries with different levels of development, and with varying political ideologies. In 1980 LAFTA was replaced by LAIA (The Latin American Integration Association) reflecting the new mechanisms adopted to encourage intra-continental trade, such as new bilateral or multilateral agreements, preferential trade for LAIA members, and greater concessions to its least developed members such as Bolivia, Ecuador and Paraguay. SELA (the Latin American Economic System), established in 1975, is a body of twenty-five member states from Latin America (including Cuba) which is primarily a vehicle for economic consultation and co-operation, but excludes U.S.A. involvement.

Brasil's increasingly influential role in the Americas is exemplified by the diplomatic optimism expressed by Henry Kissinger, the then United States Secretary of State, on his visit to Brasil in 1976:

'Brasil, emerging on the world scene, stands astride the great international challenge of our time; the gap between the developed and the developing worlds. Brasil which itself is both industrial and developing, mirrors the world in its vastness, diversity and potential. Brasil has brought to the great task of economic and social advance, to the uplifting of its people, not only its staggering resources, but its boundless energy'.

Throughout its history, Brasil has occupied an unique position in the developing world. The combined effects of an infusion of diverse cultures, rapid population growth, rapid economic growth, contrasting rates of regional development, and the transformation to a predominantly urban society, have resulted in the emergence of a distinctive nation state with marked internal contrasts.

The Brasilian 'economic miracle' is not only the result of the increasing mobilisation of indigenous resources. It has relied heavily on the application of 'first world' technologies, foreign investment and loans, and also on the participation of the multi-national corporations. Whilst Brasil has been able to maintain majority control over most public and private ventures involving partnership with the multi-nationals, it is clear that these have had a considerable influence in directing the course of economic development, as is the case in many countries. In the past Brasil's economy had become increasingly tied to those of the advanced countries, especially the United States of America—a dependence Brasil shared with most Latin American countries. In many ways these countries competed to supply the needs of the advanced countries, so that there was a reluctance by Brasil and others to move towards a more integrated and interdependent economic community in Latin America. However, as Brasil's economy has become increasingly diversified in the 1960s and 1970s, so have trading links with other developing countries become more important. When LAFTA was established in 1960, only six per cent of Brasil's exports were to member countries; by 1969 the proportion had increased to eleven per cent. However, this increase is not as dramatic as it appears, because it was mainly the result of strengthened trading links with its major trading partners of Argentina and Mexico. By 1978 the figure was still only twelve per cent. The most significant change has been the development of new export markets in underdeveloped countries in Africa and Asia, and the reduced dependence on the U.S.A.

These trends emphasise not only Brasil's relatively advanced stage of economic development within the developing world, but also, its leading role in the development of 'tropical' technologies. Many state-owned, mixed economy, and private Brasilian companies are becoming increasingly involved in the development of a number of underdeveloped countries.

In its early stages of economic development Brasil had to rely on foreign participation; but more recently Brasil has had to find answers to problems not faced by the advanced countries. These are especially problems related to the development of tropical agriculture, the processing of certain minerals, the development of alternative energy sources, and also in the manufacturing sector. Thus the economy is becoming increasingly integrated within a much wider world economy than was previously the case. There is no doubt that the considerable advances in alternative energy, and especially in the alcohol programme, will be of considerable benefit. Brasil has been forced into developing alternative sources of energy by its low proven reserves of fossils fuels, and the need to import petroleum from the Middle East. In contrast, many advanced countries have yet to commit themselves to developing similar alternatives or substitutes; consequently Brasil could well be in a relatively strong position when the world energy crisis deepens, as the world's petroleum reserves become depleted in the not too distant future.

As has been previously shown, Brasil's economic development has exaggerated, and has contributed directly to, the marked regional imbalances within the country, mainly as the result of the phenomenal growth of the industries and commercial agriculture in the South-east region. Official concern regarding this imbalance was expressed in the 1946 constitition, but the spatial concentration of industrial growth was considered advantageous throughout the 1950s and 1960s. However, more recently there has been a realisation that on the one hand the potential of the Central-west and Amazonia was virtually untapped, and that the South-east had become too dominant. Whilst the South had devel-

oped in line with the needs of its regional population, the North-east had experienced a relative and absolute decline because of its very large population and stagnant economy.

In 1970 the government launched the Programme for National Integration, which attempted to initiate the development of the interior and north by establishing highways which would promote the occupation of these areas by migrants from the North-east. Previously there had been a strong migratory flow from the North-east to the South-east. The First National Development Plan (I PND) launched in 1971, established regional growth centres, and special programmes to support this process. The Second National Development Plan (II PND, 1975–79) strengthened the existing regional development agencies, created others, and also completed the regional development strategy by defining the growth poles. It also recognised the need for the South-east to provide much of the drive necessary for the development of the other regions, by the decentralisation of economic activity, and by increasing capital investment. The plan contained the first major attempt to achieve a national urban development policy, and also set out detailed targets for social as well as economic and regional development. However, many of these targets were not reached, partly because of the energy crisis, and partly because many were too ambitious.

The Third National Development Plan (III PND, 1980–85) reinforces previous objectives, but is very different in character. It recognises that the uncertainties imposed by the world recession necessitate a flexible planning strategy, 'to fulfil the greatest object of creating a democratic and developed society' and to mobilise the 'country's great potentialities'. It states that the 'composite objective' is 'the formation of a developed and free society, benefiting all Brasilians, within the shortest period of time'. In its major objectives it stresses the need for rapid economic growth, improving standards of living, greater social justice, the need for increased political liberties, and for a policy of income redistribution in favour of the poor and low income groups. In other areas it emphasises the need to 'reduce urban hypergrowth' and to achieve a 'non-predatory occupation of the Amazon'. It also points to the need to stimulate rural areas through the development of agriculture and especially cattle rearing.

Thus the plan reflects the growing demands for political liberalisation, greater social jusice and higher standards of living, for the majority of Brasilians. Throughout the plan frequent reference is made to the need for controlling inflation which has the effect of undermining all attemps to improve the well being of the majority of Brasilians.

The plan does not contain policies for controlling population growth, but regards Brasil as having a considerable advantage over many other countries in that it has the resources and means for increasing food production, energy, and economic development. This may prove to be a mistaken view. During the 1970s many have come to believe that in the future mankind will have to discard the view that economic growth is the 'panacea', and recognise that there are limits to economic growth.

It is appropriate to conclude with a brief comment on the Club of Rome's researches into the 'Predicament of Mankind', published in 1970 as *'The Limits To Growth'*. The Club of Rome was originally an informal group of thirty individuals from ten countries, including scientists, educators, economists, humanists, industrialists and others, though it has since expanded considerably. In 1970 it began its 'Predicament of Mankind' study at the Massachusetts Institute of Technology (U.S.A.). It first defined the five basic factors that 'determine, and therefore, ultimately limit, growth on this planet—population, agricultural production, natural resources, industrial production, and pollution'. The project raises many crucial issues, and though these are related to the 'world system', they clearly have a relevance to all the countries which together form this world system.

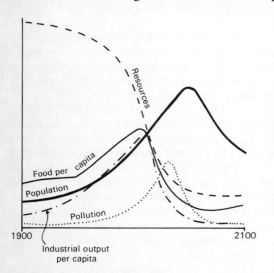

Source: simplifield from fig. 35 *The Limits To Growth* (1970)

iii. The Limits to Growth, World Model Standard Run.

The project gathered considerable data on the five factors outlined above for the period 1900 to 1970, and demonstrated that the growth of these factors was proceeding at an 'exponential' rate, that is at a constant rate of increase. This means for example that world population is increasing at an annual rate of about 2.1 per cent, so that the world population is doubling every 33 years. In their 'standard run' they assumed that there would be no major change in the physical, economic, or social relationships that have historically governed the development of the world system. They explain their results shown by the graph, as follows:

'Food, industrial output and population grow exponentially until the rapidly diminishing resource base forces a slow down in industrial growth. Because of the natural delays in the system, both population and pollution continue to increase for some time after the peak of industrialisation. Population growth is finally halted by a rise in the death rate due to decreased food and medical services'.

They state that if these conditions apply, then 'population and industrial growth will certainly stop within the next century at the latest', and conclude that every effort should be made to 'begin a controlled, orderly transition from growth to global equilibrium'. They regard a stable population as being vital in achieving 'global equilibrium.'

Relating these studies to Brasil's future, it becomes clear that three factors are particularly important—population growth, resources, and economic growth. If the number of Brasilians continues to increase exponentially as it has in the past, then there would be twice as many Brasilians by the year 2030. However, Brasil's potential resources have always been emphasised in the past. The Club of Rome carried out other 'runs', one of which assumed that the world had double the amount of resources. They concluded that in this case increased industrialisation resulted in an 'overloading of the natural absorptive capacity of the environment', that the death rate would rise abruptly because of pollution and from lack of food, and that the additional resources would become rapidly depleted 'simply because a few more years of exponential growth in industry are sufficient to consume those extra resorces'.

Even if these conclusions are pessimistic and exaggerated, it is still clear that population control is vital, and that vast resources merely delay an inevitable collapse if economic growth continues. Thus Brasil may have an advantage over many countries, as stated in the Third National Development Plan, but this advantage is only a short-term advantage.

Brasil is the land of the future, but what type of future will Brasilians achieve?

Bibliography

This concise bibliography includes relatively recent texts, articles, papers and statistical sources. The reader is referred to the most recent texts for a more extensive bibliography. All sources quoted in the text are listed below.

Askew, G. P., et al., 'Soil landscapes in the northern Mato Grosso', *Geographical Journal*, vol. 136, Pt. 2, 1970.

Baer, W., *Industrialization and Economic Development in Brazil* (Yale Univ. Press) 1975.

Bergsman, J., *Brazil: Industrialization and Trade Policies* (Oxford University Press) 1970.

BOLSA—*Bank of London and South America Review*, monthly.

Brazilian Embassy, London. Publications:
No. 3 *The Brazilian Development Model: an Experiment in Growth*, 1972.
No. 5 *Social Aspects of Brazilian Economic Development*, 1974.
No. 10 *Amazonia*, 1976.
No. 11 *Agriculture, Mining and Oil in Brazil*, 1976.
No. 12 *Transport and Telecommunications in Brazil*, 1976.
No. 13 *Brazil on the March* (II), 1976.
No. 14 *Brazil: A Geography*, 1976.
No. 15 *Brazil's Energy and Heavy Industry*. 1977.

Brooks, E. et al., *Tribes of the Amazon Basin in Brazil*. (C. Knight) 1972.

Brooks, E., 'Twilight of the Brazilian Tribes', *Geographical Magazine*, vol. XLV, no. 4, 1973.

Brown, E. H. et al., 'Geographical research on the Royal Society/Royal Geographical Society's expedition to the eastern Mato Grosso, Brazil', *Geographical Journal*, vol. 136, Pt. 3, 1970.

Butland, G. J., *South America* (Longmans) 1973.

Camacho, G., *Latin America: a Short History* (Allen Lane) 1973.

Cole, J. P., *Latin America: An Economic and Social Geography* (Butterworth) 1975.

Cole, M. M., 'Cerrado, Caatinga and Pantanal: distribution and origin of the savana vegetation of Brazil', *Geographical Journal.*, vol. 126, Pt. 2, 1960.

Cunha, Euclides da, *Rebellion in the Backlands* (translation of *Os Sertões*) (University of Chicago Press) 1977.

Cunningham, S. M., 'Planning Brazilian Regional Development During the 1970s', *Geography*, vol. 61, 1976.

Dean, W., *The Industrialisation of São Paulo: 1850–1945* (University of Texas Press) 1970.

Dickenson, J. P., 'The Iron and Steel Industry in Minas Gerais', in *Liverpool Essays in Geography: a Jubilee Collection*. Steel, R. W., and Lawton, R. (Eds.) 1967.

Dickenson, J. P., 'Industrial Estates in Brazil', *Geography*, vol. 55, 1970.

Dickenson, J. P., *Brazil: Studies in Industrial Geography* (Dawson. Westview) 1978.

Dozier, C. L., 'Northern Paraná, Brazil: An Example of Organised Regional Development', *Geographical Review*, vol. 46, 1956.

Evenson, N., *Two Brazilian Capitals: Architecture and Urbanism in Rio de Janeiro and Brasília* (Yale University Press) 1973.

Fodor's Guide to South America (Hodder and Stoughton) annual.

Forde, C. D., *Habitat, Economy and Society* (University Paperbacks, Methuen) 1964, see Chapter 9, 'The Boro of the Western Amazon Forest'.

Freyre, Gilberto, *The Mansions and the Shanties* (A. A. Knopf) 1963.

Freyre, Gilberto, *The Masters and the Slaves* (A. A. Knopf) 1963.

Freyre, Gilberto, *Order and Progress* (A. A. Knopf) 1970.

Friese, F. W., 'The calamities zones of North East Brazil', *Geographical Review*, 1938.

Furtado, C., *The Economic Growth of Brazil: A survey from colonial to modern times* (University of California Press) 1971.

Galloway, J. H., 'Brazil', in *Latin America: Geographical Perspectives*, Blakemore, H., and Smith, C. T. (Eds.) (Methuen) 1974.

Gauthier, H. L., 'Transportation and the Growth of the São Paulo Economy, *Journal of Regional Science*, vol. 18, 1968.

Gilbert, A., *Latin American Development: a Geographical Perspective* (Penguin) 1974.

Goodland, R., *The Savanna Controversy: Background Information on the Brazilian Cerrado Vegetation* (McGill University) 1970.

Goodland, R. J. A., and Irwin, H. S., *Amazon Jungle: Green Hell to Red Desert?: an Ecological Discussion of the Environmental Impact of the Highway Construction Program in the Amazon Basin* (Elsevier Scientific Publishing Co.) 1975.

Gunther, J., *Inside South America* (Greenwood Press) 1976.

Hall, A. L., *Drought and Irrigation in North-East Brazil* (Cambridge University Press) 1978.

Hanbury-Tenison, R., *A Question of Survival for the Indian of Brazil* (Angus and Robertson) 1973.

Henshall, J. D., and Momsen, R. P., *A Geography of Brazilian Development* (G. Bell) 1975.

Ianni, O., *Crisis in Brazil* (Columbia University Press) 1970.

Instituto Brasileiro de Geografia e Estatistica, Rio de Janeiro. Publications:
Anuario Estatistico do Brasil (statistical yearbook).
Atlas Nacional do Brasil, 1966.
Divisão do Brasil em Micro-Regiões Homogeneas, 1968.
Divisão do Brasil em Regiões Funcionais Urbanas.
Geografia do Brasil (5 vols.) 1977.
The Second National Development Plan (II PND, 1975–79). 1974.

Instituto Brasileiro de Siderurgica, *Anuario Estatistico* (statistical yearbook) 1975.

Instituto Brasileiro do Cafe, (Gerca) 1974:
Yearbook.
Essays on coffee and economic development (1973).

James, Preston E., 'Coffee lands in Southeastern Brazil', *Geographical Review*, vol. 22, 1932.

James, Preston E., 'Trends in Brazilian Agricultural Development', *Geographical Review*, vol. 43, 1953.

James, Preston E., 'The Geomorphology of Eastern Brazil: as interpreted by Lester C. King, *Geographical Review*, vol. 49, 1959.

James, Preston E., and Faissol, S., 'Problem of Brazil's capital city', *Geographical Review*, vol. 46, 1956.

James, Preston E., *Latin America* (Cassell) 1959.

Katzman, M. T., *Cities and Frontiers in Brazil: Regional Dimensions of Economic Development* (Harvard University Press) 1977.

Keeble, D. E., 'Models of Economic Development', in *Socio-Economic Models in Geography*, Chorley, R. J., and Haggett, P. (University Paperbacks, Methuem) 1969.

Marshall, A., *Brazil* (Thames and Hudson) 1966.

Maybury-Lewis, D., *The Savage and the Innocent* (World Publishing Co./Evans) 1965.

Meadows, D. H., Meadows, D. L., Randers, J., and Behrens, W. W., *The Limits to Growth* (Pan) 1974.

Ministry of Mines and Energy (Brasil), *National Energy Balance*, 1978.

Ministry of External Relations (Brasília) *Brazil: Trade and Industry*, monthly magazine.

Momsen, R. P., *Brazil: A Giant Stirs* (D. van Nostrand) 1968.

Money, D. C., *South America* (University Tutorial Press) sixth edition 1976.

Mountjoy, A. B. (Ed.) *Developing the Underdeveloped Countries* (Papermac, Macmillan) 1971.

Niedergang, M., *The Twenty Latin Americas* (2 vols.) (The Pelican Latin America history) 1971.

Odell, P. R., and Preston, D. A., *Economies and Societies in Latin America*: A Geographical Interpretation (John Wiley & Sons) 1978.

Passos, J. dos, *Brazil on the Move* (Sidgwick and Jackson) 1963.

Poppino, R., *Brazil, the land and people* (Oxford University Press, New York) 1968.

Prado, C., *The Colonial Background to Modern Brazil* (University of California Press) 1970.

Robinson, H., *Latin America* (Macdonald and Evans) 1977.

Robock, S. H., *Brazil's Developing Northeast* (Washington) 1963.

Robock, S. H., *Brazil: a Study in Development and Progress* (Lexington) 1976.

Roett, R. *The Politics of Foreign Aid in the Brazilian Northeast*, (Vanderbilt U.P.) 1972

Sahota, G. S., 'An Economic analysis of internal migration in Brazil', *Journal of Political Economy*, 1968.

Saunders, J. (Ed.) *Modern Brazil: New Patterns of Development* (University of Florida Press) 1971.

Smith, T. Lynn, *Brazil: Peoples and Institutions* (Louisianna State University Press), 1973.

Sternberg, H. O'Reilly, *The Amazon River of Brazil* (Steiner, Weisbaden) 1975.

SUDAM, *Amazonica: New Universe* (Ministry of the Interior, Brazil)

SUDENE, *Informa* (periodical).

Taaffe, E. J., Morrill, R. L., and Gould, P. R., 'Transport Expansion in Underdeveloped Countries', *Geographical Review*, vol. 53, 1963.

Taylor, J. A., 'Farming in Southern Brazil', *Geographical Magazine*, 1957.

Taylor, J. A., 'New Brazilians set the pace in Paraná', *Geographical Magazine*, 1972.

Taylor, J. A., 'Current Problems in Brazilian coffee production', *Geografisch Tijdschrift*, vol. 8, 1974.

Trewartha, G. T., *The Earth's Problem Climates* (Methuen) 1966.

Veliz, C. (Ed.) *Obstacles to Change in Latin America* (Oxford University Press, New York) 1969.

Veliz, C., *The Politics of Conformity in Latin America* (Oxford University Press, New York) 1971.

Wagley, C., *An Introduction to Brazil* (Columbia University Press) 1963.

Webb, R. K., *The Changing Face of North East Brazil* (Columbia University Press) 1974.

Wellington, R. A., *The Brazilians: how they live and work* (David and Charles) 1974.

Glossary of Brasilian Terms, Their Pronunciation and Meaning

Note that K, W and Y are rarely used, as there are other similar sounds. The guide to pronunciation is for Brasilian Portuguese. The symbols used in the guide are as follows:

˘ above a letter; as the 'a' in China, 'e' in broken.
′ is found after the syllable which is stressed.
italic type signifies a nasal sound.

Açude (a-soodee) a small flooded area behind a weir or dam.

Agreste (a-greshtĕ) the transitional zone of polyculture with reliable rainfall in the North-east.

Agregado (a-gre-gah doo) a tenant farmer or servant.

Alvará (al-vă-rah′) a decree.

Amarelo (ă-mă-re′loo) yellow, or yellow skinned person.

Angra (an′gră) an inlet or bay.

Baixada (bў′shă-dă) lowland.

Bandeirante (ban-day-ee-rant′) a pioneer, literally 'flag bearer'.

Belo Horizonte (be loo oo-ree-zontee) beautiful horizon (place name).

Branco (bran′koo) white or white man.

Brasil (Bră-zeel) Brasil or Brazil.

Brejo (bre′zhoo) a marsh

Caatinga (Kah-teen-gă) semi-arid scrub vegetation, literally 'white bush'.

Caboclo (kă-boo-kloo) a subsistence backlands farmer.

Café (kă-fé) coffee.

Cafèzal (kă-fe-zal′) a coffee plantation.

Cafuso (kă-foo′zoo) a person of mixed Amerindian and African descent.

Campanha (kam-pă′nyă) the southern grassland region.

Campinas (kam-pee′năs) open grasslands (place name).

Campo (kam′poo) grassland.

Candango (kan-dan-goo) a construction worker.

Capitania (Kă-pee-tă-nee-ă) a captaincy, territory granted to wealthy Portuguese in the early sixteenth century.

Carioca (kă-ree-o′kă) an inhabitant of Rio de Janeiro, literally 'white man's home' (Amerindian term).

Casa Grande (kah′ză grand-ĕ) literally 'large house', the plantation owner's mansion.

Centro-Oeste (sen′troo oestĕ) The Central-west region.

Cerrado (sĕ-rah′doo) Brasil's tropical 'savanna' grasslands.

Chapada (shah′pă-dă) a high plain, of more limited extent than a planalto.

Charqueada (shar-ké-ă-dah) a meat drying factory.

Cidade (see-dahd-ee) city.

Colono (koo-loh′noo) a colonist or settler.

Convivência (kon-vee-ven-see-ă) living together, racial harmony.

Corcovado (koor-koo-vah′-doo) the granite mountain at Rio de Janeiro, literally 'hunchbacked'.

Cruzeiro (kroo-zay′ee-roo) Brasil's unit of currency.

Do (doo) masc. **Da** (dă) fem. of the, or from the.

De (dĕ) of, from with or by.

Derrubar (dĕ-roo-bar′) to destroy, cut down.

Desenvolvida (dĕ-zen-vohl-vee-dă) developed (adj.).

Engenho (en-zhĕ′nyoo) Old fashioned mill, also used for the plantation itself e.g. **Engenho de Açucar**, sugar mill or sugar plantation.

Erva mate (air′vă mahtĕ) Paraguayan tea (Ilex paraguayensis).

Espigoẽs (ish-pee-goengsh) A mountain ridge or river divide.

Estado Novo (ish-tah′doo noh′voo) Getulio Vargas' New State, a term still in general use.

Estância (ish-tanśee-ă) a large ranch, most commonly used in southern Brasil.

Favela (fă-ve′lă) a shanty town.

Fazenda (fă-zen′dă) a large farm, plantation, or ranch.

Fazendeiro (fă-zen-day′ee-roo) the owner of a fazenda.

Feira (fay′ee-ră) a weekly fair, public market, or market town.

Flagellados (flă-zhĕ-lah-doos) literally the 'beatenones', the drought refugees.

Friagem (free-an-sh*eng*) the cold winds (waves) which bring killing frosts in southern Brasil.

Frigorifico (free-goo-ree-′fee-koo) a refrigeration factory.

Galeria (gă-lĕ-ree'ă) a gallery or tunnel.

Garimpeiros (gar-eem-pĕ-ee-roos) small-scale mining prospectors.

Gaúcho (gă-oo-choo) the cowboy of southern Brasil.

Grandes Regioēs (gran-days rĕ-zhee-oengsh) major regions.

Guanabara (gwă-nă-bă-ră) literally 'bay like the sea' (Amerindian word).

Igapó (eeg-ă-poo) swamp forest resulting from frequent flooding.

Ilha (ee'lyă) island.

Indio (een'dee-oo) indian, term used for Brasilian Amerindian.

Inverno (een-vair'noo) winter.

Jangada (zhan-gah'dă) raft.

Jardim (zhăr-dee'm) garden.

Juiz de Fora (zhoo-ees'h dĕ fo'ră) a colonial magistrate (place name).

Latifúndio (lă-tee-foon-dee-oo) the system of farming by large holdings, also reflects the society.

Lavouras secas (lă-voh'ras sĕ-kas) crops used in 'dry farming'.

Lavrador (lav-ră-dohŕ) a farmer or farm labourer.

Linha (lee'nyă) line.

Macumba (mă'koom-bă) the 'white' voodoo religion

Mameluco (mă-mel-oo-koo) a person of mixed European and Amerindian descent.

Mandioca (man-dee-o'kă) manioc or cassava (Manihot utilissima).

Mangue (man'gĕ) mangrove swamp.

Marcha Para O Oeste (mar'shă pă'ră oo oestĕ) the 'March to the West', occupation of the interior.

Massapé (mă-să-pe) the fertile heavy black clay soils of the North-east coastlands.

Mata (ma'tă) forest.

Meridional (mĕ-ree-dee-oo-na'l) southern, e.g. *Planalto Meridional*, Southern Plateau.

Minas (mee'năs) mines.

Minas Gerais (mee'năs zhe-ră'ees) Literally 'general mines' (place name).

Mineiro (mee-nay'ee-roo) an inhabitant of Minas Gerais.

Minifundio (mee-nee-foon-dee-oo) the system of farming by small holdings, also reflects the society.

Minuano (mee-noo-ă'noo) the cold dry south-westerly wind in southern Brasil.

Morro (moh'roo) hill.

Municipio (moo-nee-see'pee-oo) an urban municipality.

Natal (nă-tal') Christmas, birthday (place name).

Negro (nay'groo) Negro, black.

Nisei (nee-sii) a person of mixed Japanese and European/Brasilian descent.

Nordeste (nor-deshtĕ) North-east.

Nordestino (nor-desht-ee-noo) an inhabitant of the North-east region.

Norte (nort'ĕ) north, the North region corresponding to Amazonia.

Nova (no'vă) **Novo** (noh'voo) new.

Oceano (oh-see-ă'noo) ocean.

Oceano Atlantico (oh-see-a noo at-lăn-tee-koo) Atlantic Ocean.

Oeste (oestĕ) west.

'Ordem E Progresso' (or'den e proo-gre'soo) 'Order and Progress', the Brasilian national motto.

Ouro (oh-roo) gold.

Ouro Prêto (oh-roo pray'too) black gold (place name).

Padroēs (pă-droengsh) 'tree guides' used by the Amerindian.

Pantanal (pan'ta-nal) the swamplands of Mato Grosso do Sul.

Paraná (pă-ră-nă) a river distributary (place name).

Pardo (par'doo) brown. Census term including mameluco, cafuso and Amerindian.

Pastoril (pash-tohr-eel) pastoral.

Pau (pow) wood. **Pau-brasil**, Brasil wood.

Paulista (powl-ish-tă) inhabitant of São Paulo.

Pé da Serra (pe dă se'ră) piedmont or foothills.

Pernambuco (pair-nam-boo-koo) (place name).

Pico (pee'koo) mountain peak.

Pinheiras (pee-nyay'ee-ras) the region of the pine forests in southern Brasil.

Planalto (plă-nal'too) high plain or plateau.

Poligono das secas (poo-lee-gon'oo dăs se'kăs) the 'drought polygon' of the North-east region.

Povo (poh'voo) the common people.

Povação (poo-voo-ă-saong) village.

Pôrto Alegre (pohr'too ă-le'grĕ) literally 'lively' port or haven (place name).

Pororoca (poh'roh-re'ka) the bore or tidal wave experienced on the Amazon river.

Praça (prah'să) square or plaza.

Prêto (pray'too) black.

Quadrilátero Ferrífero (kwă-dree-la-tair'oo fĕ-ree-fĕ-roo) the 'Iron Quadrilateral' of Minas Gerais.
Queimar (kay-ee-mar') to burn.

Rapadura (ră-pă-doo-ră) brown sugar from which the molasses has not been removed.
Recôncavo (rĕ-kon-kă-voo) the structural basin and fertile land near Salvador.
Recife (rĕ-seefĕ) reef (place name).
Ribeiro (ree-bay'ee-roo) brook or stream.
Rio de Janeiro (ree'oo dĕ zha-nay'ee-roo) literally 'River of January' (place name).
'Rio Mar' (ree'oo mar) 'sea river' a term applied to the Amazon river.
Rios do açúcar (ree'oos doo ă-soo'kar) the 'sugar rivers', rivers in the North-east used for transporting sugar.
Roça (ro'să) a forest clearing, or the process of clearing forest.
Roçeiro (roo-say'ee-roo) a subsistence farmer who cultivates a roça.
Rodovia Perimetral Norte (roh'doo-vee-ă pĕ-ree-mĕ-tral nortĕ) the Northern Perimeter Highway.

Samba (săm-bă) a Brasilian dance (and music) of African origin.
São Paulo (saong pă-oo-loo) Saint Paul (place name).
Secas (se'kăs) droughts.
Selva (sel'vă) jungle or rain-forest.
Senzala (sen-zah'lă) the slave quarters on a plantation.
Seringal (sĕ-reen-găl) large rubber estate.
Seringueiro (se-reen-gay'ee-roo) a rubber tapper.
Serra do Mar (se'ră doo mar) mountains by the sea.
Sertanejo (sĕr-tă-nay'zhoo) an inhabitant of the sertão.
Sertão (sĕr-taong) plural, **Sertoẽs** (sĕr-toengsh) the remote undeveloped backlands.
Sertãoejismo (sĕr-taong-ĕ-zhee-zmoo) the 'worship of the backlands'.

Silvavilas (seel'va-vee'lăs) the new towns along the new highways in Amazonia.
Sudeste (sood-eshtĕ) South-east region.
Sul (sool) South region.
Suleiro (sool-ĕ-ee-roo) an inhabitant of the South.

Tabuleiro (ta-boo-lay'ee-roo) table-land.
Temperada (ten-pĕ-rah-dă) temperate.
Terra firme (te'ră feerm) dry land, land above the flood plain.
Terra Roxa (te'ra roh'shă) the 'red-earth' soils of the South-east plateau.
Tradiçional (tră-dee-see-oo-năl) traditional.
Travessão (tră-vĕ-saong) the frontier of cultivation as in the Agreste region.
Triângulo (tree-an'goo-loo) triangle, the 'panhandle' of Minas Gerais, down-town São Paulo.

Urbanização (oor-bă-nee-ză-saong) town planning, or the provision of urban services and amenities.
Usina (oo-see'nă) a modern sugar refinery and plantation.

Vaca (vah'kă) cow.
Vaqueiro (vă-kay'ee-roo) cowboy of northern Brasil.
Várzea (var'zee-ă) floodplain of a river.
Vazante (vă-zant-ĕ) low lying damp ground.
Velho (ve'lyoo) old. **Pôrto Velho**, old port (place name).
Vento (ven'too) wind.
Verão (vĕ-raong) summer.
Vila (vee'lă) town.
Volta Redonda (vol'tă-redon'dă) round river bend (place name).

Xingu (sheen'goo) Amerindian tribe and place name.

Zona (zoh'nă) zone. e.g. **Zona da Mata**, forest zone.

Index

Note that the index should be used together with the contents list, and lists of illustrations. Figure numbers are given in **bold type.**